The IRA
Bombing Campaign
Against Britain,
1939–1940

ALSO BY JOSEPH MCKENNA
AND FROM MCFARLAND

*The Irish-American Dynamite Campaign:
A History, 1881–1896* (2012)

*Guerrilla Warfare in the Irish
War of Independence, 1919–1921* (2011)

British Ships in the Confederate Navy (2010)

The IRA Bombing Campaign Against Britain, 1939–1940

Joseph McKenna

McFarland & Company, Inc., Publishers
Jefferson, North Carolina

Every effort has been made to trace the owners of copyright in the photographs included. If contacted, the author will be pleased to correct any errors and omissions in subsequent printings of this book.

Library of Congress Cataloguing-in-Publication Data

Names: McKenna, Joseph.
Title: The IRA bombing campaign against Britain, 1939–1940 / Joseph McKenna.
Description: Jefferson, North Carolina : McFarland & Company, Inc., Publishers, 2016. | Includes bibliographical references and index.
Identifiers: LCCN 2016000167 | ISBN 9781476662589 (softcover : alkaline paper) ∞
Subjects: LCSH: Irish Republican Army—History—20th century. | Bombings—England—History—20th century. | Bombings—England—Coventry—History—20th century. | Political violence—England—History—20th century. | Ireland—Politics and government—1922–1949. | Victims of terrorism—England—Coventry—History—20th century. | Bombers (Terrorists)—Ireland—History—20th century. | Trials (Terrorism)—Great Britain—History—20th century.
Classification: LCC DA963 .M37 2016 | DDC 363.3250941/09043—dc23
LC record available at http://lccn.loc.gov/2016000167

British Library cataloguing data are available

ISBN (print) 978-1-4766-6258-9
ISBN (ebook) 978-1-4766-2372-6

© 2016 Joseph McKenna. All rights reserved

No part of this book may be reproduced or transmitted in any form or by any means, electronic or mechanical, including photocopying or recording, or by any information storage and retrieval system, without permission in writing from the publisher.

Front cover: the aftermath of the IRA terrorist bombing in Coventry on 25 August 1939 (Simon Shaw); *inset* James O'Donovan in Dublin after arrest, circa 1941 (Irish Police Service)

Printed in the United States of America

McFarland & Company, Inc., Publishers
 Box 611, Jefferson, North Carolina 28640
 www.mcfarlandpub.com

For the people of Coventry, that they may know that the five victims of August 25 are not forgotten.

Since writing this dedication, a memorial to the dead was unveiled on 14 October 2015 in the grounds of Coventry Cathedral.

Acknowledgments

My thanks to the staff of the Social Sciences and Local Studies Departments of the Central Library, Birmingham, England. Thanks also to the staff of the National Library, Dublin; Central Library Cork; Coventry Record Office; and to Neil Cobbett and the National Archives, Kew, London.

Thanks to Denise Brackell of the *Sunday Times*, Dr. Roger Boulter, and especially to an old Republican who knew of those times.

Table of Contents

Acknowledgments vi
List of Abbreviations viii
Preface 1
Introduction 4

1. The Campaign Is Launched 19
2. More Bombs 37
3. The Railway Bombs 70
4. Prevention of Violence (Temporary Provisions) Act 77
5. Coventry, 25 August 85
6. The Arrest and Trial of the Coventry Bombers 98
7. Sentence and Appeal 130
8. The End of the Campaign 138
9. The Irish Response to the Campaign 146
10. Release, Repatriation and Reflection 154

Appendix I: The "S" Plan 173
Appendix II: Persons Convicted in Great Britain in Connection with the IRA Campaign During 1939–1940 184
Appendix III: Expulsion Orders Under the Prevention of Violence Act 1939 192
Chapter Notes 195
Bibliography 198
Index 201

List of Abbreviations

ACA Army Comrades Association
ARP Air Raid Precautions
ASU Active Service Unit
CID Criminal Investigation Department
COS Chief of Staff
DET. INSP. Detective Inspector
DET. SERGT. Detective Sergeant
DET. SUPT. Detective Superintendent
GHQ General Headquarters
GPO General Post Office
HO Home Office
IO Information Officer
IRA Irish Republican Army
IRB Irish Republican Brotherhood
K.C. King's Counsel, a senior barrister at law
LMS London Midland Scottish Railway
MEPO Metropolitan Police (London)
MI5 British Intelligence (Internal)
M.P. Member of Parliament
OC Officer Commanding
PC Police Constable
REV Reverend
RUC Royal Ulster Constabulary
UCD University College Dublin

Preface

It was one of the biggest cases of mass murder in England just prior to World War II and yet, because of the outbreak of the war just over a week later, it is largely unknown. James Clay, age 81; John Corbett Arnott, a schoolboy of 15; Gwilym Rowlands, 50; Rex Gentle, 33; and Elsie Ansell, a young woman of 21 who was to be married in a fortnight, were all killed on 25 August 1939, in a terrorist bombing in the medieval cathedral city of Coventry. Today in the ruins of the bombed-out cathedral, destroyed during the Blitz, there is a memorial with a message of reconciliation, but regarding the deaths of the five citizens of Coventry, there is nothing. Their deaths go unrecorded, these persons killed during a short-lived, misguided bombing campaign carried out by the IRA against Britain in 1939–40.

The starting point for this work, for me, was a scrapbook of news cuttings, housed in the Local Studies Department in the old Victorian Central Library in Birmingham, England. Within it was a news cutting with an illustration of a terraced house in Birmingham, revealed to be an IRA dynamite factory. I made a mental note of the fact, but did not pursue it. I suppose it must have been a few years later when I came upon a book that gave more details of this little-known campaign, not just restricted to Birmingham, but a national campaign carried out by the IRA. The book was one of a series about famous British trials, Letitia Fairfield's *The Trial of Peter Barnes and Others*, published in 1953. She, a barrister herself, Irish, and a sister of novelist Rebecca West, gave details of the Coventry bombing.

It was a curious trial, murders apart. Two men were tried, found guilty and hanged for a crime neither committed. One of them, Peter Barnes, was actually in London, some 100 miles away, at the time. The man responsible for the deaths was the "strange man," as he was known in the court proceedings, a man who was never brought to trial. As a librarian, working in the Local Studies department, I took an interest in the regional aspect of the campaign.

I was on holiday in Dublin when I discovered the name, or rather the nickname, of the "strange man"; it was Joby. The name of the bomber was one of the worst-kept secrets within the Republican movement. So many people knew about it, but were bound by the IRA oath, or just reluctant to discuss the matter, no one would divulge the secret. The Irish police also knew who the bomber was, as indeed did Special Branch in Britain, but for whatever reasons the police did not or could not pursue the matter. Dutifully, when I returned to work, I wrote out a slip and placed it in what was then an index of obscure material relating to the West Midlands. The entry read: "Coventry Bombing 25th August 1939. The real bomber was allegedly a man called Joby." Then I filed it, and forgot all about it. Some twenty or so years later, having returned to my old department, just prior to taking early retirement, I came across the slip again when looking for something else. There it was: Joby did it, but who was Joby?

Having taken early retirement, I decided to pursue the interest. J. Bowyer Bell's history of the IRA, *The Secret Army*, gave a brief outline of the campaign, and Robert Fisk's *In Time of War* placed the campaign in its historical perspective. Again, as in the past, I found that the newspapers of the day, speculation aside, proved a valuable source of detailed information. The *Midland Daily Telegraph* was particularly useful for its coverage of the campaign in Coventry, and likewise the *Birmingham Mail*, *Evening Despatch* and the *Birmingham Gazette*, for the IRA activity in that city. The *Liverpool Echo* recorded the bombing campaign in Liverpool and Lancashire. Nationally, and for political balance, I used the national dailies the *Times*, *Irish Times*, *Guardian* and *Daily Herald* to gain a nationwide perspective. Then there were the Republican newspapers, the *United Irishman* and the later *Saorise*, the weeklies of the Republican Sinn Fein party, and by extension the IRA.

Perhaps surprisingly, I found quite a lot of material available at the Public Record Office, or the National Archive as it is now known, at Kew in London. I say surprisingly because a lot of material relating to the earlier Irish-American dynamite campaign of the previous century is still unavailable, if indeed it still exists. For the 1939–40 campaign, material is available in the HO (Home Office) 45 and 144 series. Material is also available in the MEPO 3 series. In addition there are published Parliamentary Reports, and details of the campaign in Hansard, which is the day-to-day account of the proceedings in the British Parliament. Two books in particular were essential to give this work its detail. They were Uinseann MacEoin's *The*

IRA in the Twilight Years, and *Harry*, the biography of Ulsterman Harry White. Architect Vincent MacEoin, a man I met a couple of times at Sinn Fein functions in Dublin in the early 1970s, sought out the old IRA veterans of the 1930s and '40s, when he himself was a member, and recorded their stories. Without him so much would have been lost. Last was David O'Donoghue's book, *The Devil's Deal*. Though it deals specifically with James O'Donovan, author of the S-Plan, and his connection with the IRA and Nazi Germany, it did reveal the name of the "strange man," who was the then-dead Joby O'Sullivan.* So there was confirmation of what I had heard some 20 years earlier, "Joby did it." Interestingly, O'Sullivan's commanding officer during the campaign in the Midlands was Dominic Adams, uncle of the present president of Sinn Fein, Gerry Adams. Connected to him was a dark secret, which nobody seemed prepared to divulge, perhaps because of his family connection.

The intriguing question that remains concerning Sullivan and Adams is: did Sullivan panic, and abandon the bicycle that contained the bomb, as he himself later claimed? That is the official IRA viewpoint. Or did Dominic Adams order a daylight bombing in Coventry, knowing that there would be civilian casualties—which O'Sullivan then carried out? Both men are now dead, so we may never find out the truth, but the evidence does seem to suggest that Adams did order a daytime bombing, and O'Sullivan, quite a ruthless man, carried it out.

Up to the present there is no book that deals directly with this campaign in any detail, a campaign which never had a hope of succeeding. The closest are the O'Donaghue book as cited above, and Enno Stephan's *Spies in Ireland*, both of which concern themselves with the IRA's connection with Nazi Germany. Both merely give oblique and cursory references to the campaign. In contrast, this work covers in detail that which the earlier books omit. It is a record of two misguided years, when seven innocent people were murdered.

---

* There are variations in the spelling of his name. In some, his surname is given as Sullivan, and his nickname, Joby, taken from his Christian names Joe B., sometimes appears as Jobie. I have preferred to use Joby O'Sullivan, the spelling given to me by an old Republican.

Introduction

To understand why the 1939–40 bombing campaign took place, and to understand the rationale of those who took part in it, it is essential to understand what had happened—or rather what had not happened—in Ireland over the preceding years since the end of the War of Independence. Michael Collins saw the establishment of a twenty-six-county Irish Free State as but a steppingstone to an Irish Republic. His long-term strategy had been to establish secure borders for the state, then launch a twin-pronged guerrilla war against the North using the IRA and the Free State Army, thus securing a united thirty-two-county Irish Republic by 1925. His assassination and his replacement, by lesser men, meant that this did not happen. They seemed content with the status quo. For those who took part in the bombing campaign, those sixteen years between 1923 and 1939 were seen as a betrayal of everything that they believed in. The six counties that made up Northern Ireland were still occupied by the British in a Protestant state for a Protestant people. Not only were they occupied, but the Nationalists—the Catholic population—were second-class citizens in their own country. Small wonder therefore that so many of those taking part in the bombing campaign were from Northern Ireland.

Truce, Treaty and Civil War

After three years of guerrilla fighting in Ireland between the Irish Republican Army and the occupying forces of Great Britain, British Prime Minister David Lloyd George, increasingly under international pressure because of the brutal techniques employed by British paramilitary police forces, sought a truce. He proposed that negotiations should begin in London with representatives of the Dail, or Irish Parliament, to end the war.

These negotiations were opened in July 1921, and concluded in December of that year. Lloyd George offered the Irish delegates a considerable measure of autonomy for Ireland, as the Irish Free State, but reserved to Britain the custody of Irish ports, a declaration of allegiance to the British monarchy, and the partitioning of Ireland into separate southern and northern states. The alternative, he declared, was a return to "immediate and terrible war." The country was tired of war, and of the terror and the brutality and the severe restrictions on everyday life. Seeing the proposals as a way forward to eventual independence, the delegates, headed by Michael Collins, accepted the British proposals without further reference to the government in Dublin.

In the Dail the Cabinet was split. Those opposed to the Articles of Agreement, or the Treaty as it was more popularly known, held that the Republic of Ireland, as proclaimed on 21 January 1919 in the first sitting of a democratically elected Irish government, was by the will of the people a fact. Collins and those in favor of the treaty claimed that acceptance did not preclude future Republican status. They saw the treaty as a stepping-stone to that Republic. Amidst some rancor, on 7 January 1922, the Treaty was approved by the Dail by a majority of 64 to 57. It was a close decision. Of the cabinet members, William Cosgrave, and three of the signatories of the Treaty, Arthur Griffith, Michael Collins and Robert Barton, were in favor. Eamon de Valera, Austin Stack and Cathal Brugha were vehemently opposed. In protest de Valera resigned as president, and was replaced by Arthur Griffith. The pro–Treatyites were supported in the main by the press, the Catholic Church, businessmen and men of property—all those who had a stake in the country. However, for a not insignificant minority, the treaty was a betrayal of all they had fought and believed in.

Just as the Dail was split, so too was the Irish Republican Army that had brought the British to the negotiating table. At Army H.Q. seven members voted against the Treaty, and six in favor of it. Again it was close. The division extended right through the Army command. During January and February, as army barracks were evacuated by the British troops, they were occupied, in some cases by pro–Treaty, and in other cases by anti–Treaty troops. For the moment, while Army H.Q. remained united, this was not a problem, but it was obvious that both sides were jockeying for position, seizing as much as possible in preparation of a final outcome.

The provisional post–Treaty Free State government, anticipating a mandate from a war-weary people, assumed some functions of an elected Free State government, under the chairmanship of Michael Collins. They began forming a new national army. It consisted of former IRA men, and "trucileers" as they were mockingly called; these were men who had joined the IRA at the end of the war. They were officered by pro–Treaty men, who by and large were members of the Irish Republican Brotherhood. The IRB itself was fractured, but for the moment, out of loyalty to Collins, the members agreed to work together to prevent civil war. Senior anti–Treaty officers of the IRA called for an army convention to discuss the situation. They proposed that the IRA should be depoliticized by taking control of the army out of the hands of the Dail, and restoring it to the Army Executive. It was decided that each division at the convention would be represented proportionately to its numerical strength. On this basis the anti–Treatyites calculated that they would have an overwhelming majority, and could push for the continuation of the war for complete independence. Richard Mulcahy, new Minister for Defense of the Irish Free State, agreed to the convention, but was all the time adding to the newly created Free State army in order to tip the balance in favor of the Free State.

In February, the 3rd Tipperary Brigade, who were anti–Treaty, seized an abandoned barracks in Clonmel, then under nominal Free State police guard, forcing the police to withdraw. To forestall further seizures, the Free State government ordered Commandant Michael Brennan, known to be pro–Treaty, to move detachments into Limerick to take over further barracks evacuated by the British. Ernie O'Malley, commander of the Second Southern Division and an anti–Treatyite, issued an ultimatum to pro–Treaty troops in his area to evacuate their positions or be attacked. As tensions rose, de Valera appealed to Mulcahy to try to reach a solution. On 15 March the Free State Cabinet's response was to do a volte-face. They banned the forthcoming army convention. Nonetheless, despite the ban, it went ahead on 26 March. In what was considered by the Free State government to be mutiny, those participating were declared to be suspended from the army, be it Free State or IRA. Suspended or not, the anti–Treaty officers of the IRA remained in command of their troops. Meanwhile the Free State Army continued to grow. As part of the Treaty, the British government then began handing over its weapons to the pro–Treaty forces. During April the situation in Ireland became critical. Armed clashes occurred. Eight soldiers were killed and forty-nine were wounded. Civil war loomed.

Within the IRB, fractured like the rest of the country, talks took place between its chairman, pro–Treatyite Michael Collins, and the equally charismatic anti–Treatyite Liam Lynch, in a bid to prevent a war. They formulated plans to unite both factions in a covert assault against Northern

Ireland. Collins's offer to Lynch was that if the dissidents would support him now, then he guaranteed a unified thirty-two-county Irish Republic within four years. But away from these talks, and not knowing what was going on at senior level, on 13 April, the anti–Treaty Republican Army Executive established themselves in the judicial center of the Four Courts on the Liffey Quayside, right in the heart of Dublin. Other buildings, including the Masonic Hall, the Ballast Office and Kilmainham Jail, were also occupied. This was seen as a direct challenge to the Free State government, an attempt at a coup d'état.

In Britain, Lloyd George became concerned. He summoned Collins and Griffith to London to discuss the situation. The British Prime Minister threatened to reoccupy Ireland if something was not done. The British press clambered for the provisional government to deal with the Republicans by force of arms if necessary. Meanwhile in Ireland preparations were underway for an election on 16 June, and the submission of a new Constitution. This would legitimize the existing Free State government.

Despite not winning the subsequent election outright, with the support of other minority parties, the pro–Treaty faction declared that enough of the people had shown a clear mandate for accepting the Treaty, which would bring peace at last. As a result, the pro–Treaty party would remain as the government. On 18 June the army met again to discuss the new Constitution. Further splits ensued. The anti–Treaty Republicans left the Convention and returned to their garrison in the Four Courts.

On 22 June, Senior British Army officer Sir Henry Wilson, a fanatical anti–Republican, and now advisor to the Northern Ireland government in the setting up of its security forces, was shot dead in London by two London-based IRA men.[1] This proved a catalyst. Lloyd George insisted that the anti–Treatyites were responsible, and that unless Collins took swift and immediate action against them he would consider it a breach of the Treaty. While Collins hesitated, the commander in chief of the remaining British Forces in Ireland, General Sir Neville Macready, was ordered to prepare an attack on the Four Courts on 25 June. On the day before, Lloyd George issued an ultimatum to the provisional government: if they would not deal with the situation, then the British Army would. Collins prevaricated, but the arrest by Republicans of Treatyite General J.J. O'Connell forced him to act. Collins informed Lloyd George that he would comply.

About 2 a.m. on the morning of 28 June the streets around the Four Courts were suddenly filled with troops, armored vehicles and artillery. At 3:40 a.m. Commandant Tom Ennis of the provisional government forces sent in a note demanding the surrender of O'Connell and the evacuation of the Four Courts before 4 a.m. The demand was rejected. At 4 o'clock, guns acquired by the Free Staters from the British Army opened fire. The civil war had begun. After 48 hours of bombardment the Four Courts was a blazing ruin. Its garrison surrendered. Within days all other Republican resistance in Dublin had been crushed. Most of those who were not captured fled the city, including IRA Chief of Staff Liam Lynch.

Though initially numerically inferior, the pro–Treaty forces had the decisive advantage of superior armaments, transport and supplies, provided by the old enemy, Britain. They also had the support of the greater majority of the people, who just wanted an end to it all. As the war progressed, amidst reports of atrocities, the Free State forces by the end of the summer of 1922 held all the main cities, and most of the countryside. Then a severe blow was struck against the few surviving Republican guerrillas by the Roman Catholic hierarchy, who excommunicated them. In a country where religion played such a major part in the lives of the people, this was a crushing condemnation. Nonetheless, even with their forces diminished, the Republicans guerrillas fought on.

At this point the Free State government suffered two major losses. Michael Collins was killed in an ambush at Bealnablath in County Cork, on 22 August 1922. Previously, President Griffith died of a heart attack on 12 August. Griffith was replaced by William Cosgrave as prime minister (officially titled president of the Executive Council). Richard Mulcahy took over as military commander. The Republicans lost Liam Lynch, killed by Free State forces. In mid–October the Dail passed what was known by the die-hard Republicans as the "Murder Bill," which established military courts that had the power to order the execution of combative Republicans. Those caught in arms were shot out of hand, and a policy of ruthless reprisal executions followed. Now without any hope of winning , on 24 May 1923, de Valera, president of Sinn Fein, and Frank Aitken, Liam Lynch's successor as IRA chief of staff, issued the order to the "Soldiers of the Republic, Legion of the Rearguard," to "dump arms." The order acknowledged, "Military victory must be allowed to rest for the moment with those who have destroyed the Republic. Other means must be sought to safeguard the nation's right." Thus the civil war was ended, but with neither the surrender of the remnants of the IRA, or Irregulars as they were now known, nor the recognition of the Free State government's legitimacy. The number of people who met violent deaths during the war, which lasted just under a year, was almost 5,000—far more than during the two and a half years of the war against the British.

The IRA in England Forestalled

In Britain, untouched by the civil war, units of the IRA remained committed to a unified 32-county Irish Republic. The anti-terrorist branch of the British police force, Special Branch, had infiltrated the London command, and early on the morning of Sunday, 11 March 1923, instigated a series of raids up and down the country. Over 100 suspects were arrested and deported to the Free State aboard the Royal Navy cruiser HMS *Castor*. Upon their arrival in Dublin they were interned in Mountjoy Prison. The raids had been instigated following the interception of correspondence addressed to a known member of the IRA in London. These letters and other papers were passed to the Home Secretary, who ordered the arrests. Head of Special Branch, James McBrien, a man of Irish descent, assigned two detectives to each suspect, and within the first two hours alone had detained thirty-three people, including ten women, at local police stations. The 110 suspects eventually arrested were gathered together at Hunter Street Police Station in London, then taken to Euston Railway Station. There a specially chartered train carried them to Liverpool, where they were put aboard the warship.

In Parliament the Home Secretary justified his actions by reading out examples of the intercepted correspondence. One letter in particular gave some alarm, for the Home Secretary inferred that the target of one particular attack was those Members now sitting in the Commons. He read out the menacing lines: "I could not promise you grenades at present. It is impossible to keep the foundry open here. Hence, the output is very small; but I am having some aluminum light grenades made, and packed with shrapnel, which I hope, will be effective."[2]

The deportations were carried out using the Restoration of Order in Ireland Act, but the act had been used illegally. The deportees in law had the same rights as British citizens, who nominally they still were, under the Articles of Agreement which ended the war in Ireland. Their solicitors went to law, and the House of Lords later ruled that the operations had been conducted illegally. Some £50,000 was paid in compensation to the deportees. On 17 May, 90 of the deportees returned to Holyhead, the port of arrival in North Wales, where Special Branch detectives issued them free rail warrants to take them to their English homes. As they arrived, perhaps in a vindictive mood at being made to look foolish, the policemen insisted on a search of the new arrivals. Seven of the returned deportees were found to be carrying weapons, and were re-arrested. Some credence had been restored in state security.

The Rise of Fianna Fail

The civil war was over. The defeated Republicans dumped their arms and went underground to bide their time. The pro–Treatyites formed themselves into a political party, Cumann na nGaedheal, and passed a Public Safety Act giving themselves emergency powers in peacetime to deal with the IRA. In the general election of 1923 the political wing of Republicanism, Sinn Fein, led by Eamon de Valera, won 46 seats in the Dail, but were unable to take up those seats by their refusal to swear the controversial oath of allegiance to the British monarch. The government gained sixty-three seats and Labour, fourteen. Then in the summer of 1926 the pragmatic de Valera split the Republican movement by his declaration that he would enter the Dail, provided that he was not obliged to take the oath. In defense of his proposal he maintained that the Free State Dail was not the legitimate parliament of the republic. Therefore he would use the existing system to bring down the system in order to achieve full independence. The diehards bitterly opposed the proposal, but de Valera went ahead, forming a new political party, Fianna Fail.

As president of the Irish Free State, Eamon de Valera cracked down on former IRA comrades.

The Free State government, elected in 1923, was dissolved in 1927. It was an assembly in which the pro–Treaty Cumann na nGaedheal Party, led by Mr. W.T. Cosgrave, had commanded a majority among the deputies who sat in the House. In the general election of June 1927, Fianna Fail won 44 seats at the poll, plus the support of two independent Republicans. Cosgrave's party lost its overall majority, winning just 47 seats, but it could call on the support of Labour, Independents and others, and thus form a government. On 23 June the elected Fianna Fail deputies sought admission to the Dail chamber, but were denied unless they subscribed full-heartedly to the oath. This they refused to do, and were denied access. Legal proceedings were instituted in the High Court to test the validity of the exclusion. As the court adjudicated, Cumann na nGaedheal's Justice Minister, Kevin O'Higgins, was assassinated. In Republican circles O'Higgins was identified with the most ruthless aspects of government policy towards them. Though all sections of the Republican movement denied involvement, the government saw in his death a serious challenge to its authority. It introduced three bills. The first was a Public Safety Bill giving the authorities wide powers to deal with illegal organizations (namely the IRA). The other two were constitutional measures aimed at absentee Fianna Fail deputies. One bill required all candidates in future elections to make a declaration under oath that they would take the oath of allegiance and sit in the Dail, if elected. The other measure was devised to prevent any attempt by Fianna Fail to press for a referendum on the oath without first taking their seats in the Dail. This was a glorious Catch-22 situation, created by the government, but in August a Jesuitical solution was found which was equally devious. The Fianna Fail deputies would subscribe to the oath with mental reservations. De Valera sold the swearing as an "empty formality." The new deputies entered the Dail on 11 August, and pledged to dismantle the Constitution of the Irish Free State in order to bring about the cherished republic. In Parliament, Fianna Fail established alliances with the National League and the Labour Party, eventually forcing a vote of no confidence in the government. Fresh elections were held in the autumn, with Cumann na nGaedheal just hanging on.

    The Cosgrave government fought a second general election in February 1932 on the basis of its past service. Fianna Fail emphasized economic self-sufficiency, the Republican ideal and the aspiration to reconcile all sections of national opinion. Fianna Fail won 72 seats and was returned as the largest party in the new Dail. Reforging its links with the other parties, it formed the new government. De Valera now began breaking the links with Britain. Firstly there was the unilateral rejection of the oath of allegiance to the British sovereign. Secondly was the retention by an Irish government to land annuities hitherto paid to Britain. Thirdly was the expansion of industry to break the dependency on Britain for manufactured goods. Britain's response to the nonpayment of land annuities saw the imposition of substantial tariffs on Irish goods entering the British market. The dispute continued on until 1938, when in March of that year, following arbitration, Ireland agreed to make a one-off payment of £10,000,000. On the last day of the negotiations, de Valera suddenly raised the question of the return of the naval bases occupied by British forces under the provision of the 1922 treaty. Surprisingly, British Prime Minister Neville Chamberlain agreed to the proposal. It was something Winston Churchill would never have agreed to, but Churchill was still sitting on the sidelines, out of favor with his own party.

As Ireland did her best to cut her ties with Britain, new movements and new leaders sprang up on the Continent. The 1930s saw the rise of fascism in Europe. In the fullness of time Cumann na nGaedheal played nursemaid to this dark movement in Ireland. They were called the Blue Shirts. They sprang out of an organization of ex-members of the Free State Army, the Army Comrades Association. Their purported role was to protect free speech and private property, to uphold law and order and to deter communism. In August 1932 the Association opened its ranks to the public. It was all so reminiscent of Hitler's Germany; Jews and atheists were excluded from membership. By April 1933 the ACA claimed a membership of 100,000. In April 1933 the association adopted the wearing of a blue shirt. Three months later, in July, the organization changed its name to the National Guard under a new leader, General Eoin O'Duffy, who had recently been dismissed as Commissioner of Police by the de Valera administration. O'Duffy, a homosexual, with the look of a prosperous pig farmer about him, actively encouraged the use of a raised-arm fascist salute accompanied by the salutation, "Hail O'Duffy!" To some it was ludicrous megalomania—to others it was a warning of what might happen if it was not checked. In September 1933 the National Guard joined with Cumann na nGaedheal to become United Ireland, or in Irish, Fine Gael. Eoin O'Duffy became its leader, with William Cosgrave as its leader in the Dail. The rise of the Blue Shirts, it was claimed, was in response to the growing menace of the Communist IRA. They announced themselves as defenders of the Roman Catholic Church. They would ensure that Fine Gael politicians would retain freedom of speech from IRA hecklers.

O'Duffy then proposed to commemorate the deaths of Kevin O'Higgins and Michael Collins with a mass march to Glasnevin Cemetery on 13 August 1933. Special trains were chartered to carry country contingents to Dublin. At least three to four thousand uniformed Blue Shirts were expected to march. The analogy with Mussolini and his march on Rome was not lost on de Valera. Though O'Duffy strenuously denied he intended to lead a coup d'état, de Valera decided to take no chances. Arms were confiscated from leading figures in the movement. A special police force composed principally of ex–IRA men was raised and armed. Late at night on Saturday, 12 March, the government banned the march. Not sure whether it would still happen, 300 heavily armed policemen ringed the Parliament building, and 700 lined the route of the intended march. Early on Sunday morning, O'Duffy called off the march. To break the movement, the government then introduced a bill to prohibit the wearing of political uniforms, which was passed into law in March 1934. On 21 September, General O'Duffy was persuaded by the Central Council to resign from Fine Gael. The Blue Shirts, after a pathetic intervention in the Spanish Civil War in support of Franco, became a spent force.

By the raising of a special IRA-based police force to subjugate the fascists, de Valera had maintained his connection with the IRA. But the IRA's renewed assertion of its own identity under a pro-Republican government, with parading and drilling in public and their exploitation of their apparent close links to the Fianna Fail government, was a situation which no government jealous of its powers could any longer tolerate. At the 1934 commemoration of the dead of 1916 at Glasnevin Cemetery, Moss Twomey, the Chief of Staff of the IRA, read out a message from the Army Council. It declared that the small and quite unrepresentative group of armed men who made the 1916 rebellion had established "the right and authority of our nation to fight for its right to inalienable sovereign independence." Was this a challenge to de Valera's government? He decided that it was. In response to orders to refrain from public drilling and to hand in their arms, the IRA leadership refused, unless de Valera promised to turn Ireland from a Free State into a Republic within five years. De Valera had no alternative but to declare the IRA an illegal organization, as Cosgrave had done before him. He would not be blackmailed. The decision to do so was taken in June 1936 following the brutal killings of three civilians by the IRA.

Meanwhile de Valera continued to break the links with Britain. Slow but sure was his policy. On the abdication of Edward VIII, de Valera rushed through the Dail the Constitution bill (Amendment No. 27) severing the Crown from the Irish Constitution. The position of governor-general, little more than a figurehead, was abolished. De Valera now set himself the task of abolishing the Free State. Following the general election and a plebiscite in 1937, with a majority of 77 seats in the Dail, de Valera instituted a new Constitution. A new state, Eire, was created. Ireland had become a republic in all but name. The reluctance to take the final step was the belief that such a declaration might cut off the Six Counties for good. De Valera still hoped that he could bring about the unification of Ireland by peaceful means. In January 1938 de Valera met with British Prime Minister Neville Chamberlain, a meeting which led to the signing of the Anglo-Irish Agreement on 25 April. This ended the "Economic War" which had seen tariffs placed on Irish commodities entering Britain. The agreement, almost as an afterthought, saw the restoration of the British Treaty ports. If, as seemed likely, a European war broke out, Ireland could remain neutral.

The IRA Resurgent

When de Valera's new government took over following the general election of 16 February 1932, military tribunals were suspended, and the declaration orders that made the IRA and the left-wing Saor Eire unlawful were revoked. An olive branch was extended to the IRA men imprisoned under the previous administration, and they were released. After representation, work was found for a number of them within the state apparatus. This had a double benefit. It rewarded previous loyalty, i.e., their part in the war of independence, and it hopefully took the gun out of Irish politics. But there were some who could not, or would not, be reconciled to anything less than a 32-county Irish Republic. The hero of Crossbarry during the War of Independence, Tom Barry, and a rising star within the IRA, Sean Russell, mistakenly believed that de Valera would now actively declare for an Irish Republic. The IRA began to drill openly once more. In early July, Barry was invited to discuss with de Valera the formation of a volunteer National Defense Force. Barry was very much in favor, believing that such a force, made up of old IRA volunteers, would inevitably be used in an armed conflict against the North. De Valera, however, had another object in mind: the neutering of the IRA. Men joining the National Defense Force would be obliged to swear an oath of loyalty to the Free State government, and submit themselves to the authority of the Minister of Defense. Without the promise of action against the North that Barry had hoped for, the IRA Army Council rejected the proposal, and remained a separate military force.

Under what was still deemed to be a government sympathetic to an eventual republic, the IRA began to recruit new volunteers and openly drilled. It began behaving like an alternative government, a position which de Valera's government viewed with concern. The IRA's declaration of "No Free Speech for Traitors," expounded in its newspaper, *An Poblacht*, was seen by the government as a rejection of free speech, one of the fundamental tenants of a democratic society. The IRA came to be seen as a challenge to the authority of de Valera's government. That government felt obliged to act.

On 2 May 1934, Tom Barry was arrested and sentenced to jail for a year for possession of arms. The point was to show the IRA that it was not above the law. The point made, Barry was released as a good will gesture at Christmas.

In a series of incidents that followed, the IRA appeared to openly challenge the authority of the democratically elected government. In March 1935 at a General Army Convention, Barry called on the members to support military action against Northern Ireland within six months. Later that month, as a strike by tram drivers paralyzed Dublin, government troops were sent in to drive the trams, or at least to provide guards to ensure that they continued to run. The increasingly socialist-biased IRA gave its support to the strikers. The IRA attacked or sabotaged trams, and soldiers drafted in to drive the trams were attacked. The government responded by arresting 43 IRA men and associated activists, including Barry, who was sentenced to 18 months' imprisonment. The strike was broken.

Previously on 9 February, Richard More O'Ferrall, son of land agent Gerald More O'Ferrall, was accidentally shot dead when he went to assist his father, who was about to be attacked by IRA men led by James Joseph Reynolds. It was claimed that More O'Ferrall senior was on the point of evicting 121 tenants from the Sanderson estate in County Longford. The IRA men had gone to the house to give him a beating, but things had gone wrong. Reynolds was arrested for the murder, but was found not guilty at his subsequent trial. On 24 March 1936, Vice-Admiral Henry Boyle Somerville was shot dead at his home near Skibbereen, County Cork. Somerville was well known in the area for giving references to local lads who wished to enlist in the British Royal Navy. Tom Barry was held to be responsible for the action, though nothing was ever proven. Barry denied any responsibility. A month later John Egan, dubbed a police spy, was executed in Waterford on the orders of IRA GHQ. Things were getting out of hand. The government had no choice but to act. On 18 June the IRA was once more declared an illegal organization. Jim Killeen and Moss Twomey of IRA GHQ were arrested. Other senior members went underground.

Following the arrest of Twomey, Sean McBride was co-opted by the Army Council to take over as temporary head of the IRA. McBride was a meticulous man; he was an organizer, a man more given to politics than the armed struggle. It was not long before he came into conflict with the more militant Sean Russell. The men clashed openly, particularly over Russell's unauthorized preparations for a bombing attack on Britain. McBride, a bookkeeper by nature, sought to bring Russell back under control. He insisted that records be kept and expenditures be submitted. Russell had no time for such silliness. He was planning a war. McBride insisted, and being ignored, called for Russell's court-martial. Russell was found guilty of failing to account properly for funds, and was demoted.

In July 1936 the Spanish Civil War began. In black-and-white terms it was seen in Ireland as a struggle between Catholics and Communists. As with most things, it was a little more complicated than that. The democratically elected Spanish Republican government was made up of a number of disparate political parties, including liberals, socialists, communists and anarchists, all brought together in opposition to a repressive right-wing regime, supported by the Catholic Church, and dedicated to maintaining a feudal system. Once in power the new Republican government sought the compulsory breaking-up of the huge estates, offering compensation to the owners, and distributing the land to the peasants. But then anarchists began attacking the homes of the rich and destroying Catholic churches. In the face of such acts, and in a bid to restore the status quo, General Francisco Franco led a revolt in Spain. In Ireland, a very Catholic country, many flocked to join the resurrected Blue Shirts, who went off to fight for Franco. The more left-wing volunteers of the IRA saw the war for what it really was—a war between the dark forces of fascism, which threatened to sweep through Europe, and those of democracy, albeit a flawed democracy fashioned by Moscow. Paedar O'Donnell, who had been in Catalonia when the war began, returned to Dublin to urge IRA support for the Republic. Despite the IRA's policy of nonintervention, those volunteers on the left, including Frank Ryan and George Gilmore, and the younger men looking for action, went off to Spain to fight for the Republic in the International Brigade. In all some 400 Irishmen, most of them IRA men, made their way to Spain. Many never came back; 42 were killed, 114 wounded, and twelve captured, including Frank Ryan.

When the next Army Convention of the IRA was called, McBride was ousted. Tom Barry was elected Chief of Staff of the IRA. The convention then looked at two proposals: an attack on the North, favored by Barry, and Russell's bombing campaign against England. Barry's Northern campaign was given precedence. The plan was not for a progressive guerrilla campaign, but for an ambitious *coup d'état*—a large-scale invasion of Northern Ireland. Barracks were to be captured en route before the final push on Belfast. Barry returned to Cork and there enlisted the help of proven IRA Volunteers. Camps were established and men, in their hundreds, were trained. Barry went north to brief the Northern Command of the IRA. Detailed maps of the location of army and police barracks were prepared.

Links with Clann-na-Gael in America enabled the import of 500 Thompson sub-machine guns.

Finally everything was prepared, but just a matter of days before the assault was to be launched, the whole program was canceled. Cumann na mBan, the women's section of the IRA, asked to participate. Asked how they knew about it, they informed Barry that all of Dublin was talking about it. The British also knew about the intended campaign. The Belfast IRA had been infiltrated by the RUC, who were running both the local O.C. and the Intelligence Officer, men whom Barry had conversed with over the plan. Discovered to be a traitor, the O.C. was court-martialed and later executed. In the following month evidence led the investigating IRA team to discover that the I.O. was also working for the RUC Special Branch. On 26 January, he was shot four times on his way to Mass. He died the next day in the hospital. Barry and his men would have been walking into a trap. Luckily for them the invasion had been canceled.

Russell, meanwhile, his plan rejected, and without permission, left for America. He met Joe McGarrity of Clan-na-Gael, who promised him financial support. In Ireland, Paedar O'Flaherty and Tom McGill sounded out support for Russell around the country. O'Flaherty traveled to England, and upon whose authority it is not known, he dismissed the commanding officer, and replaced him with Jimmy Joe Reynolds, a known supporter of Russell's campaign. Reynolds brought Pearse McLoughlin, Mick Ferguson and Mick Welsh onto his staff. They were all supporters of Russell's plan to bomb England.

In mid–1937 Barry announced his intention to resign at the next Army Convention. He was replaced by a Dubliner, Michael Fitzpatrick. He had been on the Army Council for a number of years, and was looked upon as a safe pair of hands. In London the pro–Russell group were replaced by the former O.C. Jack Lynch, alias Buckley.

The status quo had been resumed. Under Fitzpatrick the IRA, to the frustration of many of its younger volunteers, seemed to be just marking time. They existed, but seemed to have no purpose.

In April 1938 the General Army Convention of the IRA met in Abbey Street, Dublin. Many delegates expressed their impatience at inaction. Russell's proposed bombing campaign was again raised. Tom Barry totally condemned it. It was a campaign doomed to failure, he proclaimed, just as the Fenian bombing campaign of the 1880s had been. Barry announced that he was ethically, morally and physically opposed to a bombing campaign to be carried out in England. There were enough British soldiers in the Six Counties to bomb, rather than civilians in England. To embark on such a campaign would make the IRA no better than the Black and Tans. What good would it do to leave a bomb in a cloakroom or a hotel room, and be 40 or 60 miles away when it exploded, killing some ordinary innocent person—someone like them, going about his daily business? Inevitably innocent people would be killed, and the Irish population in England would suffer retaliation, Barry argued. His and Fitzpatrick's views, though, were in the minority. The young Turks wanted action, and action now.

While it might be wrong to say that the convention was packed with Russell's supporters (he himself was not allowed to attend), his call for action had prompted additional newly founded units to send delegates. Emotional speeches and passive parades were not for the younger volunteers, nor indeed some of the older men, who had seen action during the War of Independence. They voted in a new executive, the majority of whom supported Russell's call for action. Russell, who had been court-martialed and suspended in January 1937, was reinstated and appointed Chief of Staff. Five of the twelve executive members resigned—Barry, Tomas MacCurtain, John Joe Sheehy, Sean Keating, and Johnny O'Connor—contending that the Army Council was unrepresentative of the IRA as a whole, as evidenced by the appointment of a dismissed volunteer as Chief of Staff. Barry publicly walked out of the convention over the passing of a resolution to start a bombing campaign against England. Russell was now unopposed. Many were less than wholehearted in their support of the campaign, including such leading Republicans as Paddy McLogan, Tadgh Lynch, Donal Donaghue, James Hannaghan and Frank Fitzgerald. They were asked to resign from GHQ staff, which they did. Rapid promotion of his supporters, and the co-opting of new members onto the Army Executive, ensured that Russell's plan could now go ahead. Only in the North, where the volunteers had called for action, was there no need for reorganization. Included in the Northern firebrands was the young fanatic Dominic Adams, a man drawn from a Belfast Republican family with roots in the Fenian movement. In May the Army Council adopted the campaign plan, even though no detailing had been presented. Now secure, Russell sent for his old War of Independence colleague, Jim O'Donovan, a man who knew how to construct bombs.

1

The Campaign Is Launched

James O'Donovan, the hero or the villain of the bombing campaign, depending on your point of view, was born at Roscommon in 1896, the son of middle-class parents. When he was a child of eight, the family moved to Glasgow in Scotland, and the young James attended the Jesuit-run Saint Aloysius College. The family returned to Ireland in 1913 and went to live in Drumcondra on the north side of Dublin. O'Donovan enrolled in University College Dublin's department of chemistry. From here he graduated with a bachelor of science degree in 1917. At the college he developed Republican sympathies to the extent that he was enrolled into the IRA by the president of the UCD's chemical society, Professor Thomas Dillon. Dillon gave him a special brief, to develop new explosive material for the armed struggle for independence. To this end O'Donovan succeeded in obtaining research work with the Nobel explosives company. In parallel, O'Donovan meanwhile rose within the ranks of the IRA, to become its Director of Chemicals. The Truce came, and with it the split within Republican ranks over the Treaty. O'Donovan, opposed to the Treaty, was imprisoned during the civil war. Upon his release he started up a chemical company in Dublin, but this failed, and he obtained a job as a manager with the state-owned Electricity Supply Board. In early August 1938 he was invited to a meeting with his former War of Independence colleague, the IRA's former Director of Munitions, Sean Russell.

O'Donovan, with his explosives expertise, agreed to help Russell, but in what? There was no master plan for the campaign, other than explosions taking place in England. At Russell's request, O'Donovan drafted a campaign plan as the basis for discussion. This was the S-Plan, or Sabotage Plan. It proposed taking military action against six specific targets:

1. Action against British military forces (classified as not very promising).
2. The destruction of armament factories.
3. The disruption of all civil/public utilities.
4. Key industries.
5. Commerce: banking, shipping.
6. Newspapers, particularly those defaming Irish unification, etc.

The effort would concentrate on England's public services. The prime target would be the electric grid. Apart from the dislocation of industry and business, the moral and panic effects of extensive blackouts would be very great. Equally the disruption of the public transport network would have a paralyzing effect on every branch of industrial and commercial life. Attacks, O'Donovan advocated, were to be specifically targeted against England, and not involve the Celtic countries of Northern Ireland, Scotland and Wales.[1]

The plan was accepted and O'Donovan was given control of explosives and munitions, and became responsible for the training of cadre units, who would pass on their expertise to others. When he took over, O'Donovan discovered that preliminary experiments with balloon-type incendiary, or bombs, had already begun. Paddy McGrath had been working on correlating time for acid to burn through rubber. At the same time Jim Ryan had been working on the alarm-clock electric fuse mechanism. In June 1938, Sean Russell and senior officer Maurice Twomey, seconded to the campaign, called a general meeting at Wynn's Hotel in Dublin. As well as delegates from Ireland, others already embedded came from London and the English Midlands. The plan was expounded. As a trial run, the campaign would commence with attacks upon the Six County border in November, spreading later to England.

In Britain, Special Branch was traditionally responsible for monitoring Irish Republican activity. It was regarded as the province of the police rather than the Intelligence Departments of MI5 and MI6. As such, their aim was the prevention of crime rather than the gathering of intelligence to prevent crime. It was a fine distinction, but a distinction that found them in 1939 with their guard down. In the absence of any IRA agitation on the mainland, they had relaxed their observation on an organization that had apparently been decimated by the Dublin government's crackdown, leaving it little more than a small extremist underground organization constantly harried by the Irish authorities.

In England, teams of locally based IRA men had already begun purchasing the chemicals necessary to manufacture bombs. During the late summer of 1938, three senior IRA men, Jimmy Joe Reynolds, Peader O'Flaherty and Denis O'Connell, had their car stopped in a routine check by the police in Ilford, in Greater London. Names and addresses were taken, and the car was searched. In the trunk was found a large quantity of potassium chlorate. A receipt in their possession showed that the chemicals had not been stolen, but had been purchased. There was nothing illegal in the possession of the chemical, and the men gave satisfactory answers to the police questions. They were allowed to proceed, but one of the policemen was suspicious. He reported his suspicions to the station officer, who informed Special Branch. They arranged for a covert search to be made at the various lodgings of the three men. At one of the addresses, in Dagenham in northeast London, while no arms or bomb-making equipment was discovered, a notebook was found in a jacket pocket. It contained a number of names and addresses. These were copied down, and when checked against Special Branch's card file of known and suspected IRA men, a number of matching names were found. Included was the name of Jimmy Joe Reynolds, recently appointed OC in Britain. Before the information could be acted upon, Reynolds had departed for Dublin. A short while later two other known IRA men, Jack McNeela (alias Gibbons) and Mick Ferguson, were arrested in London in a van also carrying potassium chlorate. They were on Special Branch's list. The two were brought in for questioning, then released on bail. Ferguson skipped bail, but McNeela was arrested and given four months' imprisonment for membership in the IRA and other associated misdemeanors. Ferguson was later sent back to England, where he was arrested and sentenced to ten years.

In Ireland, O'Donovan's main problem was not the explosives themselves, even though there were problems that had to be ironed out, but the lack of competent and experienced operatives. Many of the volunteers who attended his bomb-making classes lacked any previous experience of sabotage. Very few had any technical training, and many lacked formal education beyond primary school. Eoin McNamee was later to say to Uinseann MacEoin of his training: "[S]igns and symbols on a blackboard; what the blazes would I know about them, and me only past the third book in Brocderg school."

In a way, training apart, this use of new and unknown operatives—"new skins" as we would now call them—turned out to the operatives' advantage because they would be unknown to the police in England. But, and it was a very big but, O'Donovan was concerned that once these men had been trained and dispatched to England, they would have to live on their wits in order to maintain themselves in English cities, where their very accents would place them under suspicion when the bombs started going off. This was a concern shared by IRA Volunteer Sean Talty from County Clare: "I thought the plan to send over raw recruits was very cruel. I could get lost in the town of Ennis never mind the city of London: sending over lads with no experience, no resources and no proper training. The way he [Sean Russell] spoke you knew he had vast experience but did not realise that in us he would be dealing with raw country lads having no practice with explosives or anything, and yet we would be expected to live like English people in London, Manchester, Sheffield and all such places."[2] Dan Keating reiterated this concern: "There were too many people sent over who had no knowledge whatsoever of the country or where they were going. They were quickly caught, and among them there would be some useful key men."[3]

A number of the men sent over were quite naïve. There is the apocryphal tale of a couple of country lads from Cork or Mayo who went into a shop to buy a few alarm clocks to be used as a timing device for a bomb. The assistant, suspecting them, asked them to wait while she went into the stock room to check. She then telephoned New Scotland Yard.

There they were, sent over to England, so unworldly wise, and paid £3 to £4 a week, which quite often did not arrive. Sent into a world so beyond their understanding, and they were told not to mix with the Irish population, the very people who could help them. Their best hope of survival, Russell advised, was to avoid contact with the Irish population in England; to avoid all the Irish clubs and halls which would be watched by CID and Special Branch, the physical arm of MI5. To help counter British Intelligence, new unknown IRA commanding officers were sent to establish safe houses for them in many of England's larger cities. Where safe houses were not available, then what might be considered to be "innocent" houses were selected for use. These were houses with no previous IRA connections. The danger with these, particularly if they had English landladies, was that they would be aware of the coming and going of their lodgers, and any lodger not keeping regular working hours would fall under suspicion, particularly after the bombs started going off. One young man from Derry recruited in London by, it is believed, Dan Keating, then working in Mooney's Bar in the Strand, had an understanding Irish landlady. He had mixed up some "Paxo," as the explosive was known, in one of his landlady's saucepans. While he was out meeting his O.C., the landlady, discovering the mixture, disposed of it down the lavatory. Whether or not she knew what it was is open to conjecture. Not all landladies were so understanding, though, in wishing to protect their young men.

1. The Campaign Is Launched

Volunteer bomber Joe Collins was lucky—his landlady did not live on the premises—but he was very aware that others were not so lucky. In an unpublished memoir he recalled: "I had a room in Temple Street [Manchester] where I assembled bombs. It was a tenement house where the tenants were mostly unemployed men or old people. The rent was six shillings a week, there was no gas and no electricity. The room was illuminated at night by a paraffin lamp which hung from a nail in the wall. The landlady was an Irish woman, named Mrs. Murphy, who did not live on the premises. That suited me, as she didn't know whether I was working or not. At that stage of the campaign any Irishman renting a room might well be reported to the police, especially if he didn't appear to have any job. This house had been recommended to me before I arrived in Manchester by an IRA man from Belfast, Bernard McGuinness, who also stayed there. He was known to the occupants of the house and they took little notice of his comings and goings."[4]

Those who stood the most chance of success were the English-born children of Irish parents, men like Dan and Ned Stapleton, Tom Hunt and Martin Staunton, who, with their English accents, could pass themselves off as being English; or the likes of Glaswegian-accented Peter Walsh, though some in England at the time would have confused Scots and Irish. But these men were soon discovered, not by their own faults, but caught up in the paper trails of others. Thus the best potential for success was lost early in the campaign.

By the end of 1938, O'Donovan was using Killiney Castle in south Dublin, then a derelict building (but now the Castle Hotel), as his base. He spent five months training his core volunteers in the making of bombs. First, he instructed them, you mixed potassium chlorate and paraffin wax in a saucepan upon a gas stove. It was a highly combustible combination. They must make sure to use a wooden spoon or stick—never a metal spoon which could cause an explosion. They soon discovered that mixing the chemicals too frequently in a closed or unventilated room caused very bad headaches. The mix was then placed in a container, a box or suitcase. To explode the mixture required a fuse, connected to a detonator, to be ignited. For this you took sugar, sulfuric acid and magnesium—magnesium became highly flammable in contact with acid. The acid was sealed within a wax container, then placed within a balloon, though two balloons, one inside the other, or better still a condom, was to prove a more reliable device, giving the bomber a good ten to fifteen minutes or so to escape. The bomb was now complete, but inert. To activate it one had only to squeeze the balloon, breaking the wax container, to let the acid leach out. This would eat through the rubber, and coming into contact with the magnesium would flare up, melting the sugar compound surrounding the fuse, which being ignited, would travel in seconds to the detonator, which in turn exploded the device.

Once trained, these core volunteers in their turn instructed others. Joe Collins recalled the training: "I had a call from Stephen Hayes asking me to meet him in the Castle Hotel where I was instructed to attend a training class at a premises [the Green Lounge behind the Home Market shop] in Stephen's Green. Our instructor there was Paddy McGrath who was an expert in explosives. Paddy, a 1916 veteran, was later to be executed by the Free State. There were four classes each day, each lasting for about three hours, and there were anything up to nine men at every class. The training was very thorough."[5] There were also classes out in the country, as Sean Talty related to Uinseann MacEoin: "The camp was on the north side of Benumbing [County Sligo], with hazel wood all around and an empty house where we had our meals. There were 50 men in the camp: John Joe McGirl, a fresh faced blonde youngster; Micky Traynor, a low set, sheet metal worker from Belfast; Sean McCaughey, tall dark and handsome; Dick Mulready from Mullingar, a violin player; Willie Joe McCorry of Belfast, and many more. Peadar O'Flaherty was there too, in charge of it. He was a good O.C., insisting on strict discipline; a bit extreme in that he allowed no half measures. We learned all about explosives in the camp; how to make Paxo, wire up detonators, electric coils, potassium chlorate and balloons. In the camp you learned everything off by heart as though you were back at school."[6]

Christy Quearney trained men in his own home: "I was training men of the Dublin Brigade and was Company Training Officer, and I was lecturing on the making of Paxo and timing devices, such as they were then, and setting off a series of small demonstration explosions. Looking back now it was all really amateurish. The training took place wherever we could, even in my own house, although it was known to the police. Jimmy O'Hanlon, who had been a member of the Second Battalion, was known because of his expertise, as the Paxo king. E Company, Second Battalion, was an engineering company under Pearse McLaughlin. He knew all about explosives, after the blowing up of the George 2nd statue in Stephen's Green in late 1938 as a dry run for the campaign in England. He left for England in October 1938 prior to the campaign commencing."[7]

There were also training classes in London. Leo Duignan, who had arrived in England in January 1938, was seconded to an IRA company in North Acton, under the command of Jack Lynch. He remained a "sleeper" until the autumn of 1938, when he was summoned for training one night a week in the construction of bombs. Not long after he was joined in the classes by newly arrived Willie McGuinness, former OC in Dublin, Mick Fleming, Mick O'Leary, Tony Magan and Peter Walsh.

Belfast-born Harry White joined another team based in London. He recalled that one Sunday afternoon they were summoned for an explosives class held in Hyde Park. It was the only time all of them could meet, and there was nowhere else they could meet. There they sat in the autumn sunshine quite blatantly, on a bench and upon the grass, with Londoners milling all around them, learning how to make "Paxo," from paraffin wax and gelignite. The principal unit, as they were then, consisted of Lanty Hannigan, a Limerick man who was O.C.; Joe Dillon, his adjutant; Belfast-born Dominic Adams, the engineer; Gina Halfpenny from Dundalk; and Ned Stapleton, a London-born Irishman with an English accent. There was another Belfast man, Albert Price, based in Coventry, along with Gerry Kerr, Frankie Duffy, Albert McNally and Maggie Nolan, who became the principal courier.

With final preparations in hand, Russell, accompanied by Stephen Hayes of IRA GHQ, slipped quietly into England for an inspection trip. They met up with Jack Lynch, a County Cork man who had been a "sleeper" in England from 1937. He had adopted the pseudonym of Buckley. They confirmed for themselves that everything was ready. Explosives and chemicals had been collected in safe houses, and targets had been identified. Senior IRA men Moss Twomey and Jack McNeela were less sure. In the summer of 1938 they too toured England and Scotland, inspecting the units. They came away with the opinion that these units were weak and inexperienced, but felt duty bound in loyalty to Russell to soldier on.

Following his return to Ireland, Russell held a staff meeting with representatives of Northern Command, and it was agreed that northern units would run a preliminary try-out in the Six Counties, targeting British customs posts. In late November, bombs prepared in the south were moved up to the border in suitcases. The time for the attacks was set for the night of 28 November. Jimmy Joe Reynolds, a staff captain who had briefly been O.C. in Britain, and Ulstermen John James Kelly and Charles McCafferty, primed their bombs in the back room of the home of Kelly's brother Patrick, at Castlefin on the Donegal border. Their targets were to be the customs huts at Strabane and Clady. Paddy pointed out at the last minute that the bomb primed to go off at Strabane would go off just as local people were passing by on their return from the local cinema at Lifford, thus endangering their lives. So Reynolds agreed to adjust the time on the timing device. Then something went wrong. The Strabane bomb detonated prematurely. The explosion within the confined space of the cottage killed Reynolds and McCafferty, and the force of the explosion propelled Kelly through the collapsing wall. He lingered for several days before dying. In his delirium he kept repeating Reynolds's final words, "Stand back John James—there's a wee mistake!" Other customs posts along the border were successfully attacked that night, but the incident at Castlefin indicated that there were still problems with bomb construction.

Reynolds was buried in Cloonmorris Cemetery, Bornacoola, County Leitrim. Irish Special Branch men under Superintendent Glynn, and armed with Thompson sub-machine guns, surrounded the cemetery to prevent an IRA firing party from giving a last salute. Nevertheless, mingling with the crowd, the color party of six men under the command of James McCormack[8] of Mullingar entered the cemetery and fired off three rounds from their rifles before retreating across the fields and along the railway to a safe place where they hid their rifles and short arms. Soon after, using the alias of James Richards, McCormack departed for Coventry to play his part in the bombing campaign.

Six weeks before the launch of the campaign, the Army Council met in Dublin. Mairtin O'Cadhain, Dublin OC, tried to have the campaign postponed on the grounds that the IRA in England was unready. The plans were too advanced to stop now, though. O'Cadhain was outvoted, and resigned from the Council. He was replaced by a Russell supporter, Willie McGuinness. At the meeting Russell and the other five members voted to go ahead with the bombing campaign.

With the attack on the border posts, the RUC were convinced that the IRA was about to launch a major bombing campaign in Northern Ireland. They launched an investigation. Since the loss of their two key informants, information was scant. The list of known IRA activists was updated, and then on 22 December, the RUC made a mass arrest of all known suspects under the Special Powers Act. Those arrested were taken to Crumlin Road Prison and interned without trial for an indefinite period. The government of Northern Ireland hoped that the mass arrest had disrupted the campaign. The campaign, though, was not directed against Northern Ireland, but rather at England herself, and the Ulster men and women who mattered were already in England. There was some inclination in New Scotland Yard, headquarters of the British police in London, that something was going to happen, but nothing concrete. Sir Norman Kendal, Assistant Commissioner of the Metropolitan Police, and head of Special Branch, wrote, "During 1937 and 1938 informants within the Irish Republican

Army gave warning that the movement was being revivified and reorganized in preparation for an attack on Britain, aiming at forcing the fusion of Northern Ireland with Eire, and of the complete separation of the latter from the Empire."[9]

Newly appointed Willie McGuinness had been sent over to London some time earlier to form a new battalion staff there. McGuinness was a small, dapper man who dressed like an English bank clerk, complete with a briefcase. He stayed at "good class" hotels, which gave him a degree of immunity. His very "presence" gave him further immunity. He simply did not look, or behave, like a terrorist bomber. Just before Christmas twelve trained IRA men made the journey over to Britain to join the regional OCs already there. Three, Charles Casey, Seamus McGuinness and Eoin MacNamee, were sent to London; three others, Joe Deighan, Gerard Quigley and Michael Cleary, were sent to Liverpool. Jackie Kearns and Sean Fuller went to Birmingham and Coventry; Rory Campbell and Patrick Fleming to Manchester, and Peter Walsh and Sam O'Kennedy to Glasgow. At least three of these men were born in Britain and had English or Scottish accents. One of them from London, Charles Casey, had a broad Cockney accent. Perhaps this is why some of them were chosen: their ability to more easily blend in.

As the final preparations got underway, Russell contacted the surviving members of the Second Dail, which Parliament had elected prior to the Truce in the war against Britain. He sought their sanction for the IRA to declare war against Britain. Their acquiescence was confirmed in a public announcement in the *Wolfe Tone Weekly* (8 December 1938), where they, the remaining members of the Second Dail, transferred the right to establish a Republican government to the Army Council of the IRA. In reality they had no right to do so, as they no longer had that power. The Second Dail met on 30 June 1922 to dissolve itself and formally transfer powers to the Third Dail—the Free State Dail.

Russell then called an extraordinary general meeting of the Army Convention, whose 50 delegates reaffirmed their support for him. On 12 January 1939 a formal ultimatum was sent to British Foreign Secretary, Lord Halifax:

Your Excellency,
I have the honor to inform you that the Government of the Irish Republic, having as its first duty towards its people the establishment and maintenance of peace and order here, demand the withdrawal of all British armed forces stationed in Ireland. These forces are an active incitement to turmoil and civil strife, not alone in being a symbol of hostile occupation, but in their effect

and potentialities as an invading army. It is secondly the duty of the Government to establish relations of friendship between the Irish and all other peoples and to achieve this we must insist upon the withdrawal of British troops from our country and a declaration from your Government renouncing all claim to interfere in its domestic policy or external affairs. The Irish people have no cause of hostility to any European nation, even those nations whose natural development may bring them into conflict with British interests, and we are desirous of making it clear that we shall in no event take part in a war of aggression against any people or permit the nation to be regarded as having any community or identity of interest with Britain that would make us liable to attack by British enemies. The occupation of our territory by troops of another nation and the persistent subvention here of activities directly against the expressed national will and in the interests of a foreign power, prevent the expansion and development of our institution in consonance with our social needs and purposes, and must cease. Neither the Government of the Irish Republic nor the Irish people are actuated by any feelings of hostility to the people of Britain. Rather would we welcome a better understanding but this can be brought about only on the basis that each of the two peoples is absolutely free to pursue its own course unhampered by the other. We shall regret if this fundamental condition is ignored and we are compelled to intervene actively in the military or commercial life of your country as your government are now interfering in ours. The Government of the Irish Republic believe that a period of four days is sufficient notice for your government to signify its intentions in the matter of the military evacuation and for the issue of your Declaration of Abdication in respect of our country. Our Government reserve the right of appropriate action without further notice if upon the expiration of this period of grace, these conditions remain unfulfilled.

Signed on behalf of
The Republican Government and the Army
Council of Oglaigh na h-Eireann
(Irish Republican Army)

Stephen Hayes Patrick Fleming
Peadar O'Flaherty George Plunkett
Lawrence Grogan Sean Russell.

What to make of it? Lord Halifax consulted with his senior civil servants. A telephone call to Dublin brought the reassurance that de Valera's government had not declared war. Walter Tricker, the Foreign Office Clerk, filed the letter away as the work of some crank.

On Sunday, 15 January, the four days having expired, an IRA proclamation was posted throughout Ireland calling for the support of the people in the complete withdrawal of the British from Ireland. Dubliner Chris Quearney of the IRA 2nd Battalion in that city relates, "The Campaign started with a small size proclamation stuck on every lamp post on January 12, 1939. We were out at four and five in the morning reporting to the

1. The Campaign Is Launched

Hardwicke Hall [home to the youth wing of the IRA, Fianna Eireann]. George Plunkett was there, as he was a signatory to the proclamation. Recruiting became very intense at the start of the Campaign, and we rapidly acquired fine volunteers some of whom became very good officers. We had special classes arranged for potential officers. Things went well in England at the commencement, although as a concerted effort it was not on. Our lads were short of money and materials; at the same time they could not hold down jobs through having become known, so they had to be constantly on the move."[10]

On the evening before the notice was issued, an attempt was made to blow up Nelson's Column, in central Dublin, as a prelude to the campaign. Peadar O'Flaherty, allegedly Russell's right-hand man, along with Joseph Deighan and one or two others, walked down O'Connell Street to the column. As the thoroughfare would be crowded, their intention was to climb the spiral staircase to the top, place the gelignite around the statue and withdraw, telephoning the police in enough time for them to cordon off the area. Arriving at the pillar, they found that O'Flaherty had forgotten to check that it closed earlier on Saturdays during the winter months. Such lack of planning did not bode well for a successful campaign.

Two days later, on Monday, 16 January 1939, the bombs started to go off. There were seven major explosions on power stations and electrical lines. There were three in the London area; an overhead electricity cable close to Willesdon power station was badly damaged, there was an explosion outside the control room of Southwark power station and the Enfield arms factory was left without power. There were two in greater Manchester, one near Birmingham and one in Alnwick in Northumberland. Over half a million pounds' worth of damage was caused on that first night and early morning. The first explosion occurred at an isolated spot near Alnwick at 5 a.m. The bomb exploded under an electricity pylon, causing it to tilt, but not fall, thus failing to cut off the electricity supply. The sound of the explosion was heard five miles away.

At 5:48 a.m. there was a large explosion heard throughout Crosby, in north Liverpool. It was not until the following day that the cause of the explosion was discovered. Two fifteen-year-old boys playing in a field near the Leeds to Liverpool Canal discovered the remains of the bomb near an electricity pylon. One of the legs had been completely blown off and the others damaged by the blast, which had created a hole six feet deep. Besides the pylon the boys discovered a charred attaché case with a small blue alarm clock in it. The pylon carried the main electricity line between Liverpool, Warrington and Manchester on one side, and that of Liverpool,

Preston and Scotland on the other. Though badly damaged, the pylon had not been toppled.

At 6 a.m. there were three major explosions in the London area at Willesdon, Harlesdon and Southwark, where the Electricity Board's control room was damaged. The explosion created a large crater in the forecourt of the building. There were no casualties and the control station was reportedly undamaged. At Willesdon the explosion damaged an overhead cable running from the Grand Union Canal to Willesdon Power Station.

In Manchester, at the junction of Newton Street and Hilton Street, a bomb placed in an electricity manhole exploded. Albert Ross, a fish porter who was passing, was killed instantly in the explosion. This was the thing that Tom Barry had most feared: the accidental loss of innocent life. A second bomb exploded outside Williams Deacon's Bank in nearby Whitworth Street.

At Ham's Hall, Coleshill, near Birmingham, an unexploded bomb was found in one of the power station's cooling towers, and a second was found at Clarence Dock in Liverpool. At a power station at Windle in Lancashire an unexploded bomb, later disarmed, was taken away for forensic study. A fingerprint on the alarm clock was later identified as belonging to Michael Cleary, alias Mason. On the first day alone, over half a million pounds' worth of damage was caused. The attacks came as a complete surprise to Special Branch in London. They had been assured by Special Branch in Northern Ireland that the IRA, thanks to their pre-emptive strike, had been nullified.

On the following day at Barton-upon-Irwell in Lancashire an attempt was made to demolish an electricity pylon stretching across the Manchester Ship Canal. A faulty timer prevented the explosion. In greater Birmingham a second attempt was made on Ham's Hall Power Station, and bombs did explode, but failed to cause any significant damage. At Wilderness Lane, Great Barr, northwest Birmingham, a bomb severely damaged an electricity pylon, cutting off the supply for a number of hours. That same day in the early hours, a bomb exploded in the capital, at Williams Deacon's Bank, causing disruption to the gas mains. In response an all-out alert was sounded. All power stations, gas works, telephone exchanges, and radio transmitters nationwide were put under police guard. All ports serving Ireland were closely monitored by Special Branch and the CID.

At six o'clock on the morning of 18 January, armed Special Branch officers, aided by the CID and other police units, simultaneously raided the homes of known IRA men and those whose names and addresses had appeared in the address book previously found in the lodgings of the house in Dagenham. Jack Logue, Frank Burns and Dan Fitzpatrick were arrested by Detective Inspector Keeble, Detective Sergeant McDougall, and a police back-up team, at their lodgings in Mornington Crescent, Camden Town. In the house were found 88 sticks of gelignite, detonators and fuse wire. At the home of Lawrence Lyons, in Roundwood Road, Willesdon, rented in the name of Turner, Inspector William Rogers and Sergeant Covney found a 6mm rifle and 24 rounds of ammunition. Lyons himself was then traced to his place of work, at a building site near Dartford in Kent, where he was arrested. At the lodgings of James Lyons in Petherton Street, Islington, the police discovered 4 drums of aluminum powder. Brendon Kane, a butcher's rounds man, was arrested by Inspector Newton at his lodgings in Harold Road, Sutton. In his possession they found a Mauser automatic pistol. Joseph Casey, employed as a porter, was arrested by Inspector Frank Bridges. He had two Colt revolvers and a Mauser pistol with 70 rounds. He also had a letter from Gerald Wharton who lived in Camden Road. The letter, dated May 1938, read, "Owing to unforeseen circumstances I regret I will be unable to accept the position of T/O suggested at the last CC meeting. Meantime it is not advisable to arrange any further meetings at the above address as I shall be there only at irregular hours for some months." A back-up team headed by Inspector Thompson and Sergeant Evan Jones drove over to Wharton's lodgings, where they arrested him and recovered a large quantity of potassium chlorate, iron oxide, and more than 100 balloons. Each of the items could be explained away, but the combination of all three suggested bomb making. Of the balloons, Wharton, a scaffolder by trade, allegedly claimed that they were leftover decorations from Christmas. There were rather a lot. Thompson did not believe him.

In Manchester the Special Branch there met with equal success. Superintendent Page, heading up the raiding parties, arrested Michael Rory Campbell and Patrick O'Connell at a house in Alexandra Road. They found documents relating to the IRA, and maps of Greater Manchester on which were marked police stations, fire stations, military barracks and railway stations. At Parkfield Street, Rusholme, Special Branch officers arrested Patrick Deviney and Jackie Glenn. Here they found copies of IRA Battalion orders and other incriminating papers. In all seven suspects were arrested. Forty sticks of gelignite, six one-hundredweight barrels of sodium chlorate, and three incendiary bombs packed in matchboxes were recovered.

Over the next few days Special Branch followed a paper trail of names and addresses garnered from the earlier arrests. On 21 January, Manchester police raided a shop in Dryden Street, Chorlton-on-Medlock, an inner city neighborhood. Here they found a barrel of potassium chlorate, 49 sticks of gelignite, two Mills bombs, ten detonators, an alarm clock and compromising papers. Mary Glenn, a young woman of 22 who returned to the shop while the search was in progress, was arrested, as was her younger sister Nora, aged 15. The papers led to the arrest of John Gavahan of Mahony Street, Chorlton-on-Medlock; Joseph Broderick of Tintern Street, Salford; Denis Duggan of Dunstall Road, Wythenshawe; and finally Patrick Walsh of Ogalvie Street, under whose bed the police discovered a number of sealed barrels of potassium chlorate.

Four days later, on 25 January, officers of the Metropolitan Police Force, led by Detective Inspector Sidney Barnes, went to the house of Michael O'Shea at Clewer Crescent, Harrow Weald. O'Shea was arrested following the discovery of a firearm and a considerable amount of IRA correspondence, including a copy of the S-Plan. This was a major breakthrough in understanding the IRA mindset. By analyzing the plan they could second-guess what institutions the IRA might target. Later that day Detective Inspector Baker arrested John Mitchell, a garage mechanic, at Whiteside Road, Brentford.

At his lodgings in Cambridge Street, Pimlico, the IRA's London O.C., Patrick Fleming, alias Michael Preston, was arrested by Inspector Tansley and Sergeant Cooper. In the flat Special Branch discovered handguns, a ton of potassium chlorate, electric wiring, and clocks that had been modified for use as explosive timing devices His lodgings contained a wealth of paperwork. The police discovered three cipher keys labeled "GHQ only," "OC Britain only," and "For Units in Britain." When decoded, one sent message read, "Send immediately a report of all explosives and material in your area, i.e. potash, fuses, detonators (electrical and commercial), gelignite and galvanometers." Other papers included chemical details of explosives, locations of targets, including a detailed advanced plan for an attack on a power station at Brimsdown in North London, and papers relating to his position within the IRA. He also had 50 Post Office envelopes, 77 sheets of notepaper headed H.M. Government, and other official notepaper.

They found another name and address: John Healy, proprietor of the Irish Club in Kilburn High Road. Armed officers under Detective Inspector Buckle raided the club and Healy's home address in Fordington Road, West Hampstead. Here they found two tons of potassium chlorate and a ton of iron oxide. There was also a letter, dated 11 January 1939. It was addressed to the "Commandant, London Unit."

Special Branch were convinced that Preston was in fact Patrick Fleming, one of the men who had signed the declaration of war sent to Lord

Halifax. They sent to Ireland, and a Garda sergeant was sent from Killarney to identify him. For whatever reason, the Irish policeman could not—or would not—identify him. So Fleming stood trial as Michael Preston, and was sentenced to 12 years' imprisonment.

On 28 January, Peter Walsh, alias Stuart, was arrested by Detective Inspector Whitehead, at his lodgings in New Oxford Street, not far from the British Museum. Walsh, IRA Quartermaster in Britain, was traced through an incriminating invoice found at Fleming's address. It was for a typewriter which Fleming had purchased for delivery to Walsh's address. Three days after Fleming's arrest, Walsh, very wary that he too might be arrested, approached his lodgings with unease. He walked past them twice, looking up towards his rooms, but could see no signs of activity. As he entered the door to his flat he found himself confronting an armed Special Branch officer. Other armed policemen then materialized from several directions, and he was led away. The police found 39 sticks of gelignite, a 40-lb. drum of aluminum powder, 11 packets of a whitish powder, four

The tobacconist shop in Edge Lane, Liverpool. In the rooms above, the IRA stored explosive chemicals.

electric detonators, 654 rubber balloons, and a Royal Air Force uniform. Among his papers were instructions from Michael Cleary, alias Michael Mason, O.C. in Britain, written from an address in Liverpool. The orders in one of the letters stated, "If you think an operation cannot be carried out without men being arrested or civilians killed you are at liberty to call the operation off." This at least conformed with the instructions of the S-Plan lately discovered. The attacks were against property and not civilians.

Following an urgent telephone call to Liverpool, Special Branch raided the address in Great Nelson Street and there arrested Michael Cleary (alias Mason) and Joseph Walker. In their room the police discovered six electrical cables. Among Cleary's possessions was found a letter about to be sent to Sean Russell.[11] The two men were taken down to London on 7 February for interrogation at Scotland Yard. More names and addresses were found, leading the police to go to the confectioner and tobacconist shop of Thomas Edward Kelly, in Edge Lane, Liverpool. Here they found four barrels of potassium chlorate. Kelly claimed that he had been storing the barrels for two men who had paid him five shillings to do so. He had no idea what the barrels contained. At his subsequent trial, held at the Liverpool Police Court on 7 February, the jury believed him, and he was set free. Also caught up in the Liverpool raid were Peter Matthew Dowley, James Hannan, and his sons, Patrick and John Joseph. Papers at Hannan's shop led the police to a locked-up garage in nearby Lilley Road. Here they discovered an arsenal of explosive chemicals, including large amounts of potassium chlorate, iron oxide, sulfuric acid, gelignite, detonators and ammunition. Of these four, only John Joseph Hannan was found guilty, on the evidence of grains of explosive in the turnups of his trousers.

Leading on from the raid on Patrick Fleming's home, an address in Cardiff was discovered. It was the premises of Timothy Dacey, who owned a cycle shop in the Welsh capital. Welsh Special Branch visited the premises, where a search, on 28 January, revealed 20 sticks of gelignite and 16 detonators. At the Glamorgan Assize in March 1939, Dacey received 7 years for possessing explosives.

As Special Branch in London trawled through the paperwork that they had seized, more names and addresses were discovered. Papers seized from Peter Walsh threw up the names of Molly Gallagher and Margaret Edgeworth, who lived in Thornhill Square, Barnsbury, a road enclosing a small park and recreation ground. On 10 February the house was searched and Molly Gallagher, who was at home at the time, was arrested when the police discovered two hold-alls of potassium chlorate. Amongst her papers was an address book which included the name and address of Peter Walsh.

Underage, she was given three years in Borstal, a young offenders' open prison. Margaret Edgeworth, who was not at home, escaped back to Dublin.

At a house in Sixth Avenue, Manor Park, an armed team led by Detective Sergeant Arthur Cain arrested Charles McCarthy and his two sons Thomas and Daniel. In the house they found two tins of detonators, timing devices and nearly one hundred balloons. Charles's daughter protested the innocence of her father and brother Thomas, denouncing Daniel as a member of the IRA. In a simultaneous operation the police also raided a house in Ashmore Road, Paddington. Here Detective Inspector Bridges found traces of aluminum powder in two drums stored in the basement. The occupant, John Ryan, was arrested. He was tried and found guilty of possessing explosive substances and was sentenced to eighteen months.

On the 18th, Detective Sergeant Fretwell, with armed back-up, went to a flat at an address in Hargrave Park, North London. There they found Francis McGowan and James Patrick Connolly. Under McGowan's bed was found a carpetbag. The bag, when opened, was found to contain 9 brown paper parcels. The parcels contained a whitish-gray powder. Four of them contained lengths of magnesium tape. There was also a hot water bottle which contained turpentine.

The police had made a clean sweep, or so it appeared. Forty-six people were arrested. By routine police work, following the trail of evidence, they had rounded up the perpetrators of the terrorist explosions and their associates. The arrests resulted in the successful conviction of 33 of the 46; 18 people in the Central Criminal Court in London, 10 in Manchester, 3 in Birmingham, and 2 in Cardiff. This represented over 40 percent of known IRA members in these major cities. The first sentences to be handed down by a British court was at Falkirk in Scotland in February 1939. Terence J. McSherry from North Leitrim received 10 years' penal servitude for conspiracy to steal explosives and for actually possessing explosive substances. His conspirator, Samuel Kennedy, received 5 years for conspiracy to steal explosives. If the police had followed up the Scottish connection, the source of explosive substances for the bombing campaign in England, the campaign could have been severely restricted if not stopped.

There were some in Republican circles who believed that the campaign had been betrayed by an informer. Tom Byrnes, a member of the old Liverpool Brigade of the IRA, claimed that it was betrayed by "a Dublin man, a fellow called O'Neill, who they said was responsible, but I wouldn't know." In truth it was down to good policing. Special Branch had identified the principal IRA players in England long before the campaign had begun.

Once the bombs started going off, the police simply watched and waited until the bombers made direct or indirect contact with the resident IRA, then they pounced. One senior Special Branch officer was to write, "The work of the authorities in tracking down the terrorists was considerably facilitated by the carelessness which the latter displayed in the custody of secret documents.... In one instance a coded message and the cypher key were left in the same drawer."[12]

The contents of the S-Plan were potentially troubling. A copy was sent to Cecil Liddell of MI5's Irish Section. It was far more sophisticated than the usual IRA literature. The reference to a predicted outbreak of war led him to believe that it might have been prepared other than in Ireland. To Liddell it read like a German General Staff plan. Were the Nazis involved? Would the IRA act as a fifth column against Britain? MI5 began to look for a German connection. Newly established liaison between British and Irish Intelligence confirmed such a connection. Liddell discovered that links had been established between the IRA and the Abwehr by James O'Donovan.

The rest of the month of January was quiet. There were no further bombings that month. This led the authorities to believe that the campaign was over. But they were wrong. For the rest of the month, as IRA GHQ had planned, nothing happened. It was to be a time for reflection; a time for consideration. The campaign was far from over . It was to become a war of nerves.

2

More Bombs

With so many men arrested, mainly because of someone's incompetence in providing the police with paper trails, the surviving organizers were obliged to call for more volunteers. While attempts were made to provide the new recruits with safe houses and dumps, they were largely thrown back on their own initiatives to make what provisions they could to continue the campaign. Cells were supplied with bomb-making equipment by the regional O.C.s, but it was the operatives who had to find places to store the material. Some made contact with the local Irish community, but this involved compromise and risk. Storing explosives in their digs and bed-sits was often the only alternative, but this could lead to discovery by nosy landladies. How the 16-year-old Brendan Behan was discovered at his Everton lodgings was not made clear by him in his colorful autobiography, *Borstal Boy*, but discovered he was:

> Friday, in the evening, the landlady shouted up the stair: "Oh God, oh Jesus, oh Sacred Heart. Boy, there's two gentlemen to see you." I knew by the screeches of her that these gentlemen were not calling to inquire after my health, or to know if I had a good trip. I grabbed my suitcase, containing Pot. Chlor, Sulph Ac, gelignite detonators, electrical and ignition, and the rest of my Sinn Fein conjurers outfit, and carried it to the window. Then the gentlemen arrived.
> A young one, with blonde Herrenvolk head and a BBC accent shouted, "I say, greb him, the bestud."[1]

Of the incident, Dan Keating related to Uinseann MacEoin: "I was sent briefly on a message to meet Brendan Behan, who had only arrived over, in Liverpool. I was to meet him in Castle Street, but when I got there I realized there was a lot of police activity; I kept going anyway, wheeled around the corner into the next street and took the first train back to London. I knew he was caught; it was easy catching Behan because he could not keep his mouth shut."² In truth, even at the early age of 16, Behan had a drinking problem which caused him to boast of his abilities.

Harry White, in his biography, summoned up all the uncertainties facing the Volunteers:

> Sean Russell or Seamus Donovan who inspired the S plan could never have foreseen the claustrophobic conditions working over a gas cooker in a crowded doss house with prying landladies, to which we would be exposed. On top of that, supplies of explosives were irregular and uncertain. You took your life in your hand going to a call house, or even attempting from your own meagre resources to buy the components, suitcases, balloons, or alarm clocks. A mere inquiry with an Irish accent after these in a shop—it is not like now where articles are on open display upon supermarket shelves—was enough to set the alarm bells going. In the face of difficulties like these it was inevitable that casualties would be high. In the end those who got back to Ireland were the lucky ones; half of our active personnel were caught, and were imprisoned for long terms.³

Despite these setbacks for the IRA, there were now sufficient people in England to continue the campaign. Leo Duignan, who had remained a "sleeper" since his arrival in England, was now activated. His team consisted of Jim McGuinness, Mick Griffin, Pearse McLaughlin, Sean Keane, Paddy Earley, Harold Bridges and Peter Campbell. Duignan and Griffin were the bomb makers, and McLaughlin was the wire man who connected up the bombs. Early on the morning of Saturday, 4 February, two major bombs exploded in the left luggage offices of Tottenham Court Road and Leicester Square Underground Stations in London. The IRA were back. Time bombs concealed in suitcases had been left overnight. Though there were no fatalities, the explosions seriously injured two people and caused considerable damage. The ASU had less success when they attempted to blow up a cable bridge on the Grand Union Canal at Harlesdon, West London. If they had succeeded they would have flooded the immediate area, knocking out the electricity supply. The bomb blew outwards, doing little damage.

In Liverpool that same day, an unsuccessful attempt was made to blow up an outer wall of Walton Jail. Tom Byrne, in an interview with David O'Donaghue in July 2001, mentioned the attack: "We got away with things considering we tried to blow up—Jesus, when you think of it now—the wall in Walton jail because there were a couple of IRA fellows there. Our job was to blow a hole in the wall so they could get out. We did not realize the fecking walls were about that thick. All we succeeded in doing was to make a little hole in it. We did not get caught."

Another daring scheme was the proposal to bomb the ocean liner *Queen Mary*, then in dry dock pending her maiden voyage. As a clerk with the shipping company F.J. Callaghan and Company, suppliers to the Cunard line, young IRA volunteer Tom Byrne had access to the nine miles of docks in Liverpool. His proposal, which would have generated international interest if it had succeeded, was never taken up.

More concerning to the authorities, possibly, was a report in the *Times* that new plans had been discovered following an RUC raid on a suspected IRA house in Belfast. The plans related to an intended attack on Buckingham Palace, the London residence of the King and Queen. Security there was increased, and regular searches instigated. Protection in the grounds and castle at Windsor, another royal residence, was also stepped up. All visitors to the state apartments at Windsor and St. George's Chapel nearby were stopped and searched. At the Palace of Westminster, the home of the British Parliament, armed police were added to the normal strength. The same occurred at the Tower of London, where the crown jewels were housed. Both buildings had previously been targets at the time of the Fenian bombing campaign in the 1880s.

In February, Special Branch in London struck lucky. They identified a house in connection with the Underground explosions. It was the home of Sean Keane and his wife in Camden Town. The house was placed under surveillance. The police watched and waited. Leo Duignan, then living in Fulham, turned up at the house to remove explosive materials. Living with the Keanes were IRA men Willie McGuinness, Mick O'Leary and Tony Magan. As he left, Duignan was followed to the lodgings of Peter Campbell in Hammersmith. The police pounced on both addresses and arrested the occupants. There was an unforgivable paper trail which led on to the arrest of others: Pierce "Jim" McGuinness, Pearse McLoughlin and Jack Daly, as well as Jack Healey, a painting contractor who was able to acquire many of the ingredients in the normal course of his work. Another, Harry White, was lucky: he was not at home when the police raided his lodgings. White went on the run, finding new lodgings in Lambeth. Though he was never sure, White suspected that a fellow Belfast man had been followed to his new flat in Lambeth. As he approached it one afternoon someone dropped a heavy wet cloth from a balcony onto the ground just before him. As he looked up a woman leaned over the balcony and quietly warned him that the police were waiting for him in his new lodgings. He turned and walked away. Of those arrested in the February swoop, Jack Keane was able to persuade the authorities that his wife was innocent, and Jim McGuinness, who after arguing his case with considerable skill before the Recorder, Sir Gerald Dobson, was released. For the remainder, though, there was the prospect of long prison sentences.

In Coventry, early on the morning of 5 February, there were fires in four department stores: Marks & Spencers, Owen & Owen, Montague Burton the tailors, and Woolworths. The fires were the result of delayed-action incendiary devices laid the previous day. To stretch police resources further, notes were received regarding future IRA targets. The oil refinery at Bristol was mentioned, as was Bow Street Police Station with its magistrate's court. While these letters may have been the work of cranks, the police could not take the risk. Uniformed policemen were deployed as a visual deterrents. On Thursday, 9 February, two bombs exploded at Kings Cross railway station in London.

Incendiary attacks continued. In late February the IRA set fire to the Rosslare-to-Fishguard ferryboat, *St. David*. The three IRA men involved were Tom Costelloe, Garrett Cotter and Tad Drummond. They made use of a rugby excursion to Wales to set off their bombs, mingling with the supporters on the journey. They traveled with some girls from Tralee to avoid suspicion, and in the process carried a radio transmitter over to England. The group were stopped by the police, who were more concerned with controlling the surge of noisy supporters. Clearing Fishguard, they continued on to London by train. Returning that night from Paddington Station, they met up again with a crowd of rugby supporters, now making their way home. At the dock they heard of the fires that had broken out, but had been extinguished before too much damage was done. They returned safely to Ireland.

On 2 March the attacks resumed. A bomb exploded on an aqueduct of the Grand Union Canal near Stonebridge Park in northeast London. In what was obviously a concerted attack, a bomb exploded in a culvert under the Birmingham Canal Navigations, in Wednesbury in the Black Country. Though the aqueduct and culvert were damaged, the explosions were insufficient to completely destroy the two structures. By the late 1930s, the canals, though largely superseded by the railways, still remained a vital organ of the British transport network. On the night of 3 March in Willesdon, not far from Kilburn, an Irish quarter in west London, railway man Harry West prevented an explosion on a railway bridge. On the 4th there were four cases of incendiarism in Birmingham, and on the 8th, back in Willesdon in London, an unexploded bomb was found at a Central Electricity Board junction box. There was more incendiarism back in the Midlands when delayed action firebombs destroyed two railway carriages of an express train on the Wolverhampton-to-Euston (London) line on the 11 March. Then everything went quiet again.

As people began turning on their Irish neighbors, people they had known for years, in the belief that they, being Irish, they must be supporting the bombers, the London-based newspaper *Irish Freedom* (March 1939) summed up the opinion of the majority of Irish people living in England with the front-page banner headline, "BOMBINGS CANNOT WIN UNITED IRELAND." The paper went on to proclaim, "The cause of the Irish Republic, the struggle to end Partition and achieve Ireland's unity and independence ... can never be achieved by the methods of terrorism. This policy is based on the erroneous theory that terrorist acts can serve as a substitute for mass political action."

The trial of the first nine prisoners arrested after the swoop of 18 January, was announced for the 23 March. On the night before, a car exploded in a Birmingham street, setting fire to a house nearby. It would appear that the car was to be used to transport a bomb that exploded prematurely. On the day of the start of the trial, explosions occurred throughout the day in London, Birmingham, Liverpool and Coventry. In London there were five explosions at wholesale food markets, telephone and gas installations, and the newspaper premises of the *News Chronicle* in Fleet Street, in the heart of the city. In Coventry there were four explosions, at Cheylesmore, Quinton, Gosford Green and Coundon Road. Craters were blown in the pavements. While there was no serious personal injury, 600 telephone lines—about one tenth of the whole city's communications—were put temporarily out of order.

The first explosion in Coventry occurred at 7:15 a.m. at Cheylesmore. Smoke started billowing out of a telephone inspection chamber in the footpath. Soon afterwards there was a deafening roar as bricks, concrete and fragments of the iron cover were flung into the air, causing damage to factories and houses over a radius of several hundred yards. At 10 a.m. came the second explosion, a quarter of a mile away in Quinton Road, when again an inspection cover blew up, causing damage to surrounding property. Barely had the police begun an inspection of the site when a third explosion occurred. This was outside the Corporation's electricity substation in Gulson Road opposite Gosford Green. Again it originated beneath a telephone inspection chamber. The cover of the chamber, a four-foot length of concrete and iron, was flung into the air, and falling in Gosford Green, imbedded itself several feet into the ground. At 11:30 a.m. the fourth explosion occurred at the corner of Barras Lane and Coundon Road. Arriving there, the police discovered that another crater had been blown in the footpath. A large part of the inspection cover had hurtled through the air and into the roof of the nearby presbytery and housekeeper's bedroom of St. Osburg's Roman Catholic church. The housekeeper was very lucky: she had left the room barely moments before the explosion. A Corporation bus which was passing nearby had its windows blown out. Some passengers suffered minor cuts.

The police appealed for witnesses. Mr. L.B. Steadman, proprietor of the Swift skating rink, at the site of the first explosion, went to the police. He reported: "I locked up my premises somewhat earlier than usual last night. It was about a quarter to 12, and as I left I noticed a saloon car with dim lights draw up at the entrance to Cheylesmore car park. Two men got out, but immediately jumped back into the car as I stepped out into the middle of the pavement. I hesitated about informing the police because their actions seemed to me somewhat suspicious, but in the end I decided to go home."[4] Another witness, a woman living in Friars Road, also later reported seeing two men behaving suspiciously, but she did nothing either.

The trial of the first nine prisoners arrested on or after 18 January, took place at the Central Criminal Court, or the Old Bailey as it is more popularly known, before Mr. Justice Travers Humphreys. Humphreys was perhaps not entirely unbiased. He had served as junior counsel to Sir Edward Carson in the prosecution of Sir Roger Casement following the failure of the Easter Rising back in 1916. Casement was hanged. During the Irish War of Independence, Humphreys was a prosecuting counsel at Courts Martial in Dublin, where those IRA men found guilty were invariably sentenced to be hanged. If a successful prosecution of the IRA was the order of the day, Humphreys was your man, and he did not disappoint.

The prisoners were tried in two groups. The first group consisted of Michael Cleary, alias Mason, an engineer by trade, aged 29; Joseph Walker of Liverpool, a laborer aged 26; Peter Walsh, alias Stuart, a poster writer aged 25; Michael Fleming, alias Preston, a laborer aged 23; Charles James Casey, a porter aged 23; John Healy, a furniture dealer and club proprietor, aged 40; James Michael Lyons, a French polisher aged 26; and Michael O'Shea, laborer, whose age was not given in the report of the trial covered by the London daily newspapers. The indictment against them was that they "did conspire with other persons in Manchester, Liverpool, Cardiff and Dublin, and elsewhere in the United Kingdom and in Ireland to cause explosions of a nature likely to endanger life or to cause injury to property." A charge of conspiracy was a bit of a catch-all. People could be prosecuted for simply knowing the perpetrators of a crime. It was guilt by association.

Sir Donald Somervell, the attorney general, opened for the prosecution. He referred to the demand to Lord Halifax, and the implementation of the S-Plan four days later. The arresting police officers then gave their evidence. On the second day of the trial Chief Inspector Cherrill of the

Fingerprint Department at New Scotland Yard gave evidence that a thumbprint found on an alarm clock attached to an unexploded bomb recovered at Windle was that of Michael Mason. The case for the defense opened on 27 March. Four of the accused had refused to plead, nor give evidence. This did not make things easy for their barristers. Nevertheless the team persisted, casting doubt on the guilt of some of their clients. Mr. Justice Humphreys summed up and the jury withdrew to consider the evidence. After deliberating for an hour and fifty minutes, the jury returned. They found that all eight defendants were guilty of conspiring to cause explosions. Michael Cleary, alias Mason, was sentenced to seventeen years' penal servitude. Peter Walsh got fifteen years; Charles Casey, fourteen years; Michael Fleming, twelve years; John Healy, ten years; James Lyons, ten years; and Joseph Walker, who from the evidence was only on the periphery, was given just eighteen months with hard labor.

In the trial of the remainder, Gerald Wharton, who it was revealed at the trial had previously served two years hard labor in Wormwood Scrubs under the Defence of the Realm Act, but was freed at the time of the Treaty in a general amnesty, and a man in receipt of an IRA pension, was sentenced to 10 years' imprisonment. Daniel Fitzpatrick received 8 years. The remaining defendants were sentenced to terms of imprisonment, and the two youngest to Borstal training. Daniel McCarthy was convicted, but Charles, his father, and Thomas McCarthy, his brother, who were entirely innocent, were both acquitted. The next day the last of the prisoners were convicted and sentenced. Francis and James McGowan and James and Daniel McCafferty were given between 4 and 7 years' detention. Molly Gallagher from Liverpool, whose family originated from County Mayo, was sent to Borstal for three years, for being in possession of sodium chlorate at her home. In less than one week, Judge Humphreys had sentenced twenty-one members of the IRA and Cummann na mBan to a total of 152 years' penal servitude.

There was a later appeal by one of the second group, Gerald Wharton. Unable to control his bitter hatred of the IRA, Humphreys made a remark to Wharton in front of the jury, prior to their retiring: "You were a member of that gang which committed murders of British officers and others up to 1922. You are a hypocrite in my view. You are the worst and the most dangerous of the gang which is now before me," he accused. In British law, a judge simply could not make such a prejudicial comment like that. The case against Wharton rested on traces of potassium chlorate and iron oxide being found in suitcases in his home. He claimed that the cases belonged to former Irish lodgers. One of the lodgers, swept up in the police raids,

Dan Fitzpatrick, admitted that one of the suitcases belonged to him. He denied Wharton's involvement. On 12 June 1939, Wharton's case came before the Court of Criminal Appeal with Lord Chief Justice Hewart presiding. Wharton's defense claimed that Judge Humphreys had misled the jury about Wharton's present relationship with the IRA. The jury had undoubtedly been swayed by Humphreys' parting comment. The counsel for Wharton also highlighted that a guilty verdict could only be returned if the prisoner had knowingly kept the materials in his possession—a point Judge Humphreys had not mentioned to the jury. Regarding Wharton's IRA pension, which he had been in receipt of since 1935, Counsel for the Defence were able to show that the pension had only been granted upon Wharton's renunciation of taking any further part in any IRA-related activities, and his swearing of an oath of loyalty to the Free State government. On 13 June, Wharton's conviction was overturned and he was released. On 22 August, following the passing of the Prevention of Violence (Temporary Provisions) Act, Wharton was arrested and deported. Britain's vindictiveness is unmatched. Under the Irish version of the Act, any IRA man deported was immediately arrested and interned at the Curragh. In Wharton's case this did not happen. The Irish government did not believe that he was still connected to the IRA.

Five Irishmen, including Paddy O'Connell of Thurles, County Tipperary, received 20 years each at the Manchester Assize in March 1939. Another received 14 years, while one of the two who got 7 years was a woman, Mary Glenn from Claremorris, County Mayo. Her brother Jack was amongst the men who got 20 years. At Birmingham, Robert McCann got 10 years and Tom Magill got 7 years for possessing explosive substances; and at Glamorgan in Wales, Timothy Dacey received 7 years for possession of explosives.

Sifting through the paperwork acquired during the raids led Detective Inspector Whitehead and Detective Sergeant Hugh Scott to raid the home of John Keane, just a few doors down from Gerald Wharton's former address. Keane was out at work, but his landlady let the policemen in. Here they discovered a hamper packed with potassium chlorate, sulfuric acid and thirty rubber balloons. The policemen sat down to wait, and when Keane, a porter, returned home, he was arrested. That same day a team led by Detective Inspector Cooper arrested Denis and Joseph McGillycuddy for possession of gelignite, fuses, aluminum powder and an unlicensed Webley revolver at their lodgings in Burns Road, Harlesdon, London. All three men were sentenced to 10 years' penal servitude. John Murrihy was sentenced to five years' penal servitude. When the police raided his lodgings at Richmond Gardens, Shepherd's Bush, London, they discovered an empty Mills hand grenade on the top of a cupboard in one of the rooms he rented. They also found some leaflets referring to a St. Patrick's Day concert benefiting the Irish Prisoners Aid Society.

The paperwork threw up another name, John Martin. He had received chemicals from another known IRA man, John Healy, back in December. The bomb material had been delivered to an address in Acton Lane, Harlesdon, West London, but a raid on the premises failed to turn up the mysterious John Martin. A watch was put on the premises, and in the fullness of time the police were led to a house in Gower Street. The landlady confirmed that two young Irishmen lived there, a Mr. McGuinness and a Mr. Martin. Fingerprint evidence led to the conviction of Martin, at the Central Criminal Court on 5 May. The evidence against James McGuinness was weak, and he was acquitted. Martin, an engineer by trade, before he was sentenced to 10 years' penal servitude, admitted that his real name was Pearse McLaughlin. He had arrived in England in early January.

Almost as a riposte to the trial, on the night of 28–29 March, the IRA bombed Hammersmith Bridge, one of the more important bridges over the river Thames, in London. The explosion was the work of a four-man team led by Edward Connell. Using the name Chessman, Connell hired a private car and chauffeur from a local firm, Godfrey Davis Ltd. The chauffeur picked up Connell, William Browne, Samuel Fluke (a Protestant Republican from Northern Ireland) and Willie Gaughran, about 11:30 p.m.[5] Connell informed the chauffeur, Clifford Moffat, that they wanted to go to Ewell in southwest London, but first of all wanted to make a short diversion. As the car stopped, Moffatt was overpowered and bundled onto the floor in the back of the car. Browne got into the driver's seat and the car set off once more.

Somewhere in Hammersmith, Moffatt was not sure where, the car stopped and two of the gang got out. They returned shortly with two suitcases. The car was then driven to Hammersmith Bridge. Connell and Browne got out, each carrying a suitcase. They were gone but a few minutes, and upon their return, the car sped off. Barely a quarter of a mile away in Hammersmith Broadway the car came to a halt, and they waited. Then came the sound of an explosion, but only one. Connell and Browne had placed two bombs on the bridge, each containing 30 lbs. of explosives. Perhaps they had both gone off at the same time, hence the sound of only one explosion—but no. A late-night reveler by the name of Childs, a hairdresser by trade, walking across the bridge, saw sparks coming from a suitcase. Without any fear for his own safety, he climbed through the chain on the pedestrian walkway and threw the suitcase into the river below. Hitting the water, it exploded, sending a spurt of water 60 feet into the air. The other bomb exploded, causing £1000 worth of damage. Luckily Childs was protected from the second explosion.

Meanwhile the car was driven down Fulham Palace Road to Putney Bridge, where the men got out. Much to Moffatt's surprise, Connell paid him his fare, then told him to walk away. Out of sight of his abductors, Moffatt ran off to find a telephone box, but was met by a policeman on his beat. After he explained what had happened, both men then set off after the IRA men. The team had split up into twos, and the pursuers caught up with Connell and Browne, who were strolling along the road. The policeman and Moffatt overpowered the two and arrested them. Connell was subsequently tried and sentenced to twenty years for causing the explosions. Browne got ten years.

The following day, 30 March, bombs exploded in Liverpool and Coventry. In Birmingham there was an accidental explosion at the lodgings of Belfast man Gerard Lyons, alias Dunlop, at 12, Trafalgar Road, Balsall Heath, south Birmingham. He and another IRA man, Pat McAleer, were preparing a bomb when something went wrong. As it started to smoke they fled the house. The explosion, confined to one bedroom, did some damage, but not enough to prevent a police forensics team from recovering 200 sticks of gelignite and 76 lbs. of potassium chlorate from the house. The gelignite appeared to be that stolen some days earlier from the explosives cabinet at Queslett Quarry, in north Birmingham. McAleer moved to another safe house in southwest Birmingham. Lyons went down to London. At Liverpool that same night, there were three explosions, and one bomb that failed to go off at a business premise.

The next day saw an escalation of the violence. Seven bombs exploded in London. Two went off in Tottenham Court Road. Five windows were blown out; the damage to repair cost £800. As a crowd gathered, a policeman noticed a figure walking across the road who seemed to have no interest in the scene. This seemed curious, so the policeman approached him. He was red-haired and had a Northern Ireland accent. His name, he divulged, was Samuel George Fluke. He was taken in for questioning. Fluke, an IRA man, claimed he was a Loyalist, an Orangeman, born in Northern Ireland. His father had served in the Royal Irish Fusiliers and the Royal Inniskilling Fusiliers, and rose to the rank of captain. This was later confirmed by the police. His address in London proved to be the same as Edward John Connell, who had been found guilty at the Central Criminal Court in April, for attempting to blow up Hammersmith Bridge. Connell's father, it was claimed, had served under Fluke's father, and when it was discovered that Fluke had wanted to visit London, Edward Connell's mother, Catherine, invited him to stay at their home. At his trial in the Central Criminal Court, in May 1939, at which he pleaded not guilty, Fluke admitted that he knew Connell junior was a strong Republican, but had told him in no uncertain terms that he did not agree with him. It was all circumstantial, and Fluke was a Northern Ireland Protestant, with a father who had been an officer in the British Army. Furthermore he had pleaded in court, which IRA men invariably refused to do. Catherine Connell further testified that the coat he was wearing, which showed traces of potassium chlorate, belonged to her son Edward, sentenced to 20 years for his part in the Hammersmith incident. The police had obviously made a mistake, the jury believed. They found him not guilty. Released, Fluke returned to Ireland, where he was subsequently arrested in Dublin in August 1940. He was sentenced to 6 months in Arbour Hill Prison for refusing to account for his movements, and interned thereafter in the Curragh. Upon his release he emigrated to Canada, but later returned to live in Britain. He is now dead.

In Dublin, the Army Council were becoming concerned over finance to continue the campaign. It was decided that Russell himself, the only real name known in America, should go to the United States on a fundraising tour. In his absence Stephen Hayes should take over as temporary head of the IRA. At Easter 1939, Russell sailed for America, there to meet Joseph McGarrity, leader of Clan na Gael, the Irish Republican movement in exile. With its spies in the American organization, Irish Military Intelligence (G2), later estimated that £80,000 (approximately $370,000) was raised. Ammunition explosive powder and a radio transmitter were smuggled back into Ireland. Working together, the Irish and British authorities later managed to track down the IRA broadcasting station. It was raided on 29 December 1939 and put off the air.

On 1 April there was an explosion in Coventry. At about 1:40 a.m. there was a heavy explosion at the car showrooms of Newsome and Company in Corporation Street. Surprisingly, there was little structural damage, other than shattered glass. The bomb had been placed near a series of gasoline pumps, but luckily the large tanks below were undamaged. If they had been ruptured there would have been further explosions. A passing motorist saw smoke and what he took to be a small fire at the garage. He drove to the fire station to summon help. Before he reached there, however, the explosion occurred. The blast of the bomb was largely dissipated by the fact that the entrance to the garage was open on one side, and on the other by the opening onto a yard.

There were four days of quiet, then on 5 April the bombing resumed. The targets in all cases were to the transport system. In Liverpool two bombs went off, one at a railway station, the other at council buildings. Two tram and electric light standards were damaged by the explosions. Tommy Hunt, the man responsible for the Liverpool explosions, fled back to Ireland, but was later arrested and sentenced to death by the Special Military Court in Dublin, for his membership in the IRA. He was later reprieved, and spent the war years in prison. In Birmingham there were three explosions in trash bins attached to street lights and tramway standards. One, cheekily, was set off outside of the Central Police Station in Steelhouse Lane. The second was at the Great Western Railway Station at Snow Hill, and the third by the Council House extension in Congreve Street. Twenty miles or so away, in nearby Coventry, a bomb went off at 4:45 a.m. at the junction of Bishop Street and Leicester Street. Considerable damage was done to the windows and doors of the nearby Crane's Hotel. The bomb had been placed in a metal litter basket attached to a tram standard on the sidewalk outside the hotel. The windows of the hotel were shattered and the doors of the house were blown open. By a peculiar chance, the tram standard that carried the overhead power cable was practically undamaged, other than the total destruction of the litter basket. In response the police raided all the lodging houses in the Irish sections of the city. Two men were arrested, but later released after questioning. It was a frustrating time for the police. They appealed to the public for assistance. Later that month a conference of chief constables sought additional powers of arrest and detention from the Home Office.

In Birmingham on 6 April, following a paper trail, the police raided a house in Moilliett Street in Winson Green. They searched the room of Lawrence Dunlea and there discovered six sticks of gelignite, a loaded gun and twenty-six rounds of ammunition. He was taken in for questioning and subsequently charged with possession. An explosion occurred in a public telephone box in Liverpool on the night of 11 April, completely wrecking it. Richie Goss of Dundalk, operations officer for Manchester, was arrested as he waited for a bus back to Manchester. Giving his name as Cox, he was searched, but there was no evidence of explosive materials about his person. He did, however, have £12 in his pocket, money paid by the IRA for his upkeep while on operations. Refusing to divulge where the money had come from, he was charged with the illegal possession of the money and sentenced to two weeks' imprisonment in Walton Jail.

Under suspicion that he was a bomber, upon his release from prison, he was tailed by two detectives. He led them to a shop in Stanley Road,

Bootle, the home of Rita McSweeney, who was responsible for the shipment of explosives from Cork and Rosslare. Warned that the police were closing in, and before they could act, McSweeney went on the run. Goss returned to Dublin and was subsequently shot by a Free State firing squad.

On 12 April in London, the Metropolitan Police received word that that the IRA intended to blow up Catford railway bridge in Lewisham. The police staked out the bridge for several nights but with no success. Railway workers were reminded to be vigilant. On the night of 12 April there were eleven explosions in public lavatories in London, Birmingham and Coventry. But for the obvious danger to the public, the bombing campaign had become laughable. Why would the IRA want to bomb public toilets? Analysis of the explosive remains indicated that a new type of bomb, one using carbide as its principle chemical, had been used. But why public lavatories?

Some sort of incident was expected by the authorities in view of the fact that the previous Monday (10 April) had been celebrated in Dublin as the anniversary of Irish Rising at Easter 1916. It was thought, however, that any outrage would probably be timed to miss the main holiday period, to avoid the greater danger of causing personal injury. In Ireland at the Republican commemorative march to Glasnevin Cemetery, a statement by the IRA Army Council was read out, which again emphasized the IRA's commitment to avoiding civilian casualties. The six London explosions were at widely separated points. A further occurred in Birmingham, and four of the eleven explosions occurred in Coventry. These were at Gosford Green (9:50 p.m.), Greyfriars Green (9:55 p.m.), Market Street (10:00 p.m.), and Bird Street (10:40 p.m.). At the underground lavatory at Greyfriars Green, the attendant, a man named Clement, who was cleaning the cubicles, saw a fuse burning. He lifted up the parcel and placed it in the bowl of the lavatory, then flushed. A moment later, however, the charge exploded, and Clement, though not injured, was badly shaken. Seventy-two-year-old James Dryden, the attendant at the Market Street lavatory, was also shocked when the explosion occurred while he was sitting in the wash and brush-up office. The incidents drew uniformed police officers to the scenes of the four explosions, and the CID were on the scene within minutes. A number of people were questioned, but no suspects were arrested. The police developed the theory that that those responsible for the bombings traveled to Coventry, probably from Birmingham, and left immediately after the bombs had been deposited. Dr. J.M. Webster the Director of the Home Office Forensic Laboratory at Birmingham was called in to examine the bomb fragments discovered.

There were further telephone kiosk bombings up in Liverpool on the 14th. One was blown up, but an attempt on a second came to nothing. On 18 April, two telephone kiosks were blown up in London. There were no explosions in Birmingham or Coventry, though, possibly due to the vigilance of the police. Possibly linked to the inability to blow up a telephone kiosk was the discovery of a bomb on a Midland "Red" bus traveling from Coventry to Birmingham that Tuesday night. The double-decker bus was the last from Coventry that night. It left Pool Meadow at 11:10 p.m. Near Meriden, about midway along the journey, a passenger traveling upstairs was about to get off when he noticed a briefcase under a seat. He collected up the case and handed it to the bus conductor, Henry Cherrington. There was some lighthearted banter about finders-keepers, then Cherrington decided to open the case and see if there was some indication as to the owner. The passenger jokingly suggested that it might be a bomb. As the conductor opened the bag, a wisp of smoke drifted out. Looking into the bag, Cherrington noticed all the components for a bomb, as described in the local newspaper—white powder, wires and a toy balloon; it was an incendiary device. By now the bus had come to a halt opposite the Bull's Head in Meriden. Cherrington rather foolishly put his hand into the bag. He touched a piece of wire, and instantly there was "a fizz and a flash," as he described it. Alarmed, he cried out that there was a bomb aboard the bus. Telling the driver, who had come round to see what was going on, and the two passengers aboard to get out of the way, he carried the briefcase to the edge of a ditch, then kicked it in. The village bobby was summoned, and after getting everybody back to a safe distance, he telephoned the police in Birmingham and Warwick. After some questioning the driver and his bus were allowed to continue their journey on to Birmingham, where at the garage Mr. Cherrington was questioned again by Special Branch. The Midland "Red" garage appears to have been the target. In his unpublished narrative, Joe Collins, operating in Manchester, details such a coordinated attack there: "I had a report of a bus depot where anything up to two hundred buses were parked at night, so I decided that these were a suitable target. Six men were detailed to place incendiaries under the rear seats of six buses as they made the last journey of the evening back to the depot."[6]

The bomb at Meriden, which failed to go off, was examined by the police and the Forensic Laboratory staff. The next day the Chief Constable of Coventry ordered that all essential public and other services in the city were to be guarded by special constables against the possibility of more IRA outrages. Additional civilians answered the call, and they were issued with batons, whistles and arm bands.

On 26 April, in the early hours of the morning, there were five explosions in commercial premises in Liverpool city center. The first occurred at about 1:30 a.m. at Leigh and Company's premises. The second occurred soon after at Chadburn's Ship Telegraph Company, a prominent business selling surveying equipment and telescopes, located in Castle Street near to the Liverpool headquarters of the Bank of England. There was a third explosion at 2:15 a.m. at Dunn's the Hatters on Great Charlotte Street, followed by an explosion at the offices of the *Daily Post* printers on Wood Street. The final bomb went off at the Trueform Shoe Company on London Road.

At 84, Cliff Rock Road, Rednal, on the border of Birmingham and Bromsgrove, on a newly built 1930s housing estate near the local beauty spot of the Lickey Hills, the IRA established another safe house. It was as far away from the inner city Irish quarter as you could get. As a consequence, it had not come under Special Branch interest. Eoin McNamee and Sean Fuller, both based in Birmingham, used the house before returning safely to Ireland. Another of the Birmingham based IRA men, Martin Clarke, established a new "bomb factory" here at the home of the Higgins family. On the night of 3 May things went wrong again. There was an explosion, followed by two others. A fire broke out. Clarke received injuries to his face, arm and leg. Concerned neighbors telephoned the emergency services, police, fire brigade and ambulance service, believing that there had been a gas explosion. The police arrived, and discerning the true nature of the explosion, Clarke, and three women, Mary, aged 77, and her two daughters, Evelyn and Emily Higgins, were all arrested.[7] Emily was discovered to be hiding two sticks of dynamite in her blouse. Fingerprints were sent off to the RUC, and news back from Belfast revealed that the real name of the women was Furlong. They were wanted by the Northern Ireland authorities, but had fled to the relative safety of the Irish Free State. Here they were established in Dublin by the IRA at 32, North Great George's Street, where they provided a safe house for IRA men on the run. Then at the outbreak of the bombing campaign they were sent to England, to establish a safe house in the West Midlands.

Clarke was taken to the General Hospital for treatment. Later when brought before the Birmingham Stipendiary, Clarke claimed full blame, declaring, "I wish to take full responsibility for all that has happened. These people are innocent." The clerk to the Magistrate's court observed that Mary Furlong had been discovered with gelignite hidden inside her blouse. In her defense she claimed, "I thought it was a sugar stick like my sister gets for my mother." The clerk pointed out that it was clearly marked "gelignite." There was some laughter in the court at this. The four were sent for trial at Birmingham Assize in July 1939. Clarke was found guilty on two counts: conspiracy to cause explosions and possessing explosive substances. He was sentenced to twenty years' penal servitude. Mary and Evelyn were sentenced to 2 and 3 years respectively, and Emily, discovered with the gelignite in her possession, got 5 years. On the night of the explosion in Rednal, 3 May, up in Manchester there was a slight explosion in another IRA safe house when a bomb went off prematurely. It would appear to have been caused by a flawed balloon. The bomb makers fled the scene before the police arrived.

That same night about 3,000 persons attending two cinemas in Liverpool suffered tear gas bomb attacks. The first attack was at the Trocadero Cinema in Camden Street, off the London Road. It occurred at 7:30 p.m. The cinema usherette noticed a commotion in the upper circle of the cinema. People began standing up and coughing. Then a dense black smoke began to spread in all directions. The audience began making for the exits. The cinema staff now took action and guided the people outside. The fire brigade was summoned, and under Chief Officer Oakes, the fire crew took possession of the bomb. Members of the St. John's Ambulance arrived and gave first aid to those who needed help.

Rather than waste a good night out, a number of the Trocadero's patrons then went on to the nearby Paramount Cinema in London Road. They had barely sat down when a second tear gas bomb went off. Due no doubt to its being a much larger cinema, the fumes were more quickly dissipated and were less noxious. The audience was led out of the cinema in an orderly fashion. The Liverpool CID were quickly on the scene at the two cinemas. There were several common features to both bombings. In each case the bomb was contained in a small cardboard box, discovered beneath a seat, and in the boxes were the remains of what appeared to have been metal containers. None of the patrons sitting near the source of the explosions were able to describe the person or persons who had left the tear gas bombs. The witnesses described hearing a sizzling sound close to them in the upper circle just prior to the bombs going off, and a girl brushing past them, but no more detail than that.

In response to the increased terror threat in the capital, Special Branch commander Albert Canning sought an increase in establishment from its original strength of 150 officers. Police Commissioner Sir Philip Game saw the capture of the bombers as a top priority and approved the transfer of regular CID detectives to the Branch. This increase in operatives led to greater surveillance of possible suspects.

2. More Bombs

Special Branch now had a breakthrough. It was reported that a house in Sidmouth Street, off Gray's Inn Road, Marylebone, might be an IRA safe house. There were curious comings and goings. Two women officers, Majorie Urquart and Anne Winterbottom, were put on surveillance. Late at night on 3 May, two men, Patrick Dower and Joseph McAleer, left the suspect house. The two police officers discreetly followed them. They walked up towards Great Portland Street Underground Station, at the junction of Marylebone Road and Euston Road. Here they met Gerard Kirk, alias Gerard Bradford. The three men walked down Marylebone Road to Baker Street Underground Station, where they met Timothy Murray and two other men: Gerard Lyons, alias Dunlop, who had escaped the explosion at Trafalgar Road in Birmingham, and John Joseph Keane. The officers watched from a safe distance. Gerard Kirk appeared to be giving instructions. Then the suspects split up into two groups. One of the policewomen followed Dower, Murray and Keane, the other followed Kirk, McAleer and Lyons. The first officer followed Dower and the other two back down Euston Road. It was now about half past eleven. The streets were beginning to clear of people. As the suspects approached the premises of George Newman & Company, motor car dealers, Dower was seen putting an object into the firm's letterbox. A little later Murray put an object into the letterbox of Com-Motors Ltd., also in Euston Road. The three men then split up. The officer decided to follow Murray. He walked along to Edgware Road, where he spoke to two girls and a number of young men, then he continued on and entered a house in St. Mary's Terrace, Paddingtom. By now it was 1 a.m.

Meanwhile the second officer followed Gerard Kirk, Lyons and McAleer. They proceeded down into "Theatre Land," where, near the Aldwych Theatre, off the Strand, she saw Kirk take something out of his pocket. There was a conversation between them of some minutes before they set off again. They turned into Kingsway, and after looking up and down the street to see if anyone was watching, Kirk posted a small package into the letterbox of Gestetner, a company that manufactured reproductive machinery. Then the three men half ran, half walked, up the road to High Holborn. The police officer followed at a distance. As she got to the corner of the street, she noticed the three men walking away from the premises of the Crittall Manufacturing Company. At a discretionary distance the policewoman followed her quarry until about 2 a.m., when they entered a house in Acton Street, Bloomsbury. The two officers reported back to police headquarters at New Scotland Yard.

A team of police officers then followed the routes of the suspected

IRA men as described by the two policewomen. At the Gestetner offices in Kingsway, a parcel measuring six inches by three inches was found. It contained two balloons, one inside the other, filled with acid, a stick of gelignite and a detonator. The discoverer, Constable Blake, placed the package in a bucket of water to make it safe. At 5:15 a.m., Police Constable Ernest Hayward found a brown paper parcel about ten inches by three inches, lying in a window at Heal & Son's premises in Tottenham Court Road. Removing the wrapping paper he found a rubber balloon, a stick of gelignite and a fuse. After courageously separating the components of the bomb, he placed them in a bucket of water. At Henri Selmer Ltd., in Holborn, the timekeeper, Edward Buckland, found a parcel inside the shop, dropped through the letter slot. He placed it on a desk for an office worker to deal with. Later, as the staff arrived, he picked it up to hand to a salesman. It began to smolder, so he dropped it on the floor, where it burst into flame. Quickly he threw some curtains onto it to smother the flames, then stamped on the curtains. Just then it exploded, and he and the salesman were thrown to the floor. The timekeeper suffered injuries to his leg. At 8:45 a bomb exploded at the premises of Com-Motors in Euston Road. No one suffered direct injury, but a woman working next door in a tobacconist's kiosk suffered shock. In all six bombs exploded along the two routes. Two more failed to go off.

Armed Special Squad and CID detectives raided the three houses at Sidmouth Street, St. Mary's Terrace and Acton Street, and four men were arrested. As a result, three more men were arrested. When DI Frank Bridges arrested McAleer, he found two electric detonators on his person. At Acton Street, Branch men interrogated two suspects. One gave his name as Gerard Bradford, but was later identified as Gerard Kirk, a bomb maker. The other man turned out to be Gerard Dunlop, the IRA man who had fled the explosion at the bomb-making factory in Moseley, Birmingham. All seven stood trial at the Central Criminal Court in London at the end of June 1939. The charges against six of the accused—Gerard Bradford, Patrick Dower, Gerard Anthony Dunlop, John Joseph Keane, Patrick McAleer and Timothy Murray—was conspiracy to cause explosions. Joseph Malone was charged with actual possession. Bradford, Dower, McAleer and Murray were sentenced to twenty years in prison. Keane was sentenced to ten, and Malone to five years. Malone, a Belfast man, had underlying health problems. He died barely two and a half years later, on 21 January 1942, in Parkhurst Prison on the Isle of Wight. His body was returned to his family in Northern Ireland and interred at Milltown Cemetery, Belfast. Bradford's arrest and conviction was a real bonus for the police. He was the bomb maker. Bradford, whose real name was Kirk, was likewise born in Belfast, in 1915.

Dunlop, found guilty of conspiracy, was brought back into court to face further charges. The further case against him related to his time in Birmingham. He was charged with having in his possession at Trafalgar Road, Moseley, Birmingham, on 30 March, explosive substances including gelignite, safety fuse, and toy balloons, with intent to endanger life or cause serious damage to property. He was also charged with being in possession of a revolver and ammunition. A Mrs. Dunkley, who lived across the road from Dunlop, testified that on the night of 30 March she heard a loud explosion and saw smoke emanating from the house opposite. Then she saw Dunlop, alias James Michael Lyons, and another man, coatless and hatless, and with dirty faces, make off down the road. The police were called to investigate. There had been an explosion; concentrated in one corner of the room, it caused considerable damage, but the police had managed to find a small arsenal of explosives in the room unaffected by the blast. The police found two large drums of aluminum powder, 76 lb. of potassium chlorate, 170 2-oz. cartridges of gelignite, 266 rubber balloons, detonators, packages of mixed aluminum, and iron oxide, lengths of safety fuse and a number of tools ad appliances. "It was a matter of great good fortune," said Mr. Howard, the prosecutor, "that something went wrong and caused the explosion, thus bringing about the discovery of the matter."

Dunlop's fingerprints were found on a bottle in the room, and quickly matched up against his file in Belfast. Following his second trial at the Old Bailey, he was found guilty and sentenced to 10 years' penal servitude for conspiracy to cause explosions, and secondly for possessing explosive substances. During police questioning, Dunlop had revealed his true name, Gerard Anthony Dunlop. He had joined the IRA in 1937. Arrested in Belfast in 1938 for being in possession of illegal documents, he had been sentenced to three months' imprisonment. After his release he traveled south to Dublin, where he received instruction in bomb making. With his training complete, he was sent to Birmingham. Following the accidental explosion, he was ordered down to London. He was there for just two weeks before his arrest in the capital.

The bomb defused by Constable Blake at the Gestetner office had two balloons, one inside the other, to contain the acid. At the start of the campaign the bombers had a supply of good quality rubber acid containers. As these were used up, the bomb makers resorted to buying cheap halfpenny balloons from Woolworths'. The problem with these was that they sometimes contained impurities in the rubber. Whereas it would take three hours for the acid to burn through rubber in the originals, it would penetrate any of these sub-standard balloons bought in England in a matter of minutes. This may well have been the cause of the two premature explosions in Birmingham. Learning from these mistakes, the bomb-makers then began placing one balloon inside another as insurance. In the end they discarded balloons in favor of reinforced rubber condoms.

Early the next morning (4 May) in Coventry, five terrific explosions occurred between 1 a.m. and 5 a.m. They were similar in nature to the London bombs where commercial premises were targeted. Two of the explosions happened within 100 yards of the Central Police Station. The scenes of the explosions were Messers. Goodly's, furniture store in Earl Street; the Corporation Electricity Showrooms in Corporation Street; Messers. Rhodes, the china shop in Trinity Street; Messers. Anslow's, furnishers, in the High Street; and the Co-operative Society's stores in Smithford Street, where the bomb was removed from its target, but later exploded. Police officers at the Central Police Station rushed to the scene on hearing the first explosion at Goodly's store, less than 100 yards away. They found that the bomb, which had been placed in the concave window in the front of the premises, had caused extensive damage, resulting in debris being blown outwards across the road. The thoroughfare was blocked off and traffic diverted. A large number of officers were immediately dispatched to search other premises in the center of the city.

As the Corporation Electricity showrooms were known to have a similar concave window, Detective Sergeant Pendleton and P.C. Chamberlain hurried to Corporation Street. There they found a brown-paper parcel lying inside the base of the concave window. As Sergeant Pendleton picked it up, it began to fizz. He hurriedly put it down again, yelling to Chamberlain, "Run for it!" They had scarcely covered 10 yards when there was a deafening explosion, which blew both officers off their feet. Glass from the heavy canopy above the showroom, and over 100 panes of window glass, were blown upwards and outwards by the explosion. The explosion also dislodged concrete slabs in the structure of the building. Though concussed, the two police officers were not seriously injured. Thanks to Pendleton's action, the electrical equipment within the shop was largely undamaged.

The next explosion occurred at about 1:30 at the glass and china store of Messers. W.H. Rhodes in Trinity Street, where P.C. Rollins had made a desperate effort to remove a bomb that had been dropped behind the front protecting door of the premises. The policeman tried to fish out the bomb with his baton, but was unable to do so. He blew his whistle to summon aid, then decided to run to the fire station for help. Before he had gone many steps, the bomb exploded with great force. It completely wrecked the enclosed arcade front of the shop, shattering windows, buckling and twisting bronze frames and smashing scores of English cut glass crystal and pottery pieces within. Shortly after the Trinity Street explosion, Sergeant Wright and P.C. Jones climbed the protecting gateway which led to the arcade front of the Co-operative Society's Smithford Street store. There they found another parcel bomb. They threw it out onto the open street where it would cause less damage. As it crashed onto the street, it immediately blew up with a deafening roar. With the exception of a few broken panes of glass in nearby properties, no real damage was done.

The final bomb went off just before 5 a.m., at the premises of Messers. John Anslow Ltd. Here the bomb was placed behind some wooden hoardings that had been erected during the refurbishment of the shop. P.C. Kwayser, who was on the other side of the road and approaching the shop, was blown over. The explosion shattered windows and flung the hoardings across the road towards the stricken policeman. A bronze pilaster, which had only just been erected at the shop front, was considerably damaged. Temporarily deafened by the explosion, Constable Kwayser was soon restored to health. Coventry's policemen had shown remarkable bravery in the performance of their duty.

Later that morning, in an unconnected case, a group of men and women, arrested under the Explosive Substances Act of 1883, faced trial at the Birmingham Assize held in the Victoria Law Courts in Corporation Street. The evidence against them was weak. Of their number, only John McGeough was eventually found guilty of the lesser charge of possessing ammunition with intent to endanger life. He was given a sentence of 5 years' penal servitude.

Cinemas now became the subject for attacks. This curious little campaign began with the releasing of tear-gas bombs in two Liverpool cinemas on 3 May. Fifteen people were treated in a hospital for eye and nose irritations. On 29 May there were three attempted arson attacks on Birmingham cinemas and a second tear gas explosion at another Liverpool cinema. Twenty-five people had to be hospitalized, but there was no material damage done. On the 31 May there was a tear-gas explosion in the lavatory of a cinema in London. This was followed on 1 June by two further tear-gas bomb assaults on London cinemas. One was successful, the other a failure. Then for the moment the attacks on cinemas ceased.

Early on the morning of 12 May, five bombs went off at business premises in Manchester. The first two explosions took place in an unoccupied shop in London Road, and in the window of a bicycle dealer in Peter Street.

The third was in the front doorway of a jeweler's shop in Market Street. The fourth occurred in a shoe shop in the same road, less than 200 yards away. The damage was chiefly confined to shop windows that were shattered. No one was injured. While a thorough search of all shop doorways was being made, two officers found a balloon bomb which had been dropped through the letter slot of a motor car showroom in Deansgate. A bucket of water was obtained and poured through the slot by Detective Sergeant Lennox to render the bomb harmless. As he did so, the bomb burst into flames, then exploded. Window glass was blown out onto the pavement and road. Shortly after the first explosion, a policeman on duty in Market Street saw a man running along a neighboring street and gave chase, but lost him. Following on, the CID and uniformed police officers instigated a series of raids on the homes of where "IRA sympathizers are known to live"—or Irish people, as they were also called. All Irish people now came under suspicion, even those who had served in the Forces during World War I. This was the retaliation against the innocent that IRA leader Tom Barry had predicted.

The team of bombers were led by Joe Collins, former operations officer in London, but now operations officer for Manchester. He was already on the run, and had narrowly escaped from London prior to the police raiding his lodgings. Special Branch knew his alias and had a good description of him. This was circulated to all major cities in England. Collins had moved to Manchester, staying at a doss house in Temple Street before moving to Charlton-on-Medlock, a fading lower middle-class suburb of the city. Days earlier a member of the team, John Duggan, had been sent to Liverpool to obtain gelignite from an IRA arms dump based in a bookshop in Scotland Road. The man in charge there was Joe Deighan, from County Armagh, one of the original bombers dispatched just before Christmas 1938. Deighan had formerly been working in England some time before, and was familiar with England and the English way of life. He had arrived in Liverpool in 1936 and was appointed O.C. to replace George Stannard. He was recalled to receive instruction in bomb making, then sent back to Liverpool. Fellow IRA man Pat Hannon, himself brought up in Liverpool, described Deighan as "a budding intellectual, well educated, a competent Irish speaker with a ready grasp of history; he later was a journalist in the *Irish Press* [the newspaper set up by de Valera]. His appointment was popular with the younger group now forming the unit and looking forward to an action that would force England to yield up the six Counties."[8] The dynamite shops were situated in the two main streets of Manchester, Market Street and Piccadilly.

Collins's luck ran out. Arrested under the alias of Connor McNessa, he and John Duggan stood trial at Manchester Assize in July 1939. They both received sentences of 20 years. Collins was replaced as operations officer in Manchester by Jackie Griffiths, who was later shot dead in Dublin by Irish Special Branch officers. Collins served his time at Parkhurst on the Isle of Wight, one of England's toughest prisons. He was eventually released in 1948.

Deighan himself narrowly escaped arrest on 27 July 1939. He had become aware that he was being followed, no doubt in the hope that he would lead Special Branch to others in the team. Through a friend Deighan obtained a ticket on the Liverpool-to-Dublin ferry. An hour or so before sailing, he and the friend, Tom Martin, wandered down to the Liverpool docks, and just as the gangplank was about to be removed, he dashed aboard the ferry. The police who had been following dashed aboard too in order to arrest him, but for whatever reason, the captain refused to allow them to remove Deighan. All they could do was to warn him not to return to Britain. Upon his return to Dublin, Deighan was subsequently arrested and interned in the Curragh along with his mentor, James O'Donovan. After his release, Deighan became Irish-language editor of the *Irish Press*. His memoirs were published in Irish in 1962 as *Ag Scaoileadh Sceoil*. Deighan was replaced as O.C. Liverpool by Mairtin Standuin.

Though members of the Liverpool unit were suspected of IRA membership, the police struggled to find the evidence against them. They were often followed by Special Branch and detectives from the Liverpool police force. Sometimes as many as six detectives would be put to tailing a suspect. The IRA men were very vigilant, and soon became aware that they were being tailed. It almost became a point of honor for the suspects to outwit their trailers, sometimes suddenly cycling up an alleyway too narrow for a pursuing police car to follow, or jumping on and off tram cars when they were still in motion. Mairtin Standuin, the new O.C., who worked in a branch of Irwin's grocery shops, was so closely watched that he had to leave and get work at the docks. Here, much to his surprise, his fellow workers, including some English workers, were eager to help him by keeping watch on the movement of the detectives. Indeed, one Englishman, Vincent Crompton, actually joined the IRA.

The Liverpool unit was based at a bookshop in Scotland Road, called "98," its name commemorating the rise of the United Irishmen in 1798. It was run by a veteran Fenian, Peter Murphy. All the material was stored upstairs in his shop. There was gelignite, potassium chlorate, detonators, and a rifle. "If the police come," old Peter Murphy once joked, "all I can do is set fire to the place." There were other smaller dumps in Canny Street and in Crompton Place in the suburb of Huyton. Liverpool was the chief supply center for London, Birmingham, Coventry and Manchester, as well as Liverpool itself. Among the Liverpool IRA were members of the women's division, Cumann na mBan. They were employed as carriers and messengers. They included Rita McSweeney, as mentioned above, Una Walsh, Kitty Carroll, Maire and Rose Sweeney, Maggie Nolan (who married Dominic Adams, the Coventry O.C.) and Margaret McDonnell. The men included Mairtin Standuin (born in Liverpool in 1918), Tommy Hunt, Sean and Pat Hannon, Charlie Dineen, Tommy McDermott, Leo Morgan, Peter Dowley, Seamus Murphy, and Thomas McDonagh-Byrne, the grandson of Peter Murphy.

Rita McSweeney, daughter of a staunchly Republican family from Dungarven, county Waterford, was the chief transport officer in England. Being a woman, she was less likely to be suspected. She had control of one of the largest explosive dumps in Liverpool, based at a house in Canning Street. She regularly traveled to Dublin to establish contacts and to organize the entry of supplies. Bob Foley, who worked aboard the B.&I. ferries on the Dublin-Liverpool run, brought over the supplies and liaised with Rita. She also had contact with Terence McSherry, who brought explosives down from Glasgow in Scotland. These either came from Ireland through Ardcrossan, or were from raids on Scottish quarries and military magazines. McSherry was later arrested and sentenced at Falkirk Assize to 10 years' penal servitude for conspiracy to steal explosive substances. Under the alias of Barbara Jones, McSweeney was herself arrested in Wales, along with Dick Timmons, who was using the alias of Richard Cohen. He was responsible for an explosives dump in Fishguard, the Welsh terminal of the Rosslare ferry. The two were tried at Carmarthen Assizes in November 1939. McSweeney received a sentence of five years for possessing explosives and ammunition. Timmons got fifteen years for possessing explosives. Charlie Dineen was arrested down in London. He was transporting chemicals from the Liverpool dump. When arrested he cheekily gave his name as Herbert Moore. The real Herbert Moore was head of Liverpool CID, Special Branch. Dineen was tried at the Central Criminal Court in London and sentenced to ten years. He was released following the end of World War II.

In May, three explosions occurred in underground public lavatories in London. The explosions took place at Marble Arch, at the Harrow Road-Edgware Road junction and at Hammersmith Broadway. In each case gelignite was used. The times of the explosions, 8 p.m., 8:05 p.m. and 8:20 p.m.

suggested that one group of IRA men was responsible, and that they drove from one point to the other in a private car. The damage was not serious, and no one was injured. The police put a watch on all underground stations over the next few days. They interviewed the likely suspects, i.e., any Irishman they could find in the vicinity, but no arrests were made. Guilt by association was now becoming prevalent. Twenty-year-old Sheila Gallagher was dismissed from her government job in the Home Office, following the arrest of her sister on an explosives charge. Her sister was subsequently released. Sheila's trade union, the Civil Services Clerical Association, successfully petitioned the Home Secretary, Sir Samuel Hoare, to have her reinstated.

Royal Marines, who guarded the Royal dockyards, were normally unarmed, but were now issued with side arms. The decision to arm the Marines was made when the naval authorities received what purported to be a threatening letter from the IRA. Unauthorized civilians entering or leaving the yards came under very close scrutiny, and all cars entering or leaving the Royal yards were stopped and searched.

Also in early May 1939, an IRA team up in Glasgow raided a dynamite store along Garngad Road, and escaped with approximately 570 sticks of gelignite. From a safe house in Beech Grove, Glasgow, the team, consisting of Michael O'Hara, Edward Gill and John Carson, were able to supply the IRA units in England. O'Hara himself took a suitcase of gelignite down to Liverpool, where at the railway station he handed it over to [?] Michael Cleary; but he, suspecting that he was being followed, dumped the case, which was discovered and handed over to Special Branch in the city. The gelignite in the case was wrapped up in a sheet of used brown paper. Unwrapping the parcel, police discovered a name and address on the inside. It was, "Miss J. Gardner, 37, Duke Street"—but without the name of a town or city. There was nothing for it but to trace every Duke Street in the United Kingdom, with the matching name of Gardner. Glasgow Special Branch found the answer. They raided the house. The address led them to another, the Assembly Hall, 132, Trongate. On 14 May the police raided that address and arrested a number of men, including O'Hara, Gill and Carson. Their lodgings were searched and 540 sticks of gelignite were discovered, along with 500 detonators and 160 feet of fast-burning fuse. At their trial at Glasgow High Court in August 1939, all three men were tried, found guilty and sentenced to ten years apiece. Nine other men arrested at the time were freed without trial. By good detective work, and again following a paper trail, the police were beginning to get the upper hand.

On 16 May the police made a number of raids on suspected IRA safe houses in the north. Arrests were made and the police seized 8 lbs. of potassium chlorate, two powder fuses, 26 sticks of gelignite, two sticks of saxonite, fuses, a revolver and ammunition, 29 balloons and street maps of Manchester, Salford and Liverpool. An unexploded bomb discovered on a bus in Liverpool was linked to this cache.

On 19 May 1939 the two IRA men, Peter Campbell and John Leo Duignan, arrested in February, were sentenced at the Central Criminal Court in London, to 10 years' penal servitude for possessing explosive substances. They had been found with 10 bundles of gelignite, a 5-lb. pack of gelignite, 103 detonators and 4 balloons. Discovering the address in Connaught Road, West Kensington, the police, finding that they were not at home, secreted themselves in the room next door to their flat. As he arrived home, the police allegedly heard Campbell saying to Duignan, "There's plenty of jelly for us here." The police burst in and arrested the two men, discovering the bomb-making equipment in the process. Duignan, the police found out, had arrived in England in 1938. Campbell, much to their surprise, was an American, born in New York of Irish parents.

In a coordinated incendiary attack on 19 May, the IRA targeted hotels in Blackpool, Southport, Morecambe and Harrogate in the north of England, and Eastbourne, Brighton and Southend-on-Sea, along the south coast overlooking the English Channel. Four of the fires in the north were at the Carlton Hotel, Blackpool; the Victoria Hotel, Southport; the Grand Hotel, Morecambe; and the Imperial Hotel, Eastbourne. The Yorkshire incident was at Harrogate, and another fire occurred along the Kent coast at the Kingscliff Hall Hotel, Cliftonville, near Margate. In every case but one, the suspect gave a Birmingham address, which proved to be false. It was a prearranged attack by IRA units up and down the country. Hoteliers and boardinghouse keepers were warned to be on their guard, especially when dealing with Irish people.

On 19 May, Birmingham City Police made eight arrests in the city in connection with an explosion at a house in Manchester back on 2 May. The bombers had fled to Birmingham, but left enough evidence in the house for the police to track not only them, but also other IRA units in different parts of the country.

The Liverpool IRA penetrated the King's (Liverpool) Regiment's Seaforth Barracks on the night of 22 May. A bomb of 20 sticks of gelignite was thrown through the window of the gymnasium. It was faulty, though, and did not explode. Quickly discovered, it was immediately placed in a bucket of water to await the Army's bomb disposal team. A man on a racing cycle was seen hurrying away from the barracks about the time of the intended outrage. His description was circulated by the local police force. He was never knowingly caught.

On 29 May there were a series of arson attacks on cinemas in the center of Birmingham. Four incendiary devices went off in the Paramount Cinema in John Bright Street. As a result of the incident, a search was made by the police of other cinemas in the city. As a result of this, two unexploded bombs were discovered in the Gaumont Cinema in Steelhouse Lane. They had been placed on the floor underneath the seats. The following morning, cleaners at the West End Cinema in Suffolk Street discovered two balloon-type incendiary bombs which had been lodged in the back of the tip-up seats. They had exploded, but the seating had actually smothered the devices. In Liverpool on the night of the 29th, twenty persons were taken to the hospital after a tear gas outrage at the Tatler Cinema. The bomb exploded in the center of the stalls, and the whole building was quickly filled with fumes. Many people were overcome and needed first-aid treatment. Witnesses claimed that a little earlier a young man in a gray suit rushed away from the scene. Other witnesses spoke of the suspicious movements by a young woman. The police discovered a second device that had failed to go off. It was a commercially manufactured tear gas bomb, the type used in America to quell riots.

At the Paramount Cinema in Birmingham, the bombs in the front row of the back circle went off at 9:42 p.m. People in the upper circle were alarmed by a vivid flash and a flame that shot up to a considerable height. Almost instantaneously the others went off. Panic was averted when a member of the audience, Mr. Bertram Potts, exhibiting coolness and a presence of mind, stood up and told his fellow cinemagoers not to panic, and suggested a calm and orderly withdrawal, which is what happened.

Four unexploded bombs were found in Coventry city center letter boxes on the morning of 30 May. Shortly after 8 a.m., in the course of his duties, a postman collecting letters from a pillar box in Broadgate came across a small brown paper parcel that had no name and address. Following procedure, he put it in his haversack, and at the end of his collections he returned to the central Post Office with it. Here it was unwrapped and examined. It was a bomb. There was gelignite, a balloon containing acid, a detonator and flash powder. Gingerly the bomb was placed in a fire bucket filled with water. The police were informed at once, with the result that postmen and police came upon a number of other unexploded bombs in pillar boxes and letter boxes in business premises. Difficulty was added to the task of discovery, because this was a holiday period when most shops and offices were closed. Other discoveries were made at the premises in the High Street of the Halifax Building Society and the Royal Insurance Company's offices next door. A further explosive parcel was found in the letter box of the Coventry Education Committee's Juvenile Employment Bureau, also in the High Street. Caretakers and others had to be hurriedly summoned in order that the search might be completed.

The bomb in the letter box of the Coventry branch of Royal Insurance Company was discovered when the manager, a Mr. P.D. Kinsey, went in to work. He saw a plain brown paper parcel among the mail. There was no name or address. At first he thought it was a hoax. Then he noticed traces of powder on the packaging. Realization dawned that it might well be a bomb. He carefully carried the package to a water basin in the company's toilets, filled the bowl with water, then lowered the package into the water. The police arrived and the package was found to contain four sticks of gelignite, a detonator, and a rubber balloon containing acid.

The bomb in the Halifax Building Society's office letter box was found only a few minutes later by the caretaker, who was also a member of the Auxiliary Fire Brigade. He rendered it inactive by placing it in a bucketful of water in the yard at the rear of the premises. Further down the High Street, the Juvenile Employment Bureau was locked for the holiday. From their file of caretakers within the city, the police found their man, and after he unlocked the door, yet another unexploded bomb was discovered. It too was rendered harmless.

It was the end of May, and despite the bombing campaign's continuing, the authorities had their successes.

At the Central Criminal Court in London, Peter Campbell, John Duignan, John Foley, Michael Griffin, Cormac McGarrigle, Denis McGillycuddy, Francis McGillycuddy and John Murrihy, as mentioned above, were all sentenced to long terms of imprisonment for possession of explosives and conspiracy to cause explosions. The McGillycuddy brothers were arrested at the home of John Keane, who himself later received a custodial sentence of ten years for possessing explosive substances. Keane's wife, Ellen Mary, was temporarily lodged in Holloway, the women's prison, before deportation. She herself had been quite active in the campaign. Her flat over a shop had been used to shelter IRA men, and she herself had transported explosive chemicals, though this was unknown to the police at the time.

Harry White, who had fled England after a couple of narrow escapes at the hands of London Special Branch, was induced to return as Operations Officer of Manchester. He was to replace Jackie Griffiths, who himself had narrowly escaped capture. White was well aware of the risks he ran.

The Manchester unit had been decimated, and links to suppliers had been destroyed. Nonetheless he returned. He traveled by boat to Liverpool, and from there by train to Manchester. His contact was a Mrs. Coffey, who had a small drapery shop in Chorlton. White knocked on the door, and Mrs. Coffey let him in. Quite rightly she suspected that the house was under police observation. She got him away that very night, by dressing him up as a local door-to-door insurance collector, with a bowler hat and umbrella. He walked out of the shop and was away. His new contact was Jack McCabe, the local O.C. With their supply line to Glasgow destroyed, McCabe established a contact with Belfast man, Jimmy McGowan, in Leeds. Unknown to him the Leeds house was likewise under police observation. McCabe was followed back to Manchester, and following a whole series of raids, was himself arrested, and given twenty years for causing an explosion.

The month of June, with its almost 18 hours of daylight, was the enemy of the bomber. Lots of people were out and about. There was greater risk of discovery when planting bombs. Nonetheless the campaign continued, but it was not the campaign envisaged by James O'Donovan when he drew up the S-Plan. Instead of electrical installations and road and rail communications, the campaign had degenerated into leaving bombs in letter boxes and litter bins, public lavatories and telephone kiosks. This got worse when IRA volunteers were reduced to cutting the wires in telephone kiosks. This was hardly going to force the British out of the Six Counties. Even the young volunteers could see this. They were becoming frustrated at this halfhearted campaign. Young Tom Byrne, a Liverpool IRA man, put forward a proposal for attacking the Cunard ship, the *Queen Mary*. She was in dry dock undergoing repairs and refurbishment. Such an assault, bombing the *Queen Mary*, would have attracted the world's press, but he was told no. Others were all for political assassinations, but again this proposal was turned down. So it was back to dropping incendiary bombs into pillar boxes. On the night of 9–10 June there were eighteen cases of firebombing at post offices and pillar boxes in London. There were nine cases in Manchester at the central sorting office. There were four cases in Birmingham; two in a mail van and two in the Central Post Office in Victoria Square. There were a further two cases in mail carried aboard the mail train from Birmingham to Euston Station in London. At the cathedral city of Lincoln, fifteen incendiary packages were found, and a further twelve at Leicester, four of which burst into flames. In London the bombs were found in letter boxes at Broadwick Street, Soho; Wimpole Street, Lincoln's Inn Fields; Coram Street; Tavistock Square; Woburn Square; Bedford

Square; Langley Street, Long Acre; Tufnell Park Road, Holloway; Chancery Lane; Faringdon Road; Junction Road Post Office, Holloway; Cricklewood Broadway; and Peters Street, Kentish Town. It was a concentration within central London, but given the numbers would probably have required two or three bombing teams, possibly up to ten operatives. The *Birmingham Mail* of 10 June, which covered the local outrages, announced that "a special watch will be made on pillar boxes during the weekend," thus unintentionally undermining the police operation.

On the face of it, it was a simple procedure: drop the incendiary package into a letter box and walk away. While the prime directive was, and always had been, to avoid loss of life, it was the bombers themselves who ran a risk. The usual procedure was for the bomber to wait outside an hotel or railway station, or any place where they would not draw attention to themselves. The bomb maker or some other member of the team would deliver the incendiary bomb, already primed. If the timing device was sulfuric acid in a balloon, then the bomber would have to place it at a prearranged target as soon as possible, given the unstable nature of the bomb. A group of six Irishmen based in Harlesdon, north London, engaged in such incendiary bombing, came under police observation. On the late evening of 24 June two of them, Thomas Nelson and Patrick Donaghy, were observed placing time-delayed incendiaries into pillar boxes. They were smartly arrested and later sentenced to twenty years' imprisonment.

That same night, on 24 June in another part of London, the bombing campaign entered a new phase—a phase that was a departure from the S-Plan. It appeared to be a deliberate attempt on human life. At 10:50 p.m., as people were emerging from West End theaters and cinemas, the first of four serious explosions occurred in central London. In addition the capital also suffered a number of incendiary attacks. The first bomb went off in Piccadilly Circus, followed by explosions outside Lloyd's Bank, also in Piccadilly Circus; the Midland Bank on Park Lane, and finally a branch of the Westminster Bank, were also attacked. Some seventeen people were injured in the attacks, including a seventeen-year-old boy who was blinded in one eye. The damage caused amounted to £1,000. The first bomb had been placed in a manhole. It broke the windows of premises in the vicinity, and shattered the front of a tobacconist's shop. A man standing at the entrance of the nearby Underground Station was blown off his feet and fell backwards down the steps. The explosion at Lloyd's Bank, on the corner with Sackville Street, broke windows for some seventy yards round about. At the Midland Bank in Park Lane the door of the bank was blown across the road and ended up against the railings of Hyde Park. Two other unexploded bombs were later discovered: one on the curb at Piccadilly, and the other in a public lavatory at Oxford Circus.

Thomas Hawkett, who worked in the men's lavatory in Oxford Street, spotted a suspicious parcel left behind in a cubicle. Correctly suspecting that it might be a bomb, he picked it up and dumped it into a bucket of water. He then hosed it down, knowing that this would render the gelignite useless. He then stood and watched as the brown paper covering tore, and the fuse and charge floated to the surface. The police, who were checking for other bombs, arrived and took it off his hands. Meanwhile another unexploded bomb was discovered at the curbside in Piccadilly. Detective Inspector Robert Fabian of the newly formed Vice Squad, based at Vine Street police station, approached it.

> Stooping to examine it, my heart began to move with wild excitement. The parcel was not merely fastened with string—there were two black strips of ominous adhesive tape, and to the touch it was as hot as a tea urn. It was a bomb!
> I shouted to the two nearest CID men, Sergeant Burgess and Constable Saul: "Keep the crowd back. I think there's another bomb!" I picked up the brown paper parcel gingerly, dry lipped looked round for a bucket of water, while Burgess and Saul coolly shoved the crowd back. There was no fire bucket, and the parcel seemed to get hotter as I grasped it. Somebody needed to do something quickly—and with a strange lonely dread I realized that it was up to me to do it! I knelt on the pavement, took out my pocket knife and cut the string, the adhesive tape, unwrapped the brown parcel at one end—pulled out something that felt like a sausage wrapped in greased paper.... It was gelignite—yellow, softish like marzipan, smelling sickly greasy. Another yellow, wrapped sausage ... another ... seven plump 4 oz. sticks of Polar Ammon Gelignite. I placed them at intervals along the pavement, so if one exploded the others might not catch its detonation. From the eighth stick of gelignite a pencil fuse stuck out. I sliced the pasty explosive with my knife and removed the fuse. I pulled out from the parcel two more plump sticks of brown gelignite, making a total of 40 ozs. Then at the bottom of the parcel was a heap of gray powder and in it a green rubber balloon, with a wax brown cylinder inside it. I pulled this apart, blistered my hands with acid.[9]

The fire brigade arrived but they had no water buckets, so Fabian, Burgess and Saul gathered up the bomb components and gingerly carried them to the yard of the nearby police station, where they dunked them in red fire buckets.

In the other incendiary attacks, Madame Tussaud's Wax Works was targeted. A balloon bomb exploded in the chamber of horrors. A waxwork of Henry VIII was destroyed, but a bomb in the Red Riding Hood tableau, placed in the wolf's bed, failed to go off. As the bombs started to explode, people panicked and ran. One German student who had run from the scene found himself at the mercy of an angry crowd who felt sure that he was a bomber. He was eventually rescued by the police. After some brief questioning he was released. Some thirty Irishmen in the vicinity were also stopped by the police, and taken to the police station, but were all later released. The preponderance of Irishmen in England at the time was due to England's recruitment in Ireland for workers in its munitions factories. Elsewhere that evening, police surveillance resulted in the arrest of two men, Patrick Donaghy and Thomas Nelson, who were caught in the act of dropping incendiary bombs in pillar boxes.

For his prompt action, Thomas Hawkett was awarded £5. Detective Inspector Fabian was awarded the King's Police Medal for Gallantry, the police equivalent of the Victoria Cross, and £15. The bombings were publicly condemned by the Roman Catholic Archbishop of Westminster, Cardinal Arthur Hinsley. Perhaps somewhat surprisingly, the cardinal received a letter of rebuke from James O'Donovan, author of the S-Plan. He reminded Hinsley that his countrymen had subjected the Catholics of Ireland to a recurring campaign of murder, arson and despoliation. Despite the rebuke, Hinsley's condemnation was echoed up and down the country by priests in their pulpits—especially Irish priests working in England. No help was to be given to the bombers, they informed their congregations.

Detective-Inspector Robert Fabian courageously defused an IRA bomb in Piccadilly, London, for which he was awarded the King's Police Medal for Gallantry.

IRA man Harry White up in Manchester, having survived a large-scale roundup by the police, was constantly on the move, and doing his best to obtain new supplies in order to continue the bombing campaign. He was sent a number of newly trained men to replace those lost. One was a nervous young man from Belfast, named Brady. White and young Brady selected a large department store in the center of Manchester as their next target.

On the afternoon of 11 July, White prepared the

bomb. He put the acid into the prepared wax container and sealed it. Then he inserted the container into the balloon. Five sticks of gelignite were tied together with a detonator, and then he inserted the fuse. At the end of the fuse White taped a little bundle containing potassium chlorate, sugar and aluminum powder, all surrounding the balloon which enclosed the wax container. The inert bomb was carefully put into a cardboard box and the lid placed over it. The sensitive corner containing the wax tube was carefully marked, so that when the time was ready it could be pressurized, thus breaking the wax seal and setting off the bomb.

After mixing the "Paxo," White had a terrific headache. He left young Brady to parcel up the bomb. White's instructions to Brady as he passed it over to him for tying up was, "Don't tie it too tight." Moments later White looked over at Brady. He had drawn the string far too tight on the package. As White dashed over to open the package, there was a flash; the wax container had been crushed, and the acid had leaked. The curtains started to burn. White shouted to Brady to get out, the bomb was about to explode. Everything was now ablaze. Down the stairs the two of them fled, and up the road, where they leapt onto a moving tram. From the city center they caught a bus to Blackpool—anywhere would have done, just to get themselves out of Manchester. By then the fire brigade had been notified and were on the scene, as were the police, and soon after, Special Branch. With the fire put out, they began collecting evidence and talking to neighbors. Temporarily safe in Blackpool, White noticed that Brady's trousers were badly burnt. Such a thing would not go unnoticed. He found him somewhere quiet to sit, then went off to buy him a replacement pair. From Blackpool the pair traveled to Liverpool, and from there to Glasgow, from which they eventually crossed the sea to Belfast. From there they traveled south to Dublin in the Irish Free State.

3

The Railway Bombings

In July 1939 the IRA began attacking railway stations. Bombs were left overnight in waiting rooms and left-luggage offices. Early on the morning of Sunday, 3 July 1939, seven bombs exploded at railway stations throughout the Midlands, doing considerable damage to office fittings and luggage. Luckily no one was seriously injured. The stations effected were Birmingham New Street, Derby, Leicester, Nottingham, Stafford, Coventry and Milverton (Warwick).

As the bombs started going off, telephone calls were quickly made to all railway stations around the country ordering the staff to search left luggage for other explosive devices. The quiet little station at Milverton between Warwick and Royal Leamington Spa, so out of the way that it is astonishing that the IRA even discovered it, suffered as badly as the more well-known stations. The explosion occurred about 5:45 a.m., and completely wrecked the parcel store and booking office. All the station's windows were shattered. Wreckage blocked the staircase on the down platform, forcing people later in the day to cross over the track at the end of the platform. Fortunately no one was injured, and the prompt action of the Leamington Spa Fire Brigade saved the station building from fire.[1]

In response to the news of the explosions at other Midland railway stations, a search of all luggage in the cloakroom at Coventry central station was ordered. As staff approached, smoke was seen coming from under the doors of the cloakroom. A moment later flames were seen through the glass-partitioned door. Some members of staff were sent off to get firefighting appliances, while another member dialed the emergency number, and called for the fire brigade. Barely five seconds later an explosion occurred. Above the cloakroom were the bedrooms occupied by twelve girls who were the station's refreshment room staff. Four of the girls were on weekend leave, but the other eight were in bed. They were woken by the blast and the falling plaster from the ceilings. Luckily again none of them were seriously injured. The manageress of the station's refreshment room, Miss Moore, led all the girls to safety. "There was no panic," she later told a local newspaper reporter. "We were all badly startled, but the girls were splendid, although we were all shaken up."[2]

Subsequent police investigations revealed that the bomb had been deposited in a suitcase left the previous night. Forensics revealed that the bomb was of the usual IRA type: gelignite, a detonator and fuse, and acid in a rubber balloon. So violent was the explosion that a hole was blown right through the two-inch concrete floor of the cloakroom, making an opening into the cellar below. The brickwork of the cellar was also damaged. Thick plate glass from the two big windows fronting onto the station yard was hurled as far as the Park Road junction with Eaton Road, a distance of about 60 yards. Anyone passing by at the time would have been seriously injured, if not killed, by the death-dealing shards of heavy glass. The counter, behind which the case had stood on the floor, partially screened the glass-paneled public entrance doors on the platform side, but even so, glass from the doors was flung some 30 yards across the track to the opposite platform. The heavy wooden double doors also opening onto the platform were split, and nearly all of the ceiling in the cloakroom was brought down. Suitcases in all parts of the room were ripped open, their contents strewn all over. A lock on one of the cases was found deeply imbedded in the one part of the ceiling that remained intact. A drum and a cello, which were among the instruments deposited in the cloakroom by members of the popular Jack Jackson's Band, following their last performance of the week at the New Hippodrome on Saturday night, were completely destroyed.

Early that same morning another explosion occurred at Leicester's main station. A suitcase had been left in the ticket collector's booth by a man who had arrived on the 7 p.m. train from Birmingham on the previous evening. The ticket collector that morning, Charles Venn, was talking to a member of the public. He was querying the delayed arrival of an excursion train from the seaside resort of Brighton, along England's southern coast. Venn noticed smoke emitting from the case. Then a flame shot out towards him, and there was the sound of a fuse hissing. In alarm both men, realizing what was happening, fled for their lives. As they dashed away in opposite directions the booth burst into flame. Then there was an enormous explosion, the sound of which echoed and re-echoed around the old Victorian station. Fragments of woodwork, a chocolate slot machine, and glass were hurled through the air, towards staff and passengers. Gaping holes appeared in the high ceiling of the hall, and whole sections of boarding were torn from the train arrivals and departure boards. Windows high up in the walls and in the glass roof were blown out by the concussion. The interior of the station was covered in suffocating clouds of dust and smoke. A taxi driver on the rank outside was just entering the station as the bomb went off. Glass crashed down from the roof above him. He and two companions following were almost pushed over by the pressure. Composing themselves, they dashed outside, and while one telephoned the emergency services—police, fire brigade and ambulance—another dashed over to his cab and set off with all haste to the city police station.

Ticket collector Charles Venn suffered a severe gash across his back, a cut on the bridge of his nose, and bruising. After leaving the hospital where he was treated, and perhaps still in shock when interviewed by the local newspaper, he said his main concern was over his peaked railway cap. "My cap has gone and I haven't seen it since. So I suppose that must have been blown to shreds."[3] Lucky though he was, the station should have been packed at the time of the explosion with holiday travelers disembarking from the Brighton train. Lives were undoubtedly saved because it had been delayed by 45 minutes.

Two weeks later, on 17 July, a massive explosion wrecked the parcels office of Wolverhampton Low Level Station. The bomb exploded at 5:33 a.m., as the town slept, hurling glass and debris all over two rooms and the adjoining platform. The force of the explosion was so strong that it blew out the windows of a parked railway carriage nearby. The police later revealed that the bomb had been placed in a small weekend case deposited at the parcels office the previous night. A porter, who was barely 15 yards away from the scene at the time of the explosion, revealed that he had just gone through the platform door of the parcels office when he saw a vivid flash, followed by a terrific explosion. Glass flew about in all directions in the rooms and out onto the platform. The police and fire brigade were summoned to the scene. The porter had a narrow escape, as he revealed to a reporter from the local newspaper, the *Express and Star*: "A few seconds more and I would have been in the room—and maybe I wouldn't be here telling you this," he reflected.

In London, Special Branch had identified 24-year-old Gary Jones, alias Gray, as the possible new OC London. For the time being they were content to keep him under surveillance, and see who he might lead them to. One of the houses he visited was that of engine driver Charles Woods, situated in Wembley. Woods did not have a police record, but his wife Ella May did. She was an ardent Republican. On 22 July, Detective Inspector

James Holmes and Detective Sergeant Cain, with uniform back-up, raided the house. A quantity of bomb-making equipment was found. In the garden shed was discovered an unlicensed Webley revolver, and when the newly dug back garden was explored, explosive chemicals were discovered. A second Special Branch team raided the flat of sisters Ann and Rose Conway, another haunt of Gary Gray. He was there when the police entered the premises. Some two hundred sticks of gelignite were discovered, as well as detonators. A paper trail led them to a house in Brunswick Square, Saint Pancras, which led to the arrest of Patrick Donaghy, Herbert Moore, Thomas Nelson and Edward Stapleton. Here further detonators and bomb-making paraphernalia were found. At the September Central Assize, Charles Woods was acquitted of all charges and discharged,. Ella May, his wife, was not. She and the others were sentenced to between 10 and 20 years for conspiracy to cause explosions and possession of explosive substances.

Just as the police were beginning to congratulate themselves that they had rounded up the IRA cells in the capital, four days after their arrests, two bombs exploded in left-luggage offices at two of London's major railway stations, King's Cross and Victoria Stations. One man was killed and 15 people were injured in the explosion at King's Cross Station. The dead man was Dr. Donald Campbell, aged 30, a lecturer at Edinburgh University. He was returning with his 27-year-old wife from a postponed honeymoon. It was at 1:40 p.m. on Wednesday, 26 July. Three attendants were busy in the left-luggage department. There were a dozen people grouped around the counter. A porter wheeled in three trunks from a car standing in front of King's Cross Station. Just then the bomb exploded. There was a blinding flash! The whole station shook, and in the high vaulted glass roof the shattering roar echoed and re-echoed. Broken glass fell from the roof. The blast of the bomb knocked people to the floor. Some of them had their clothing ripped off. Others further away momentarily staggered under the force, and then, fearing a second explosion, ran for the exits. Baulks of timber hurled through the air; one piece hurtled 60 feet onto platform number 6. Women screamed. There was pandemonium. A pall of smoke and dust filled the station.

After a brief moment of shock, there was a dead silence. Then people began to run into the station to see what they could do to help. Sixteen men and women lay injured on the ground. Nurse Anne Kemp of the St. John Ambulance Brigade, hearing the roar of the explosion, ran into the station to offer what help she could. She acted instinctively, her training coming into play. William Kent, one of the cloakroom attendants, was bleeding badly from a wound to his right arm. She tore off his tie and made a tourniquet of it to stop the bleeding. She called for water to be given to the less seriously injured. In front of the wrecked cloakroom she found Dr. Campbell. Both his legs were shattered. Using the station's first aid kit she applied two rubber tourniquets.

Ambulances, their bells clanging, now began arriving. Doctors and nurses were rushed to the scene. Campbell, now in a semiconscious state, was sent off to the hospital first, to the Royal Free Hospital in nearby Pond Street. Passing trucks and taxicabs were commandeered to take away the injured. Mrs. Campbell was taken by ambulance to St. Pancras Hospital. Her injuries were not as serious as had at first been thought, and she was taken to see her husband, who tragically had already died. Chief Inspector Ivor Rees, explosives expert from Scotland Yard, Divisional Detective Inspector Slyfield, a Home Office expert, and police photographers began a detailed investigation at the scene. Staff and passengers were questioned. At the same time, Special Branch men raided a house nearby that had been under observation. Five men were taken to Cannon Row Police Station for questioning.

At 9:30 p.m. that same day, barely eight hours later, a bomb exploded in the cloakroom at Victoria Station in London. There was a loud roar which reverberated around the station. When the police arrived they found platform 15 strewn with debris and broken glass. A pall of smoke and dust was escaping through the broken glass roof. Five railway workers were injured. Two were detained in St. George's Hospital. The case that had held the bomb had been left on the previous day by a woman, an attendant remembered. The police now also had a description of the suspected perpetrator of the King's Cross explosion. He was aged about 30, 5 foot 11 inches in height, a tanned complexion, low forehead, straight nose, broad high cheeks, and deep-set eyes. His hair was thick, dark brown, brushed back and parted at the side. He was wearing a dusty brown sports jacket with gray flannel trousers. He walked with a slouch. That night a warning went out to all police forces in Britain. Hundreds of police were dispatched to guard their local railway depots.

The number of officers on duty at the House of Commons was strengthened, in view of the known threat to Parliament. All visitors not known to the police had to produce identification. In the House, M.P.s heard the second explosion while they were discussing the Anti-Terrorist Bill. They were so angered that the Third Reading was rushed through the House in 5 minutes. The bill completed all its House of Commons stages in exactly one hour after the explosion at Victoria.

In the Irish Senate, Prime Minister Eamon de Valera roundly condemned the bombings. If the Irish government could not deal with the perpetrators of the bombings, then a state of anarchy and civil war would develop in Eire. "We cannot allow any body of people to take action involving the loss of life or limb in the name of this Government either here or anywhere else," he declared.

Instructions were issued the next day to all London stations regarding the stricter inspection of packages handed in at left-luggage offices. People depositing cases and packages were requested to open them for inspection. Plainclothes detectives were sent to all London stations to keep watch on passengers boarding trains for Liverpool and other northern towns. Railway officials who regularly traveled between London and the ports of embarkation for Eire were questioned about any suspicions they had of recent arrivals from Ireland. An intensified lookout was maintained at all ports for suspicious characters.

On the night of the London bombings there were three huge explosions in Liverpool. The first bomb, out in the suburbs at Moghull, blew up a swing bridge spanning the Leeds to Liverpool canal, causing it to fall into the water below. The second bomb completely wrecked the front and large sections of the inside of the Central Post Office. The third explosion, lacking any real impact, went off in a park. No injuries were reported in any of the three explosions. At 11 a.m. on the morning of 27 July at Down Holland, near Ormskirk, also in Lancashire, two farm laborers found 74 sticks of gelignite attached to a pylon, They disconnected the bomb's wiring, then ran to the house of their employer, who telephoned the police. The wires had connected the gelignite to a battery and an alarm clock, timed to go off at 1 p.m., just two hours later.

The Liverpool police force, who had identified a number of suspect bombers based in the city, now decided to act. In particular they had their eye on Joe Deighan, who unknown to them was the O.C. of the Liverpool brigade of the IRA. He was one of the first bombers trained by Jim O'Donovan. After losing the arms dump in Edge Lane, earlier in the campaign, Deighan had managed to establish a second dump at a bookshop along Scotland Road. He had been identified some weeks earlier, after members of the London Special Branch had followed a suspect up to Liverpool who made contact with Deighan. The police then kept Deighan under surveillance, in the hope he would lead them to others, but the explosions of the previous night now forced them to act.

Deighan was an astute man. He had survived seven months by being cautious. He very soon became aware that he was being tailed, and accordingly warned the other bombers not to contact him. A friend of his, Tom Martin, surreptitiously booked a ticket for him on the Liverpool-to-Dublin ferry. Deighan, who had been very quiet over the previous few days, suddenly, on the afternoon of 27 July, emerged from his lodgings and ventured out into the city. Believing that he would lead them to the other bombers, the police stayed their hand, and did not arrest him. Deighan and Martin wandered around Liverpool before moving towards the docks, the police following from a distance.

The two suspects arrived at Princes Landing Stage, the terminal of the British and Irish Steam Packet Company. Martin handed Deighan the ticket, and just as the gangway was raised, Deighan made a dash up it and onto the ferry, where he presented his ticket. The police raced across the dock and up the gangway with the intention of arresting Deighan, but the ship's officer, the ship being Irish, refused to allow them to make an arrest. The police had to settle for a warning, shouting from the dockside, for Deighan not to return to Britain.

Deighan had escaped them, but the police were now on the point of being given special powers to prevent such men from even entering the country. They had had some successes through old-fashioned police work and the use of "touts," or police informers, as the statistics presented to Parliament showed. Sir Samuel Hoare, the Home Secretary, addressed the House of Commons and revealed that between January and the beginning of July 1939, there had been 127 IRA attacks. One person had been killed and 55 injured. Police successes included the successful prosecution of 66 terrorists, the seizure of 1500 sticks of gelignite, 1000 detonators, 2 tons of potassium chlorate and ferrous oxide, 7 gallons of sulfuric acid, and 4 cwt. of aluminum powder.

4

Prevention of Violence (Temporary Provisions) Act

Almost from the beginning of the bombing campaign there had been calls in Parliament for legislation to deal with the terrorists. Back in 1883, Parliament had passed the Explosives Substances (Temporary Provisions) Act to deal with the Clan-na-Gael bombings, and it remained on the Statute Book despite having only been intended as a temporary measure. The act enabled the courts to try men caught in the possession of explosives. What it did not do was to allow the police to act in a preventative manner regarding suspects, especially when there was insufficient evidence to bring about a prosecution. This would go against the very nature of British justice as codified under the Habeas Corpus Act of 1679. An innocent man could not be arrested and imprisoned. Under the Aliens Act of 1919, a non-British resident could be deported, but citizens of Southern Ireland, as former British citizens, enjoyed the same rights and liberties as existing British subjects.

In order to deal with the bombers, new legislation was required. At a joint meeting called by the Home Office, the unanimous view held by MI5, Special Branch and Chief Constables was that the growing menace of the IRA could not be met by existing legislation. A large amount of public money was being spent on guarding vulnerable places. In a cabinet meeting on 5 July 1939, the head of MI5, Sir Vernon Kell, suggested the internment without trial of suspected members of the IRA, with a panel to deal with appeals. Realizing that there would be Parliamentary objections, certainly in peacetime, if this was presented as a bill, Home Secretary Sir Samuel Hoare, a former MI5 officer, proposed the deportation of suspects already in Britain, and the exclusion from entry of people who were suspected of being members of the IRA or Cumman na mBan, the women's branch of the organization. Hoare pointed out that after the Piccadilly outrages the police had arrested a dozen men whom they felt sure were guilty persons, but of whom they had been unable to secure the necessary evidence, and after two or three days, had to let the men go. Deportation of these suspects would have been the ideal solution. This seemed to be the answer, but, and this might prove a sticking point, could the government deport a resident? By a resident this would mean someone who had put down roots and had lived in Britain for a number of years. After some discussion in cabinet, a nominal figure of four or five years' residency in Britain was decided upon. As a sop to the Opposition in Parliament it was suggested that a committee would be formed to listen to appeals. Attached to the intended legislation was a memorandum which pointed out that the Eire Government had passed a far sterner act on 14 June than that proposed by the British government. The Irish Act was directed purposefully against the IRA. Clause I dictated: "Every person who usurps or unlawfully exercises any function of government whether by setting up, maintaining or taking part in any way in a body of persons purporting to be a government or by any other action or conduct whatsoever shall be guilty of felony and shall be liable on conviction thereof to suffer penal servitude for a term not exceeding ten years or to imprisonment for a term not exceeding two years." De Valera insisted that while he did not propose to prosecute those guilty of disorder and terrorism in England, when it came to defiance of Irish law, an open challenge to the existing Irish government, there would be no temporizing.

Part III dealt with "unlawful organizations" and gave the government power to issue a suppression order against any body which "advocates or encourages or attempts the procuring by force, violence or other unconstitutional means of an alteration in the constitution," or "raises or maintains a military or armed force." In July the IRA was declared an unlawful organization. In the Senate of the Dail the Taoiseach, Eamon de Valera stated: "No one can have any doubt as to the result of the campaign in England, and no one can think that this Government has any sympathy with it. I would like to make an appeal to the people who are carrying on the campaign to ask them how they could hope to have a decision by means of this kind.... I do believe that a number of them are animated by high ideals but I believe that they are misreading Irish history and are making no allowance for changed circumstances."

Evidence that the IRA were turning towards more dangerous practices—for instance, the bombs that went off at Piccadilly on 24 June, as people were emerging from the West End theaters—led the authorities to

4. Prevention of Violence (Temporary Provisions) Act

fear that the IRA might be turning at any moment to deliberate attempts on human life. With that prospect in view, on 24 July, the Prevention of Violence Bill was presented to the British Parliament. The bill proposed to give the Home Secretary powers to exclude and deport persons whom he was satisfied were connected to the IRA, or alternatively to cause them to register with the police. The police themselves were given additional powers of search and detention for a period up to five days.

Punch cartoon, 2 August 1939. With the passing of the Prevention of Violence Act, the police were given greater powers to deal with IRA terrorism.

In presenting the bill, Hoare referred to the S-Plan and outlined the terrorist statistics to date. There had been a total of 127 outrages perpetrated since January 1939. Of these 57 had occurred in London, and 70 in the provinces. One person had been killed and 55 seriously injured. To date 66 persons had been convicted of terrorist offenses. The police had seized 55 sticks of gelignite, 1000 detonators, 2 tons of potassium chlorate and oxide of iron, 7 gallons of sulfuric acid, and 4 cwt. of aluminum powder. To ginger up support, he explained that up to the present the bombers had restricted themselves to damaging property, but recently he had been notified that they were about to intensify the campaign with no regard being paid to the loss of human life. The IRA, he informed Parliament, was now being "closely watched and actively stimulated by foreign organizations."[1] This was a coded reference to German Intelligence. In fact, war with Nazi Germany was barely seven weeks away.

Then, as a final thrust to concentrate minds, he informed the Members that plans had been discovered of an attempt to bomb the Houses of Parliament itself. Previously IRA attacks had been on property alone, but such an attack might well cause serious loss of life. The police had information that the campaign would no longer concentrate upon the destruction of property alone. Several threats recently received indicated that the campaign would become more ruthless and would show no respect for human life.

While most saw the necessity of such an act, it was the wording in certain clauses that disturbed the more liberal members. For instance, Dingle Foot, a member of the Opposition, pointed out the draconian power that the House would be conferring upon the Home Secretary, particularly with such wording as "if the Secretary of State is satisfied." The Home Secretary would become the sole judge. There would be no hearing, and no appeal. What if false charges were brought against an innocent man? He would not be able to establish his innocence. In response, the government, as it had always intended, agreed that an appeal system should be set up. Dennis Pritt, a Labour Party back-bencher, expressed his concern that such an act should not diminish the liberties of others, or be made a precedent for diminishing those liberties. Even the introduction to the bill sparked controversy. It read: "An Act to prevent the commission in Great Britain of further acts of violence designed to influence public opinion or Government policy with respect to Irish affairs; and to confer on the Secretary of State extraordinary powers in that behalf; and for purposes connected with the matters aforesaid." "The Bill," Pritt pointed out, "will make a very nice precedent for leaving out, in a few years' time, the words 'in respect to Irish affairs' and substituting 'in relation to anything.' It almost

4. Prevention of Violence (Temporary Provisions) Act

goes out of its way to destroy our liberties," he observed. Sir Samuel countered that the proposals in the bill were perhaps more acceptable than the alternative, of internment without trial.

These concerns aside, the bill was passed into law with a substantial majority of 218 votes to 17. The Act came into force on 29 July 1939. The main clauses, which were to prove effective, following some moderation, were 2 and 4:

> (2) If the Secretary of State is reasonably satisfied that any person in Great Britain is concerned in the preparation or instigation of such acts of violence as aforesaid or is knowingly harboring any other person so concerned, and that he is not a person who has been ordinarily resident in Great Britain throughout the last preceding twenty years, or in the case of a person under the age of twenty years throughout his life, he may make under an order (in this Act referred to as an "expulsion order") against that person requiring him to leave Great Britain.
>
> ...
>
> (4) If the Secretary of State is reasonably satisfied that any person is attempting or may attempt to enter Great Britain with a view to being concerned in the preparation or instigation of such acts of violence aforesaid, and that he is not a person who has been ordinarily resident in Great Britain throughout the preceding twenty years, or in the case of a person under the age of twenty years throughout his life, he may make an order (in this Act referred to as a "prohibition order") against that person prohibiting them from entering or being in Great Britain.

Those who could not be deported through long residency were covered in clause 3:

> (3) If the Secretary of State is reasonably satisfied that any person in Great Britain is concerned in the preparation or instigation of such acts of violence as aforesaid, or is knowingly harboring any other person concerned, he may make an order (in this Act referred to as a "registration order") against this person requiring him to register with the police particulars of his full name and address and to notify any changes in those particulars, to be photographed and measured in accordance with the regulations in force in relation to this act.

Clause 3 appeared to be quite benign, but the wording belied the reality. Once named a person could appeal, but the suspect was not given details of the specific allegations, thereby making it difficult to rebut the claim against him. Independent advisors were permitted to interview the suspect and make submissions on their part, but again without knowing the cause of the registration order, it was difficult to make a case in his defense. So in short, a person could be guilty of a crime, without knowing that a crime had been committed. It was very Kafkaesque.

Special checks were imposed on Irish workers in arms factories and military facilities. Strict controls on the movement of people between Britain and Ireland were put into place. Nineteen expulsion orders against suspected IRA men were signed by Sir Samuel Hoare on 28 July, eight of them within 30 minutes of the Anti-Terrorist Bill's becoming law. Up to midnight, eight of the men had been interviewed by the police. One agreed to leave the country; the other seven took advantage of their right to object and were locked in Brixton Prison until their cases could be considered. The one who agreed to leave was James Joseph Walsh, alias Murphy, the so-called "slouching man" suspect in the King's Cross explosion. He had been arrested two days earlier by a young police constable who recognized him from the description, and was taken to Cannon Row Police Station. His apartment was searched, but no evidence was found. He appeared in two line-ups but could not be positively identified. The police had no case. Walsh agreed to be deported.

On 3 August the first six deportees arrived in Dublin. Thereafter the number continued to climb. Some returned of their own free will, in most cases just before the police called. In all, 119 people were deported, 14 people were prevented from entering Britain, and 21 people were obliged to register with the police. In Coventry some 400 premises were searched within a few days of the passing of the Act.

The Liverpool unit of the IRA were all lifted in one night. Following the January raids by Special Branch, the unit was barely 15 in number, and following the surveillance on Joe Deighan all, or nearly all, the members had been identified. Tom Byrne, a young member of that unit, recalled: "In one night the entire unit was arrested. They were taken straight to the boat. The Scottish Borderers took me away. You were stuck in a van and they took you down to the boat and that was it. They came for me at my house. My parents weren't very pleased—my mother was very upset—but they knew what was going on.... The other guys were all on the bloody boat. I don't think we had any money; we certainly weren't in the bar having a drink. Half of Liverpool's Irish were on the boat as well. They were all going back to Ireland."[2]

For the first time the Irish authorities began providing information that led to the arrest of individuals in Britain. They also asked the British to share intelligence regarding those deported back to Ireland. Then from 1 June 1940, suspects were no longer deported, but interned in Britain under the Defence of the Realm Act, section 18b. The thinking behind this change in policy was, if they were not interned in Ireland upon their return, they might well form the basis of a fifth column in Ireland and

4. Prevention of Violence (Temporary Provisions) Act

assist any German invasion. Of particular concern was Rineanna Aerodrome in County Clare (now Shannon Airport). There was a small German colony based nearby who were involved in the construction of a hydroelectric plant along the river. The fear was that in conjunction with the IRA they would seize the aerodrome, allowing German troops to fly in.

In Chicago, On 13 August, Sean Russell issued a defiant speech against Britain (*Daily Mail*, 14 August 1939, p. 11): "The bombing by our army will continue. No concession can be got from England except by use of arms. There are between 500 and 1,000 at present engaged in England in the bombing campaign. The aim of it is to hamper the public services—lights, telephones, gas mains. You can do a town a greater injury that way. Our men try to put people to the maximum inconvenience without taking lives. The last thing we want to do is to take lives.... As for de Valera and the Irish Parliament, they're compromisers. They deal with the enemy. But our fight is not with them. It is with the British. The bombings will certainly continue."

On 15 August there were two explosions in Lancashire hotels at the holiday resorts of Southport and Fleetwood. An Irish couple, "said to speak with a pronounced Irish accent," booked a double room at the Southport hotel in the name of "Mr. and Mrs. Hirst of London." The woman was estimated to be about 27 years of age; her companion was about 30. Some 6 hours later the bomb went off. Searching the wreckage the police found fragments of a celluloid doll, a fuse and a metal container. The newspapers speculated that the doll was used to dispel suspicion in any search of the room. In the second explosion a young woman of about 23 booked into the Fleetwood hotel. She signed herself in as "Miss Hull of Skipton in Yorkshire." She left her suitcase in the room and went out for a walk. The bomb went off about the same time as the Southport bomb. The room was wrecked by the explosion, which hurled glass from the windows 20 yards across the promenade. A hole was blown in the adjoining bedroom. Two pieces of a metal canister were found in the bedroom as well as metal fittings and a suitcase handle. The girl was described as wearing a green mixture costume, with loose-fitting coat and a blue cone-shaped hat which she left in the bedroom.

In Ireland the Dail began cracking down on the IRA. On 14 August there were a number of police raids in the Dublin area. George Plunkett, a senior member of the IRA, was arrested. So too were Joe Clark, editor of the *Wolfe Tone Weekly*, a mouthpiece of the IRA, and several members of the Dublin unit, including Myles Heffernan, who was caught with IRA documents in his house. On 22 August two proclamations were issued putting into force parts of the Offences against the State Act, setting up special criminal courts and giving the government the power to arrest, detain and search subjects. On 25 August the Military Tribunal was set up in Dublin. A series of raids on the homes and offices of known and suspected members now followed. The police raided 16, Rathmines Park, a house that had been used for some time by IRA GHQ staff. Here they discovered Stephen Hayes, acting chief of staff of the organization, along with senior members Larry Grogan, Paedar O'Flaherty, Willie McGuinness, Patrick McGrath and Matty Tuite. Throughout the country Irish Special Branch began picking up known and suspected IRA men and interning them.

5

Coventry, 25 August

Prior to the start of the campaign, in October 1938, a number of specially trained IRA men were dispatched to England. To avoid detection they were given strict instructions to avoid contact with other IRA members already based in England, men who might well be under Special Branch surveillance. Their mission was to establish safe houses and munitions dumps. Initially trained in London, among those sent to Coventry in the second wave was Belfast-born Dominic Adams, who replaced Sean Fuller as O.C. in the West Midlands. Adams, a committed IRA man, was a member of D Company in the Lower Falls. He had first come to the attention of the Northern Ireland authorities while still a teenager, when he was arrested in Belfast along with Michael O'Kane and Robert Sloan, for possession of a revolver following an anti–Imperialist rally in November 1932. He was picked up by the RUC in the following year, along with James Steele, during a roundup of known IRA men and sympathizers, and sentenced to three months' imprisonment for failing to answer questions put to him by the police. To avoid further arrest he crossed the border and traveled south to Dublin, where he was unknown to Irish Special Branch. He took part in a number of bank raids and other robberies in order to raise money to finance IRA activities.

In 1938 Adams volunteered to take part in the bombing campaign in England. Sent to the West Midlands, Adams found lodgings in Meadow Road, Coventry, half a mile or so west of the city center. In March 1939, Adams, using the alias of Norman, acquired a Corporation allotment[1] on a piece of land at the rear of Armfield Street, off Stoney Stanton Road, in northeast Coventry. He ordered a wooden shed from a local timber merchant. When it arrived on site, he asked a Mrs. E. Toms, whose garden at 17, Armfield Street backed onto the allotments, if he could leave the sections of the shed at the end of her garden for a couple of days. This she readily agreed to. On the Sunday after the delivery, Adams and three other unidentified IRA men (possibly including Harry White and Albert Price, who were known to be in Coventry in March) erected the shed, which measured some eight feet by six feet. Adams had established a bomb factory. Over the next few months the other allotment holders often observed men working on the plot, in and around the shed, but curiously very little work was done in clearing the weeds and thistles that had accumulated. Barely six square yards of land were turned over for cultivation.

In May 1939 James McCormack, using the alias of Richards, was sent up to Coventry to join the new active service unit under Adams. Prior to this he had been operating in London. He also found lodgings in Meadow Street, at number 17, the home of the Hewitt family: Joseph, Mary and Mary's mother, Brigid O'Hara. The family had come over from Belfast some three years earlier, and had no known Republican connections, as they were to testify a little later. In his biography, though, Harry White was to contradict this: "I travelled to Coventry which had lost its O.C., and where I ran into Albert Price. I met a couple of other lads there including Jimmy Morgan. We were stopping with Mrs. O'Hara from Belfast, afterwards charged with Barnes and McCormack." On 11 June the whole family moved from Meadow Street to 25, Clara Street, in east Coventry. They took McCormack, or Richards as he was known, with them.

Shortly after, a third Irishman arrived in Coventry. He was Joseph B.

25, Clara Street, Coventry. The IRA assembled bombs at this quiet suburban address.

O'Sullivan, known familiarly as "Joby." A new IRA active service unit was now in place. Sullivan, from Cork, the son of a bacon shop owner in Coburg Street, was the bomb maker. The team was supplied with gelignite and chemicals from Liverpool, and by early July, IRA men were regular visitors to Clara Street. They frequently brought suitcases with them. When they arrived McCormack either took these men into the front room and shut the door, or took them upstairs to his bedroom at the back of the house. On one occasion Mary Hewitt saw McCormack take white powder from a suitcase that had been left for him, and make it up into a paper parcel. She felt sure that the powder was explosive, and spoke to her husband. He reassured her that explosives did not come in white powder form. One visitor for sure was Gary Jones, alias Gray, alias Halfpenny, the London OC, later arrested in London on 22 July. McCormack, reading the newspaper some days later, observed to Mrs. O'Hara, "I see one of the boys have been picked up in London and he has been sent to prison. He called here, his name is Jones."[2]

About the second week in July, McCormack prepared a hiding place in the cupboard under the stairs. Without permission he took up the tiles and burrowed down into the foundations. Mrs. O'Hara saw what he was doing, and asked him what was going on. Quite blatantly he said, "This is for a bit of a dump." She was not quite sure what that was, but spoke to her son-in-law.

On Sunday, 13 August, as O'Sullivan and McCormack were preparing a bomb at the shed on the allotment, McCormack carelessly dropped a lighted cigarette on a floor littered with grains of potassium chlorate, which burst into flames. He tried to stamp out the flames, scorching his trousers in the process. The fire got out of hand. Both men fled from the shed and ran across the allotments. From the upstairs bedroom window of a house backing onto the allotment, a neighbor, Mr. George Walker, spotted the two men running away. He noticed smoke coming from the shed and a red glow could be seen through the shed window. At 4:45 p.m. the bomb that was being prepared exploded. The shed was blown to smithereens, leaving a crater on its site two feet deep and three feet wide. It scattered an area of some 20 yards round about with a whitish powder (which subsequently proved to be potassium chlorate), fragments of rubber balloons and particles of metal. Windows of two or three adjoining houses overlooking the allotments were shattered. Mr. W.G.H. Thomas of 21, Armfield Street gave an account of the explosion to the *Coventry Herald*: "I was walking along Old Church Road near Foleshill Road with my mate when I heard a tremendous noise. My mate said, 'That was a gas main blowing up.' I thought it was somebody blowing up tree stumps with explosives, and we both hurried back to see what had happened. We found that one of the windows at my home had been broken, and all the neighbors were looking at the hole left in the ground."[3]

Two 15-year-old girls, Gertie Bonser and Vera Pearson, were walking down the pathway that ran alongside the allotments when they saw the two men running towards them. As the taller of the two men ran past the girls he bumped into Gertie, but ran on without stopping to apologize. The girls watched as the two IRA men ran into Bell Green Road, where they were seen to jump onto a moving tram car. Both girls managed to get a reasonable look at the two men, and were able to give descriptions. Both men were between 30 and 40 years of age, they said. The taller of the two was wearing a navy blue suit and was clean shaven, while the shorter man had a gray suit with a chocolate-colored shirt and tie with no waistcoat. He had a moustache. They were fairly accurate descriptions.

With the shed and its contents destroyed, it became essential for the bombers to obtain fresh supplies. Adams contacted the OC for Britain, then based in London. On 21 August he sent Peter Barnes up to Coventry to establish contact. Cautiously he carried no bomb-making equipment. It was a preliminary visit to ensure that the Coventry team were still at large, and that he was not walking into a police trap. Barnes was told to ask for a "Mr. Norman," whom he would find at 25, Clara Street, just off Binley Road. About one o'clock, Barnes, a slim-built Irishman dressed in a light brown tweed suit, approached the house. There was a man standing at the open front door. It was McCormack. He was expecting the visitor. Barnes asked him if he knew a Mr. Norman. A Mr. MacMahon had sent him, he informed the man. It was a fairly innocuous conversation to anyone who might have overheard it. McCormack invited his visitor in. The Hewitts were out, but Mrs. O'Hara was in the garden with her grandchild. As they talked, Mrs. O'Hara entered the house. McCormack introduced the two of them. "This is Mr. Barnes," he said. "He has come from London." Mrs. O'Hara made them all a cup of tea.

While they were talking, Mary Hewitt came home from work. It was her half-day. Sometime a little later, Barnes asked Mary if she would do an errand for him. He asked her if she could buy two flour sacks for him. He needed them urgently but did not know where to buy such items in Coventry. She agreed, and Barnes gave her a one-pound note. She went to Celia's, a baker's shop at 98, Walsgrave Road, a ten-minute walk away or so. Here she bought two bags, which cost two shillings, and obtained a receipt as she thought the price was rather high, and Barnes might think that she was

5. Coventry, 25 August

cheating him. Dropping them off with the change, Mary Hewitt took her newly arrived cousin Barney Davey down to the Labor Exchange, where he registered for employment. Barnes pocketed the receipt. When she returned, at about half past four, Barnes was still there. McCormack said to her, "The bags you have got are no use." They were not fine enough. Mrs. Hewitt agreed to return them and get Barnes's money back, if she could not get the desired flour sacks. Her mother agreed to go with her. They took the baby in its pram. While Mary Hewitt remained outside with the baby, her mother went into the shop. Mrs. Downs, the proprietor, regretted that she did not have the desired sacks, and readily returned the money. The family returned home, and Barnes was given his two shillings change.

Some time later Barnes approached Mrs. O'Hara and asked, "Would you do a message for me?" She asked what it was. "Go and get me a long shape suitcase." She agreed, and he gave her a ten-shilling note. She trudged down to Forey's in Gosford Street, bought a suitcase for seven shillings and sixpence, and was given a receipt. As it was about to rain, the shop assistant wrapped the case in paper. Returning home once more, she gave the case, the change and the receipt to Barnes. He left the house about half past three, taking the suitcase with him.

The next day, Tuesday, 22 August, McCormack left the house in Clara Street about 1:30 p.m. to walk into town to meet with Dominic Adams. They met at the Hippodrome in Hales Street, and then the two men walked up to Smithford Street and the shop of the Halford Cycle Company at number 29. Adams, wearing a sports jacket and flannel trousers, with a gray pullover, then put on a pair of spectacles, to confuse any future identification. While McCormack remained outside, Adams went in and purchased a tradesman's carrier bicycle with a basket on the front. The cost was £5 19s 6d. Adams only had £5 on his person, he claimed, which he paid as a deposit, promising to return on Friday to pay the remainder and take away the bike. The shop assistant took details of his name and address, "Mr. Norman, Grayswood Avenue, Coventry," which subsequently proved to be false, and gave him a receipt for the deposit.

On the morning of Thursday, 24 August, Joby O'Sullivan, carrying a bag of tools, turned up at Clara Street. McCormack and he went into the front sitting room, McCormack closing the door so that they would not be disturbed. An hour or so later O'Sullivan left. That evening he returned, and about 7 o'clock Barnes arrived from London carrying a suitcase full of potassium chlorate. All three men spent some time together in the front room, before Barnes left shortly before 8 o'clock to catch the 8:30 p.m. train back to London.

Early on the morning of Friday, 25 August, the Hewitts left for work, leaving Mrs. O'Hara to look after her grandson. Sometime after half past nine, O'Sullivan returned to Clara Street to finish making the bomb. McCormack took him up to the front bedroom to complete the task. A small hardwood block was screwed to the back of the clock under the winder. Two holes were drilled beforehand upwards through the block, and upon being fixed, a positive and negative wire was passed up through each hole. On top of the block was screwed a piece of metal linking one terminal to a two-volt battery. The other terminal was on top of the block, and a gap, which was closed with a penny soldered upon the alarm winder, pressed down like a hammer when the alarm went off. The device had to be wedged firmly within a small timber box so that it could not move. Accidental contact by the positive terminal would result in a premature explosion.

By about ten past twelve the bomb was complete and parceled up. At half past twelve McCormack left the house and walked into the town to pay the 19s. 6d owed, and collect the bicycle. Shortly after, Mary Hewitt returned home for her lunch. Sullivan was there. He appeared anxious. He asked Mary what time it was. "Ten to one," she answered." "I wonder what is keeping Richards; he is very long," said O'Sullivan. Just after one o'clock McCormick returned with the new bicycle. "I've got the bicycle," he announced. "Where have you put it?" Sullivan asked. McCormack informed him that it was parked in the alleyway behind the house. The two then went upstairs to retrieve the "small parcel, like a boot box tied up." McCormack instructed O'Sullivan to go out the back way, through the garden and out into the alley. There the bike was waiting. Sullivan put the bomb in the carrier and set off.

The night before, down in London, a team of Special Branch officers raided 32, Leinster Gardens in Bayswater. The street had been under surveillance for some time, following information received. Officers from Scotland Yard's Special Branch had been checking on all thefts of gelignite and underworld sources of supply. There had been a series of raids on quarries in Derbyshire and the West Midlands. A suspect house was identified in Birmingham, where 60 lbs. of gelignite had temporarily been hidden before being taken to a lodging house in Leinster Gardens, London. A police team headed by Detective Inspector Robert Fabian raided the suspected lodging house, but there was no one there. Searching the room, the detectives found a torn-up letter that had been thrown into the fire, but had failed to burn. It mentioned a meeting place for the next evening. As it was not in his district, Fabian passed the information to Inspector Leonard Crawford.

5. Coventry, 25 August

The meeting place identified in the letter was a café. Crawford did not know what the IRA men looked like. Placing a detective in the café would arouse suspicion if he was just sitting there waiting, so a policewoman agreed to go there at the appointed time. At the police station the detectives waited. Then the telephone rang. It was the policewoman. She had talked to the men. One had even bought her a cup of coffee. Then she divulged their new address: it was 32, Leinster Gardens, only doors away from their old address.

The police raided the premises. As the police went in, they discovered five men descending the stairs carrying three bombs to be loaded on carrier bicycles in the downstairs hall. Two of them were grabbed, but the other three bolted back up the stairs. They attempted to escape through a skylight over the roofs. Crawford, leading two junior colleagues, went after them. After a brief scuffle, the IRA men were overcome and handcuffed. The five men—Daniel Crotty, James John Evans, John Gibson, Daniel Jordan and James O'Regan—were all arrested, and later charged with the explosions that had occurred on 24 June. Three five-pound bombs were discovered. Carefully Crawford himself dismantled the bombs and made them safe. Paperwork discovered indicated their targets to be the Bank of England, Westminster Abbey and New Scotland Yard, the headquarters of the Metropolitan Police Force. The bombs were timed to go off at half past two in the afternoon. In the flat, women's hatboxes were also discovered, containing partly made time bombs.

Back in Coventry, the next day, Joby O'Sullivan cycled along Binley Road and left into Far Gosford Street, and on into the city center, his time bomb ticking away. The target was allegedly an electrical power plant. It has been written that the bomb was set to go off at 2:30 a.m. the following morning. This clearly was not the case. The analog clock settings would not permit such a function. The setting was 2:30 p.m. It was due to coincide with the three London bomb settings. The four bombs were set to go off at the same time as a "spectacular."

Along Jordanwell, Earl Street and into the High Street, Sullivan cycled. Time was ticking away.

He turned right into Broadgate. There were two public clocks: one that straddled the road, and one above the shop of H. Samuel Ltd, "The Empire's largest jeweller." It was just before half past one. He had just over an hour to get to his target, which is believed to have been the main Royal Mail sorting office in Hartford Street with the telephone exchange just behind it. Then, for whatever reason, he pulled up outside of Astley's shop. He dismounted and parked the cycle, its pedal resting on the curb in front of a parked car. Then he walked away. It was half past one, and the street was crowded.

Joseph Mazengarb, an engineer, was crossing the road towards Burton's men's tailor shop next door to Astley's. He saw O'Sullivan dismount and park the cycle. Mazengarb looked at the bike; it was a brand-new tradesman's cycle. It had a carrier at the front containing a parcel. He particularly noticed the sign on the rear mudguard: "Keep tyres hard." Ronald Johnson also noticed the cycle with its notice. He wandered into Burton's, re-emerging at a quarter past two. The cycle was still there outside Astley's shop. At half past two, Robert Kinsella, a Coventry man, was approaching Burton's. The bomb went off at 2:32 p.m. There was a terrific explosion. Kinsella was thrown to the ground. Inside Astley's shop, the manager, Alexander Ballinger, who was standing about two yards behind the shop window, was knocked off his feet by the force of the pressure. He sustained cuts to the face, hand and knee, as the glass came flying towards him.

Less fortunate were those standing outside. Five people were killed in the explosion. They were Elsie Ansell, aged 21; James Clay, aged 81; Gwilym Rowlands, aged 50; Rex Gentle, aged 33; and John Corbett Arnott, aged 15. The body of Miss Ansell was terribly mutilated. She was unrecognizable. There was scarcely any face left. It had been blown away, together with the front portion of her skull, exposing a lacerated brain. The right shoulder was blown almost completely off, and the lower part of the right hand and wrist were badly shattered. The little and ring fingers of the right hand were blown off, the right hip and the right buttock were partly blown away, the right knee and the right leg were shattered and pulverized, and the right foot was torn and lacerated. The left hand and the engagement ring finger were left. It was her engagement ring that was used to identify her. Gwilym Rowlands died of hemorrhage due to multiple injuries. He sustained multiple puncture wounds on the face, skull, chest, arms and legs. The injuries of the other three were of a similar nature. In all almost 50 people were injured by the explosion, and 43 premises were damaged.

Following the police raid in London that previous night, paperwork led an armed Special Branch team under detective Sergeant Hughes to a lodging house at 176, Westbourne Terrace, barely a fifteen minute walk away from Leinster Gardens. When the police arrived at 7:45 p.m., the caretaker, Edward March, showed them up to an attic room on the fourth floor. The room was empty. A preliminary search of the room led to the discovery of three small packets of white powder, which subsequently proved to be potassium chlorate. There was also a guidebook to Glasgow and a map of London. The policemen sat down to wait the occupant's

5. Coventry, 25 August

The aftermath of the Coventry bombing. Note in the foreground the bicycle that had held the bomb that killed five people.

return. At 8:50 the suspect entered the room. Hughes addressed him: "Are you Peter Barnes?" "Yes," he replied. "We are police officers," Hughes continued, "and have reason to suspect you of being in possession of explosives and being concerned in causing explosions in Coventry." Hughes formally arrested and cautioned him. Barnes admitted that he had been to Coventry, adding, "but coincidences can happen."

He was then searched. In his left outside jacket pocket was found a letter addressed to "Jim Kelly, 25, Parnell Square, Dublin."[4] Complete with poor punctuation and spelling mistakes, it read:

> Dear Jim,
>
> I am sure your wondering why I did not write but I no you will understand how tings are. I am still here in London I am very lookey so far T.G. I got it very hard after coming over. I did not meet the man I was to meet. He was gone so I had to go to Liverpool the next day and I did not meet any one there either so I was a week and did not meet one. I was nearly mad so then I met one and he told me all was gone but himself so I had to fix up things for myself. We got over a few then and got things fixed up what I am on. I go from one place to the other and bring the S—believe me it is hard but I got way well so far. I am after coming back from Coventry tonight 11.30 so by the

time you get this the Paper should have some news. Of course I do not when I will be picked up. I am sure you can see by the papers how things are. I would advise you to think of coming over now and it looks like war. It may be good for us. Some of the boys think that anyway but don't know. Well Jim I do hope your kid is all right by now and I hope you were able to get the money fixed up all right as I am right for money so far. If I don't luse them after this job then I will be fixed very bad for it costs me 5/6 a night for bed and breakfast and I grub out for the day, so it cost some to stay here. Well Jim, I will say no more this time for it is very late and I have to be out very erely in the morning. You no I cant give you any address. Tell Kenny I was asken for him an I could not write to him. I may be going over to Dublin soon. There may be a letter there from you. I got one the day I left so no more. I will write you agen if I can. I would love to get a letter from you but I cant. So cheers for R from your old pal.
Dixon.

In addition, two slips of paper were also found. The first read, "Euston to L'po. 12,10–4.5; 12.30–4.22, 12.45–5.45." The other read, "L'po. to Euston 8.10–12.10, 9.15–12.30." They were railway timetables between London Euston and Liverpool. A third slip of paper contained an address in Leeds. It was checked by the Yorkshire police but without result.

A third address led the police to 115, Warwick Avenue in London, some 500 to 600 yards away. It was the home of Sarah Keane, who lived with her married brother and his wife. When questioned, she revealed that she was the fiancée of Peter Barnes. The house was searched and in Miss Keane's bedroom were discovered the Coventry receipts for the suitcase and the sacks. Barnes had inadvertently picked them up at Clara Street, and later having discovered them in his pocket, handed them over to Miss Keane for safekeeping. From the time when Sean MacBride was head of the IRA, all receipts had to be kept and handed in at headquarters so that repayments could be made. The receipts were to link Barnes to the Coventry explosion.

The day after the explosion, Saturday, 26 August, the editorial in the *Midland Daily Telegraph* appeared under the heading "Murder." It was a carefully thought out piece; the anger felt by its writer was controlled:

> Men who placed a high explosive bomb in the carrier of a tradesman's bicycle, and propped the machine against the kerb in crowded Broadgate yesterday afternoon while they made their escape, murdered five Coventry citizens and caused varying degrees of injury to some sixty others. They murdered a bride-to-be who was believed to be selecting her wedding ring; they murdered an intellectual known among his friends as a man of utter kindness; they murdered a youth on the threshold of life, and two other men in their prime. These are ugly words, but Coventry is in an ugly mood, and we feel no

inclination towards the use of discreet phraseology. Up to mid-day today Coventry City Police had not indicated in what direction their suspicions lay. We feel justified in accepting what small risk of error there may be; we accuse the Irish Republican Army of perpetrating this horror. If we are wrong the IRA should dissociate itself from this terrible crime.

At the time of the fatal outcome of the recent explosions in some of the London luggage offices we expressed the view that IRA bombers could only be regarded as potential murderers. Soon after there emanated from IRA circles something which sounded almost like an expression of regret, for it was said the timing mechanisms misfired. Will any one have the affrontery to suggest that the high explosive bomb left in the tradesman's bicycle yesterday took human life by accident? Even if the bomb had been timed to explode at 2.30 a.m., instead of 2.30 p.m., the perpetrators must have been aware that the unlighted bicycle would not have been allowed to stay in Broadgate for 12 hours. That bomb was intended to explode when it did. This senseless mass murder must be made to recoil heavily upon the organization responsible. The recoil of political antagonism has been immediate, but Coventry will not be satisfied that even the restrictive measures already taken against the IRA terrorists are sufficient. The authorities are justified in taking the view that anyone found in the possession of explosive materials under circumstances which point to their intended use as bombs is a person prepared to do what was done in Coventry yesterday. The only possible penalty for such an offence is the penal one.

The police in the city had been extremely active. Members of the CID and Special Branch worked through the night making enquiries and visiting numerous premises. Officers carried out a close scrutiny of persons traveling from Coventry Railway Station, from only minutes after the explosion. They visited public houses, hotels, boarding houses and lodging houses, and carried out the biggest search ever conducted within the city. As the above editorial was being set up in type, the police in Coventry named their chief suspect, Dominic Adams. At 11 a.m. they issued the following statement: "Coventry City Police urgently desire to interview a former Irish resident by the name of Dominic Adams. This man is described as looking about 30, height 5ft. 7ins., to 5ft. 8ins, fresh complexion, black hair, blue eyes, broad thick nose, long face, active looking appearance. Has a small scar below the left eye. He originates from Belfast and is a labourer by occupation. He has used the name of Norman." Adams was no longer in Coventry. Even before the explosion he had fled the city by train. Likewise O'Sullivan had also fled Coventry, warning McCormack to do so too.

Sullivan caught a train to Leicester, and from there bought a ticket to Holyhead and passage to Ireland. He realized quite rightly that any Irishman with a ticket from Coventry or Birmingham would be stopped and questioned by Special Branch officers based at the Welsh port. So it proved. Passengers from different parts of the country bound for Ireland were given only a cursory glance. Normally IRA bombers settled back into their shadowy lives, and prepared to strike again, but not so Adams and O'Sullivan. They both fled. This might tend to confirm O'Sullivan's later statement that the bomb was timed to go off at 2:30 in the afternoon when it was inevitable that there would be casualties. They got out before the explosion—before the police dragnet began—leaving Barnes and McCormack to face the consequences.

Throughout the afternoon and evening of the 25th, forensic teams carefully examined the site of the explosion. A team from the Forensic Laboratory in Birmingham arrived, as did two Scotland Yard explosives experts. The most important finds among the debris were parts of a tradesman's bicycle: the frame, a brake lever, and parts of the metal carrier. The cycle was new. It had an identification number. Inquiries established that it was newly purchased from a local dealer, Halford's. This fact, in conjunction with the information received from the Leinster Gardens raid, of the intended use of bicycles as bomb carriers, seemed to confirm that the bicycle was the source of the explosion. The parts were taken away for analysis.

In the aftermath of the explosion, the Irish population in Coventry came under suspicion. Tensions ran high. "They must have known something about it," was a theme often expressed. Over 400 Irish homes were raided by the police in the search for the bombers, but without success. The majority of the Irish in the city, for their part, openly condemned the actions of the bombers. There were a number of letters published in the newspapers from Irish people, such as the one below:

> Sir—We would like to express our sympathy with the relatives and friends of those who were murdered on Friday last by the bomb outrage in Broadgate, and we sincerely hope that those who were responsible for their deaths will speedily be brought to justice, for as an Irish family living in Coventry for the past eleven years, we have nothing but praise for all English people. We have always found them ready to lend a helping hand when needed: that also includes my workmates.
>
> This is the land of my adoption, and now the dark clouds of war are over us we shall stand by it, come what may. We again tender our sympathies to the bereaved, as we know how we ourselves should feel towards those who are responsible for such a murderous act.
>
> Yours faithfully
> Thomas Gailey
> 120, Moor Street, Earlsdon
> Coventry. August 29.

Such letters of sympathy were not to save the Irish people living in Coventry from verbal and physical assaults. Understandably the people of Coventry were angry, and in the absence of the perpetrators, any Irish person, even though they had been neighbors for years, became targets. Bernadette Devlin, in her autobiography, *The Price of My Soul*, records such treatment: "My father set off for England to earn enough money to get married. It took him three years. He left Northern Ireland in 1939. He, his brother, and another young man had work waiting for them in Coventry, but the night they arrived, August 25th 1939, there was an IRA attack in the city: a time bomb in the carrier of a bicycle left parked in a busy street exploded and killed several people. And because my father and the others were Irish, no one would give them lodgings. After wandering around for several hours they were given beds in the Salvation Army."[5]

The Midland Daily Telegraph, the local newspaper for Coventry, reported in its headlines for 28 August, "Widespread feeling against Irishmen," and it reported that people in factories had called for the dismissal of fellow Irish workers. The *Telegraph* was quick to point out that "the vast majority of [Irishmen in Coventry] were entirely innocent of any sympathy with the IRA." There was no protection for Irish prisoners in English jails, though. They were beaten up by fellow prisoners, and also by their jailers. It is reported that in Dartmoor, Britain's most feared jail, eleven IRA prisoners held there were so badly beaten that they had to be hospitalized.

6

The Arrest and Trial of the Coventry Bombers

The police in Coventry raided boarding houses in districts where Irish workers were known to live, in a bid to discover the perpetrators of the outrage. The Hewitts were Irish. It was inevitable that at some stage they would be visited by the police. Using good old-fashioned detective work, though, Special Branch had a good idea of what part of the city they should be searching. They had already followed up the clue of the Coventry receipts found in Barnes's possession. Even before the explosion of the 25th, neighbors had reported the suspicious goings on at 25, Clara Street to the police. At midday on Monday, 28 August, Chief Inspector Cyril Boneham of the Coventry City Police, Detective Inspector Barnes of the Special Branch, and a number of other armed officers raided the terraced house of the Hewitts. As she opened the front door, Mrs. O'Hara was instantly recognized as the woman described by Celia at the cake shop who had purchased the flour sacks. Boneham had established a link between the London IRA cell and Clara Street. The police were invited in. Boneham asked, "Are you the tenant of these premises?" Mrs. O'Hara replied she was not: "The tenants are Joseph and Mary Hewitt." The lodger, James McCormack, or James Richards, as he was known to the family, confirmed this: "That is right," he said. As the police began a search of the house, Mary Hewitt arrived home for lunch. She too was questioned. The search continued. A set of tools was found, including a soldering iron, a piece of solder and two pairs of pincers. With them was found a little setter for the back of an alarm clock. Curiously, when "Richards" was searched, a second setter was found in his pocket. When questioned why he had it in his possession, he answered, "The kiddy has been playing about with it; I suppose I must have picked it up." Out in the coal shed behind the house, a suitcase was found. It was a strange place to leave a suitcase.

6. The Arrest and Trial of the Coventry Bombers

There was enough suspicion to justify the detention of all of the inhabitants of the house with a view to further questioning. They were all arrested and taken to the central police station. At 3:30 p.m. "Richards" made a statement to the police. He detailed his early life, his arrival in Coventry, and what he had done in the city since his arrival. He made no mention of any IRA involvement. He spoke about the flour sacks as part of an overheard conversation. No mention was made of Peter Barnes. The following morning, with no real evidence as yet to hold them, they were all released on bail until 5 September, when they were told to report back. As a precaution, a covert watch was kept on the house and its suspects, particularly the two men, who were followed.

A forensic report came back. Traces of potassium chlorate were present in the suitcase found in the Hewitts' coal shed. On Saturday, 2 September, the two Hewitts, Mrs. O'Hara, and the lodger, "Richards," were all arrested under the Prevention of Violence (Temporary Provisions) Act, and placed in custody. The following day a further search was made at 25, Clara Street. Traces of chlorate were found in a trench coat hanging up in the hall, and on a chair. The two women, concerned that they would be implicated in the Coventry bombing, made statements to Chief Inspector Parker and Inspector Barnes, regarding what they knew. Mrs. O'Hara identified Dominic Adams by name. Adams was long gone, though, as was the "strange man," Joby Sullivan, whom she described: "The strange man was about 25–26, about 5ft. 4in., fair hair parted in the middle and brushed straight back, rather long face, and fairly well built. He was dressed in a slate blue suit."[1]

On 5 September, all four prisoners were charged with offenses under the Explosive Substances Act of 1883. On 13 September, in a police lineup, Frank Andrews, assistant at the Halford Cycle Company's shop at 29, Smithford Street, identified "Richards" as the man who had collected the tradesman's cycle on Friday, 25 August. Reviewing the evidence, the Public Prosecutor decided on 27 September that the facts justified a charge of murder against the prisoners. Peter Barnes was transferred from London to Winson Green Prison to stand trial with the others. The trial at the Birmingham Assizes was set for December 1939.

The four-day trial opened on 11 December 1939 at the Birmingham Assizes. It was held in the dark oak-paneled room of criminal court number 5, before Mr. Justice Singleton. The lead counsel for the Crown was Mr. Richard O'Sullivan, K.C., an Irish Roman Catholic, well acquainted with the political and historical background to the case. The line of questioning had been carefully prepared for the prosecution by Chief Inspector Parker of New Scotland Yard. There were no loose ends. Every point that the defense might make had been anticipated.

All five prisoners were brought up into the dock. The Clerk of Assize addressed them: "Peter Barnes, James Richards, Joseph Hewitt, Brigid O'Hara and Mary Hewitt, you five prisoners stand charged upon this Indictment with the murder of Elsie Ansell upon the 25th August last." They were asked how they pleaded. They all pleaded "Not guilty." From a legal point of view the question was, is the charge against the accused properly one of murder? The ancient rule of English law indicated that when a person commits a felony act in a way which is known to be dangerous to life, and life is indeed lost, that is murder—even if death was not intended. The other, very contentious issue, was the rule of "common purpose." The proposition was that if two or more persons agree to commit a dangerous crime which results in death, all the persons in the conspiracy are guilty of murder, not only the person who did the actual killing. The next point was whether the five prisoners should be tried together. Mr. Justice Singleton decided that they should.

Mr. O'Sullivan began with the opening speech for the prosecution. He outlined the case and the evidence that would be presented by the Crown. It was a very detailed account; Chief Inspector Parker had done his job well. The first witness called was Detective Constable Gibson. He was followed by press photographer Alfred Reynolds, and he by Detective Sergeant Law. These three individuals gave evidence regarding the authenticity of the photographs taken at the scene of the atrocity. Shown to the jury, many of the photographs were so horrific that they were never published.

The case then moved to the bicycle that had carried the bomb. Several witnesses were called who testified that they had seen the cycle. Mr. Douglas Jenkins for the defense asked one witness, Alfred Mazengarb, "When you saw this cycle being ridden you took the opportunity, did you not, of looking at the rider?" "Yes," Mazengarb answered. "Are you quite satisfied," Jenkins continued, "that the rider of that cycle was not one of the three men sitting here today?" "Yes," the witness answered. It was an important point. Though the law of "common purpose" prevailed, Jenkins had put it into the minds of the jurors that none of the men on trial was the actual bomber. This might influence the jury in their final decision.

The case then moved on to the actual explosion and the witnesses to it. The full horror of the explosion came across in the evidence of Police Constable Cooper, who had been on duty in Broadgate when the explosion occurred. He was examined by Mr. Ward for the prosecution.

"There on the pavement by Burton's shop did you find a man and a woman lying on the pavement underneath the window?"

"Yes," Cooper replied.

"Was the woman the lady in this Indictment, Miss Ansell?"

"Yes," came the reply.

"What do you say about the body of Miss Ansell?"

"She was lying on her left side with her knees drawn up, her right leg was pulped and her face was unrecognizable."

"Was she dead?"

"I formed the opinion that she was dead."

Ward paused to let this comment sink in. Then he made the connection between the dead body and the nearby wreckage of the bicycle. Other witnesses were called regarding the identification of the other bodies. Again Ward came back to Elsie Ansell when he interviewed mortuary attendant Frank Walduck.

"Was the body of the girl said to be Miss Elsie Ansell brought to the mortuary on the same day?"

"Yes."

"Were you present when it was identified by Mr. Beck?"

"No, he did not identify her; he identified her by her engagement ring."

"The girl was unrecognizable?"

"Yes."

The police surgeon, Dr. William Elford, was called. Ward asked him the cause of death of Miss Ansell. "Laceration of the brain and haemorrhage from various organs." Elford gave a graphic description of the body, so graphic in fact that Mr. Justice Singleton intervened, "I think that is enough."

Other witnesses were called regarding the damage done by the explosion. Then the case moved on to the bicycle that had carried the bomb. Harry Deaves, foreman at the Birmingham Bicycle Company, where the cycle was made, was able to identify it as a Halford "Karriwell" cycle. There for the moment that was it. The case now turned to the remains of the bicycle. An explosion originating in the cycle's carrier, it was ascertained, would produce the bicycle wreckage as found.

Mr. O'Sullivan for the prosecution then took up another strand of the case. The landlord of the house and the previous tenant were questioned about the pit discovered under the stairs. It was ascertained that no such pit previously existed. Mr. Ward for the prosecution put questions to the neighbors regarding the comings and goings at Clara Street. They recounted that the Hewitts had received a number of visitors unknown to the neighbors.

O'Sullivan and Ward then made the connection involving the two women in the plot, Mrs. O'Hara and her daughter Mary Hewitt. Mrs. Cecilia Downs, baker and confectioner, identified Mary Hewitt as the woman who had purchased two large flour sacks. Mrs. Mabel Howard, a shop assistant, identified Mrs. O'Hara as the woman who had bought the suitcase. Going off at a tangent for the moment, Sarah Keane, Barnes's fiancée, was questioned about sachets of chemicals discovered in Barnes's room. They were chemicals used in the process of bomb making. She was aware of them, but not of the chemical make-up. Miss Keane was questioned about the letter found on Barnes, and she was able to verify that he had written it. She also confirmed that her fiancé had journeyed up to Coventry. Mrs. Ethel Gorse, who lived in Clara Street, was next called. She verified that she had seen Barnes on the day before the explosion. O'Sullivan had made the connection between Barnes, who had explosive chemical, and 25, Clara Street in Coventry. So ended the first day of the trial.

Day two, Edward Henry March was questioned. He confirmed that Barnes was the occupier of the flat at 176, Westbourne Terrace in London, where the sachets of explosive chemicals were found. He was followed by Detective Sergeant William Hughes, who with other officers raided the flat. Hughes told the court of the discovery of the chemicals. They were subsequently handed over to Mr. Dupre, the government expert at Woolwich Arsenal, for identification. When Barnes returned to the flat, he was arrested and searched. In his inside jacket pocket was the letter that confirmed that he had been to Coventry on the previous day.

Attention now turned to the bicycle's purchase. Frank McRobb Andrews, shop assistant at the Halford Cycle Company's shop at 29, Smithford Street, now gave evidence. He wrongly identified Barnes as the purchaser, whereas it had been Dominic Adams. He was adamant, though, and in the process had linked Barnes with the explosives discovered in his flat, to the bicycle used to convey the bomb to Broadgate. Andrews then correctly identified McCormack as the man who paid off the money owing and who took the bicycle away. When Andrews was questioned by Mr. Jenkins for the defense, it transpired that Andrews had not actually dealt with the original purchase of the bicycle. It had been his colleague, Mr. William Brown. Brown testified next. Barnes was not the man he served. He had attended two police lineups, one in London and one in Coventry, but had been unable to identify Barnes. So Barnes was not conclusively linked to the purchase. McCormack (Richards) was, however. He was identified by another assistant at Halford's, Mr. W.C. Hawkins, as being the man who took the bicycle away on Friday, 25 August. The next witness was Mrs. Ada Clarke, who lived opposite the alleyway where the bicycle was left by McCormack, prior to the bomb's being loaded into its basket. She was asked if any of the accused men was the man who rode off on the fateful afternoon. She could not identify any of them.

Detective Inspector Sydney Barnes from Special Branch, Scotland Yard, was next questioned by Mr. O'Sullivan regarding the police raid on 25, Clara Street. He detailed the discovery of tools found in the scullery of the house. The implication was that they were the tools that had been used in the construction of the bomb; but then the implication was neither here nor there, for lots of people had tools of a similar nature in their homes. Then Barnes reported the discovery of a brass setter for the back of an alarm clock, found near the tools. The detective was asked, "Was there a clock in the house which that key or setter would fit? "No," the policeman answered with emphasis. He then went on to talk of the discovery of a suitcase in the outside coal store, which was sent on for analysis.

O'Sullivan then went on to ask the Special Branch man about the two ladies of the house, and the purchase of the flour sacks. Mr. Justice Singleton momentarily intervened for clarification, and Mr. O'Sullivan then gave details of the purchase and retention of the receipt. Barnes was then asked what happened after the five accused had been arrested. Mary Hewitt, he said, made a voluntary statement regarding all she knew. The prosecution requested that it be read out. Having seen the statement, the defense were concerned that it might compromise her husband. In English law at the time, a woman could not be compelled to testify against her husband. After some legal wranglement, it was decided that the statement should be read out to the jury, on the proviso that any comment of Mrs. Hewitt regarding her husband should be excluded. Mr. O'Sullivan then continued with his questioning of Detective Barnes. The policeman then duly read out Mary Hewitt's statement. She detailed the purchase of the flour sacks, who did what and when. The prosecution then attempted to blacken Mary Hewitt's character by connecting her to the IRA in Belfast. At the time of her wedding, the local branch of Cumann-na-mBan, the women's branch of the IRA, had sent the couple a card wishing them a long and happy marriage. Also found in Mrs. Hewitt's belongings was an Easter lily card, associated with the 1916 Rising in Dublin. The defense pointed out that the sending of such cards was a normal occurrence within the Nationalist community, and nothing should be read into it. The wedding card was simply that: friends sending a wedding present with a card with good wishes attached.

Detective Constable William Sykes of Coventry City Police was next called. He gave evidence that when he and the other officers went to Clara Street they searched McCormack (Richards). In his right-hand trouser pocket was found a second setter for an alarm clock. The excuse given was that the Hewitt's young child had been playing with it and he, Richards, had picked it up. Sykes then told the court that he had later taken the setter, along with the suitcase found in the coal shed, to the West Midland Forensic Laboratory in Birmingham for examination.

In custody, McCormack made a voluntary statement to the police, which Sykes wrote down. The statement was then read out to the court. It detailed his early life and how he came to Coventry. It included the day-to-day events leading up to and following 25 August. There was no reference to visitors received. The purchases of the flour bags was nothing to do with him. Mrs. O'Hara had asked her daughter to buy the bags, and that was that.

Cyril Boneham, chief inspector in the Coventry City Police, was next called. Mr. O'Sullivan for the prosecution questioned him. He related that he had been in charge of the raid on 25, Clara Street. They had found a suitcase in the coal-house which he had given over to Detective constable Sykes. O'Sullivan then questioned him about his interview, and the written statement of Joseph Hewitt. Again it was fairly innocuous. There were questions about the pit dug under the stairs, and Hewitt's involvement. Not being satisfied, Boneham told the court that he had formally arrested both Hewitt and Richards with possessing explosive substances. Upon being charged, Boneham related, Richards had said, "You did not find any potassium chlorate on me."

Mr. Justice Singleton interrupted, "Had potassium chlorate been mentioned?"

Boneham replied, "Potassium chlorate had not been mentioned at that stage, my lord."

To emphasize the point, Singleton said, "Richards, then, you say, was the first to mention potassium chlorate?"

"Yes," Boneham confirmed. He then informed the court that both Mary Hewitt and her mother were subsequently charged with possessing explosive substances.

Kathleen Rowe, a policewoman with Coventry City Police, was next called. She had been dealing with Mrs. O'Hara following her arrest. Mr. Ward for the prosecution questioned her. Constable Rowe told the court

6. The Arrest and Trial of the Coventry Bombers

that after her arrest Mrs. O'Hara had asked to speak to the senior police officer involved in the case. Chief Inspector Parker was called, and Mrs. O'Hara made a voluntary statement to him. Chief Inspector Parker was then called to the stand. He confirmed that he had taken a statement from her. Upon instruction, the Clerk of the Assize read out the statement. There were some damning comments. Richards, she claimed, had informed her, "I am an Operating Officer from Dublin." She told of how Irish fellows called at the house and asked for Jim Richards. There was more. One day in conversation with Richards he had said to her, "I see one of the boys have been picked up in London and he has been sent to prison. He called here, his name is Jones." She related that Richards had introduced her to Peter Barnes when he had called at the house. It was Barnes who had asked her daughter to buy two flour sacks. It was Barnes who had asked her to buy a suitcase for him. Mrs. O'Hara in her statement detailed the few days before the explosion. She mentioned Dominic Adams by name. She related how Barnes had returned to the house with a suitcase containing "white powder." On the day of the explosion, Mrs. O'Hara said, Richards had told her, "I am going for the bicycle which Adams ordered." Then she made reference to the actual Coventry bomber:

> I asked him where he was from and he said, "I came straight from Dublin." He was about 28 or 29 years old, about as tall as Richards, but a bit stouter. I would not know him again. He came back on Friday morning, the day of the explosion, and did some more work with the tools. Richards was in the room with the stranger and I noticed that the parcel had been moved from under the sink. After Richards went out to get the cycle the strange man stayed upstairs in the front room. He stayed there till Richards came back. He and Richards were then in the front bedroom for a few minutes. Just before Richards came back the stranger came downstairs and asked me what time it was. I told him one o'clock. At that time Richards came in and the stranger said to Richards, "Did you get the bike?" and Richards said, "Yes, it is in the back street." After this both men came down the stairs together and Richards said to the stranger who was carrying the parcel I had seen under the sink, "Go out the back way."[2]

At the end of the reading Mr. Justice Singleton reminded the jury of the law. The statement was only evidence against the maker of the bomb and not evidence against the other accused. It was rather like instructing the jury to ignore all the intriguing references to Richards—but of course they had heard them. Mr. Lyons for the defense asked that his objection to the reading of the statement be duly recorded. As such, he was laying down a marker for a future appeal.

The examination of Chief Inspector Parker continued. His evidence now related to Mary Hewitt's further statement. Upon direction, the Clerk of the Assize read it out to the court. There were references to Richards and his visitors at Clara Street, to white powder and a suitcase. Mrs. Hewitt also gave a description of the bomber: "The strange man was about 25–26, about 5ft. 4 ins., fair hair parted in the middle and brushed straight back, rather long face, and fairly well built. He was dressed in a slate blue suit." Her statement gave details of the fatal day:

> I said to Richards, "Are you going out, Jim?" He said, "Yes, I am going out to get a bicycle." He left the house and came back about 25 minutes later. While Richards was away the strange man came downstairs. He seemed to be agitated and said, "Isn't Richards a long while?" The time was then about 1 o'clock and Richards came back. Both men came into the kitchen and Richards said, "I've got the bike." I went upstairs to see what they had been doing in my room. I saw a parcel wrapped in brown paper and tied with string lying on the floor in the centre of the room. The tools had been cleared away. I did not go near the parcel. I was upset as I knew what they had done and were going to make an explosion., but I did not know where.[3]

Mr. Justice Singleton again pointed out the law, but again the jury had heard the statement which implicated Richards and the unnamed bomber.

Almost as a parting shot, Mr. Lyons, in defense of his client, asked Chief inspector Parker, "It is a fact, is it not, that Mr. Hewitt was at this time engaged in regular work at Coventry with the Randle Company?" In essence, was Joe Hewitt at work at the time of the bombing? "Yes," Parker answered grudgingly.

Next came another policeman, Detective Sergeant Edward Cowpe-Pendleton, also from Coventry City Police. He testified that he had taken a number of objects to the West Midland Forensic Laboratory in Newton Street, Birmingham, for analysis. There were no questions. Alan G.R. Whitehouse, staff chemist at the Forensic Laboratory, was then sworn in. He had examined the remains of the bicycle, the suitcase, a trench coat found in the hall at 25, Clara Street, and an old tea chest. All the items tested positive for potassium chlorate traces. Mr. Lyons cross-examined, trying to suggest that one did not necessarily have to be a bomber to possess the chemical. Mr. Whitehouse conceded that this was so. It was used as a disinfectant, and was freely available over the counter. It was also used in some tooth powders. Mr. O'Sullivan re-examined the chemist. "Would a suitcase be needed usually for disinfectant purposes?" "Unusual I would say," Whitehouse responded.

The next witness was another scientist, Frederick Harold Dupre from the Explosives Department of the Home Office. He had received the three envelopes of white powder discovered in Peter Barnes's flat. Tested by him, they were identified as potassium chlorate and sodium carbonate. Mr. Dupre was then asked by Mr. O'Sullivan, "You have had a considerable experience in home-made bombs?" "Yes," he replied. "Could a delay action bomb be constructed by using an alarm clock?" "Yes," Dupre agreed. "It has been done frequently recently." When prompted, he gave details of how this was accomplished. O'Sullivan had Exhibit 35 held up for all to see. It was the winding key from an alarm clock. Exhibit 41 was also held up. "And they have come from the same clock?" O'Sullivan asked. "Yes," Dupre agreed.

O'Sullivan then turned to the question of the use of fine sacks or pillowcases to hold potassium chlorate. Dupre explained that because the chemicals used were very fine, a fine weave, such as that used in a pillowcase, was needed to prevent the chemical from escaping. Mr. Lyons for the defense asked whether other chemicals could be used for explosives, and Dupre agreed they could. Lyons's line of questioning led nowhere. It all came down to the use of potassium chlorate. Thus ended the case for the prosecution.

The defense now put forward its case. It opened with one of their barristers, Mr. T.H. Winning, who represented Bridget O'Hara and Mary Hewitt. He submitted that there was no evidence on which a jury could find either of his two clients guilty of murder. He quoted past cases which he considered to be precedents. Mr. O'Sullivan for the prosecution put the case that the women should be tried. Mr. Justice Singleton listened, then questioned, and in the end decided that the two women did have cases to answer: "I think the case is one for the jury."

Mr. Dupre was recalled briefly. He was cross-examined by Mr. Lyons, K.C., barrister for Joseph Hewitt. At best it could be said that Lyons muddied the waters, implying there might have been cross contamination.

Then Peter Barnes, "the bagman," was called to the witness stand by Mr. Jenkins, his barrister. In English law the accused could refuse to testify, and remain silent. To put him in the witness box was a gamble. Barnes was not an educated man. Jenkins carefully led him in his testimony. The opening question was rather curious. "You are a single man, and, as far as you know, you are 32 years of age?" Did he not know his own age, or was this some peculiar legal form of question? Barnes answered, "Yes." Jenkins asked him why he had come to England. He replied that it was with the intention of finding work, marrying his fiancée, Miss Keane, and settling down in England. Jenkins then turned to the sachets of explosive substances found in his flat. Barnes said that he had bought them in the street from a girl. She had claimed that they "were shampoo powders and tooth paste and bath salts. They had a scented smell." When he showed them to Miss Keane, she had suggested that they were not much use, but he could put them with his shirts to make them smell nice. There was no suggestion that Barnes knew that they were explosive substances, his barrister stated.

Jenkins then asked Barnes why he had gone to Coventry. Unable to find work in London, Barnes explained, he had come across a man by the name of MacMahon, who suggested that he should try Coventry. He gave him the address of a man called Norman.

"Was that the Monday of the week you were arrested, the 21st?" Jenkins led.

"Yes," Barnes agreed.

Jenkins then asked Barnes about his suitcase that had been seized by the police, and in which traces of potassium chlorate were found. Barnes claimed that he had loaned the suitcase to MacMahon, the man who had suggested that he might find work in Coventry. It was hardly a convincing tale the Irishman told. Barnes informed the court that he had agreed to loan his case, on the understanding that it would be returned in the fullness of time. In the meantime MacMahon gave him ten shillings to buy a new case. Barnes was then asked about his first trip up to Coventry. He related that he had gone to the address given to him by MacMahon, to meet a man called Norman. There he met Richards. Richards claimed no knowledge of anyone called Norman, but nonetheless invited him in for a cup of tea. After drinking his tea, Barnes claimed that he had asked Mrs. O'Hara if she would go out and buy him a suitcase, which she did. Returning, she gave him two and sixpence change plus the receipt. Jenkins then asked Barnes if he knew anything about the purchase of flour sacks, to which he replied he did not. Barnes, according to his testimony, then caught the 3:30 p.m. train back to London.

"When next did you see MacMahon?" Jenkins asked.

"The following Thursday I met him at my digs."

"Did you tell him what had happened when you were in Coventry?"

"I did."

"That you could not find Norman?"

"Yes."

"What did he say?"

"He said if I went down that evening that Norman would be there.... And I will give you a letter to him and you are sure to see him."

"What was done about the suitcase?" Jenkins asked.

"I gave him the new suitcase and the half crown and he gave me back mine."

This loan of a suitcase, and its use by the mysterious MacMahon, was brought up to suggest to the jury that he, rather than Barnes, had used it to transport the explosive chemicals, traces of which were later found.

"Did you go down to Coventry again on the Thursday?" Jenkins asked.

"Yes, I went down that evening and got there about half past six."

"Who did you see there?"

"I went and knocked at the door and I was admitted by Mrs. O'Hara."

"Had you got a suitcase with you or not then?"

"Yes, I had mine."

"Had you any clothes in it?"

"An overcoat, a hat and a suit of pajamas."

"Were you anticipating staying in Coventry?"

"No."

"What were you doing with your pajamas?"

"Because I knew I would not be going back to my digs that night. I was going to 115, Warwick Avenue."

"You were going to the house where your fiancée was living?"

"Yes."

The whole thing with the suitcase and pajamas was a little bizarre. A point that the prosecution picked up on in later cross-examination. The thing with a lie is that you keep it simple and uncomplicated. The prosecution team, after years of practical experience, easily recognized a lie, and this was obviously a lie.

They bided their time to cross-examine the prisoner.

Jenkins then returned to Barnes's time in Coventry. "Did you see Richards?"

"Yes. I asked him to know if Norman came since, was he there? He said, 'No, somebody must be making a fool of you.'"

"Did you take any chlorate in a packet in your bag?" Jenkins asked.

"No."

"To your knowledge has there ever been any chlorate in your bag?"

"Not to my knowledge."

"Do you know anything about the purchase of any bicycle?"

"None whatsoever."

"Did you go with anybody or by yourself in Coventry to buy any bicycle?"

"I did not."

Jenkins then asked his client about his return to London that Thursday night, and what had happened to the letter addressed to Norman.

"What did you do with the letter?" Jenkins asked Barnes.

"I had arranged for to meet MacMahon when I got back to Euston Station, and tell him how I got on. It was sometime after ten when I arrived in London and he was waiting for me at the bus stop when I came out from Euston Station."

"Had he got a bag with him or not?"

"Yes, he had a suitcase and overcoat."

"Have you any idea where he had been or where he came from that night?"

"No."

Barnes then went on to testify that he was fed up, and told MacMahon that he was going to return to Ireland and try to find work there. MacMahon asked him to hand-deliver a letter, which Barnes eventually agreed to do. This was the letter discovered on Barnes when he was arrested. Initially he had said to the police that he had written it, but now he claimed it was MacMahon's letter which he had copied out. It seemed far-fetched that he would copy the original letter and then agree to take the copy. The whole process appeared unnecessarily complicated—too complicated for a man of Barnes's limitations.

"No further questions, My Lord," and with that, Jenkins sat down.

Richard O'Sullivan for the prosecution rose. He theatrically looked through his papers, then looking up posed a direct question: "Barnes, do you agree that this crime at Broadgate was an inhuman crime?"

Barnes could only answer one way. "Yes, it was a terrible crime."

O'Sullivan continued, "And for the commission of that crime it seems that potassium chlorate was needed?"

"I don't know."

"Did you bring potassium chlorate to this house, 25, Clara Street, on Thursday?"

"No I did not," Barnes replied.

"You have said that you have never had potassium chlorate. On 25 August you were arrested and your clothing taken to the police."

"Yes."

"Have you heard the evidence that there were traces of chlorate on the dungarees, on the trench coat that you had, and on your hat?"

"Yes."

"Can you account for traces of chlorate being on each of these articles of yours?"

"No, unless they were put into the case after MacMahon had taken it back to me. Perhaps he may have used my case for carrying powder."

O'Sullivan then asked about the contents of the case, the articles of clothing. They were quick-fire questions, designed to confuse. Barnes seemingly managed to answer them. Mr. Justice Singleton appeared to be confused, though, and sought clarification. "What had you in your suitcase when you went to Coventry?"

"A set of pajamas, an overcoat and my hat."

"It would have been almost as easy to wear the trench coat and the hat and put the pajamas in your pocket, would it not?" Singleton queried.

"No, I threw them all in. I was after getting my suitcase back from MacMahon."

"Was it a big suitcase?"

"No, it was a small one," Barnes replied.

Singleton seemed satisfied at this and allowed O'Sullivan to continue his cross-questioning.

"You never told your lady friend, as you call her, that you had ever been to Coventry?"

"No."

"Why not?"

"I went to see if I could get the job first. I did not know if she would be satisfied, me going so far away from her or not."

"You have told us in your opinion you had been made a fool of?"

"Yes."

"You understand what it is to make a fool of another, do you?"

"Yes."

"You are not trying to make a fool of these gentlemen of the jury, are you?"

"No, I am not," Barnes defended.

O'Sullivan returned to his questioning regarding Barnes's trip to Coventry and not informing Miss Keane. "Was it because you were engaged on some work of which you did not want her to know?"

"No, I was never engaged on any work. I am not a member of the IRA or anything like that."

O'Sullivan then questioned the witness over the discovery of the sachets of potassium chlorate found in his flat. Barnes's explanations seemed improbable. O'Sullivan then turned to the other discoveries found in his flat. There was a guidebook of Glasgow, which Barnes claimed had been given to him by a man on the ferry coming over. There was a map of London, which perhaps could be explained away, as Barnes was living in London and would have needed a map to navigate the city. O'Sullivan asked him, "Did you ever go to Liverpool?"

"No, I did not."

Then why would the prisoner have a scrap of paper in his possession with details of trains from London to Liverpool, and vice versa? O'Sullivan asked. Barnes's excuse was weak: "I often take them down when I am waiting for a train." O'Sullivan continued with his questioning of how illogical it would be to write down the times of trains for no obvious reason. "What were they for?" O'Sullivan asked.

"I used to take down the time trains would come and go. I had no interest in them."

So ended the cross-examination for that day.

On Wednesday, 13 December, the cross-examination of Barnes by O'Sullivan resumed.

"Have you ever been to Liverpool?" O'Sullivan asked once more.

Barnes's answer was again "No."

O'Sullivan commented upon the expense of railway tickets. How could Barnes, a known unemployed man, afford to pay out so much money for repeated journeys up to Coventry and back? Barnes explained that he considered it an investment, as he believed a job of work would come out of it. O'Sullivan now turned to the mysterious MacMahon, and asked Barnes to fill in the details of how he knew the man. O'Sullivan then questioned him whether MacMahon was the sort of man who carried a suitcase. After all, Barnes had implied that MacMahon might have used his suitcase to transfer potassium chlorate. Why had Barnes bought a new suitcase in Coventry, and not in London? The explanations were all so improbable. Why had Barnes taken a suitcase with him all the way to Coventry and back, whereas his flat and his fiancée's flat, where he intended to stay the night, was barely 500 or 600 yards away?

"Well, it was late at night when I got back," Barnes offered as an explanation.

"You prefer to carry this suitcase all the way down to Coventry and back rather than spend five minutes on your return journey carrying it round to 115, Warwick Avenue?"

"It was convenient."

"It was convenient?"

"Yes."

O'Sullivan then progressed to the actual visits to Coventry. "On both occasions when you went to Coventry you went to see a Mr. Norman?"

"Yes."

"And the first person you met at Coventry was Mr. Richards?"

"Yes."

The prosecutor then went on to ask about the flour sacks. Mrs. O'Hara claimed in her statement that Barnes had asked her daughter to buy some for him.

"Did you ask anyone in that house on the Monday to go and get some flour sacks?" O'Sullivan asked.

"I did not," Barnes responded.

"Did Richards in your presence ask anyone to go and get some flour sacks?"

"Not that I heard."

"Did you open the parcel containing the sacks that day when it came back?"

"No."

"Were you there when the parcel was opened?"

"No, I did not see any parcel at all."

"Did you say, 'These are not right; they are not the right ones'?"

"No, I did not."

"Did you ask Mrs. O'Hara if she would take them back and change them for white calico bags?"

"I did not."

That line of questioning being exhausted, O'Sullivan turned to the purchase of the suitcase. This time the response was positive. Barnes admitted that he had asked Mrs. O'Hara to buy a suitcase for him. Then it came down to the receipts. Both had been found in the possession of Miss Keane, who had agreed to look after them for Barnes.

"You told us you got receipts for the suitcase and the sacks—two receipts."

"I got the receipt for the suitcase. I do not know nothing about the receipt for the sacks."

"Did you in fact have it?"

"Yes, I must have."

"Did you in fact get back from Mrs. O'Hara the two shillings for the sacks which she had paid them?"

"No, I did not hear anything about the sacks at all."

O'Sullivan then returned to the suitcase that Barnes had taken up to Coventry.

"Did you, while you were there, deliver to them a lot of white powder from your suitcase?"

"No."

"Would it be right to say that the suitcase seemed rather heavy, or the contents of it?"

"No."

Then the cross-examination returned to the mysterious Mr. MacMahon. Was their meeting upon Barnes's return to London by chance? Where was the original letter written, the copy of which was found in Barnes's possession.

"Standing in Warwick Avenue?" O'Sullivan asked incredulously.

"Yes," Barnes answered.

"In the light, I suppose?"

"Yes."

"And both of you with suitcases?"

"Yes."

The whole concept of the scene presented by O'Sullivan appeared ludicrous. The prosecutor was toying with the witness. O'Sullivan asked if Barnes had written other letters recently. Barnes admitted that he had.

"Did you tell the police officer when you were arrested that this was only a letter you had written to a friend?"

"Yes."

"Was that true?"

"No. I did not think it was necessary for me to explain to him."

It was a little lie, but it was a lie. O'Sullivan then went on to read the letter out loud, blurring the distinction between Barnes's activities and those written about in the letter.

"'I got it very hard after coming over.' You say you had come over about the beginning of the month, and this is dated 24 August?"

"Yes."

So was the "Yes" in reference to life being hard after his arrival, or was it yes to the date of the arrival?

"'So I had to go to Liverpool the next day.'" O'Sullivan continued. "Is that why you had had in your possession in your writing the trains to and from Euston and Liverpool?"

"I know nothing about Liverpool."

So it continued; O'Sullivan read out a sentence or two of the letter, then asked Barnes to comment. "'I go from one place to the other and bring the S-' Do you know what the S means?" O'Sullivan asked.

"I do not."

He read on. "'Believe me it is hard but I gotway well so far. I am after coming back from Coventry tonight 11:30.' That was true?"

"Yes."

So there it was, the crossover between Barnes's activities and those referred to in the letter; or was Barnes just confused by the way the question was put?

"So far as you know it was not true of Mr. MacMahon?"
"I do not know."
"So far as you know he was not there?"
"No."
"When you came to the passage, 'I am after coming back to Coventry tonight,' was that the first time that you knew Mr. MacMahon had been to Coventry that day?"
"Yes."
"Has Miss Keane ever seen MacMahon?"
"No, she has not."
"Have you made any attempt to find MacMahon?"
"No."
"So far as you know, have Richards, Hewitt, Mrs. O'Hara or Mrs. Hewitt ever seen MacMahon?"
"Not to my knowledge."
"I suggest to you that MacMahon has no existence."
"Yes he has. I am telling the truth about him."

Mr. Justice Singleton then interrupted. "Can you tell me where your suitcase is now?"
"The police have it," Barnes replied.
"Is it this one that is produced?"
"No, I do not see it in court. It is a small suitcase."
"Still, big enough in which to take a hat, an overcoat and your pajamas?"
"Yes."

Then the judge went over the same ground about the convenience or inconvenience of taking the suitcase all the way up to Coventry and back. His questioning was apparently to satisfy himself that he had got the facts right himself.

"If you went from Westbourne Terrace to Warwick Avenue it was only 500 or 600 yards, you say?"
"Yes."
"When you walked from Coventry Station to Clara Street, if you walked, how far is it?"
"It took me about half an hour to get across."
"You carried the suitcase all the way round and then brought it back to Coventry Station and then from Coventry to London?"
"Yes."

Was Mr. Justice Singleton slow on the uptake, or was he inadvertently directing the jury? He then asked about the mysterious Mr. MacMahon.

"Where did you meet him [after your return from Coventry]?"

"He met me at the bus stop in Euston Station across from the station."

"Your arrangement was to meet at the station?"

"Yes, he told me."

"He had not been to Coventry, had he?"

"I do not know whether he had or not."

"He was a friend of yours, or you were friendly with him? If he was going to Coventry that day there was no reason why you should not go together?"

"No."

"He told you to go, you say, and he would meet you when you came back?"

"Yes, that night."

"So you knew he was not at Coventry?"

"Yes, as far as my knowledge went."

"And it was he, you say, who asked you to write the letter saying, 'I am coming back from Coventry tonight at 11:30'?"

"Yes."

There were no further questions. Barnes stepped down from the witness box and returned to the dock.

The next witness called was James McCormack, or as he was still known, James Richards, for he had not as yet divulged his real name. Like Peter Barnes, he was questioned by his barrister, Douglas Jenkins.

"When did you first see Barnes?"

"On Monday, 21 August 1939. It was about three o'clock in the afternoon."

"Had you ever seen him before?"

"No."

"Tell us how it came about that you saw him and where it was."

"I was standing at the door at the doorstep outside where I was staying at 25, Clara Street when Barnes came to the door. He told me that he was sent there by some man in London for to meet a man at 25, Clara Street that was to get him a job. He mentioned the man's name but I cannot remember it. I told him there was nobody stopping at 25, Clara Street, only myself. He asked me then where he could get a cup of tea. He was already after introducing himself as Peter Barnes so I told him I would take him inside and get him a cup of tea."

Jenkins then went on to question his client about the suitcase. "Was there anything said about a suitcase?"

"Yes, he was about half an hour in the house and he asked Mrs. O'Hara would she buy him a suitcase."

"Is his account accurate as to what happened about that?"

"Yes."

"Was anything said about buying some flour bags?"

"Not in the room that he was sitting in when I sent Mrs. Hewitt for two flour sacks. I was in the kitchen at the time."

"Would Barnes know anything about that?"

"No."

"About what time did he go?" Jenkins asked.

"It would be somewhere around five o'clock or the half hour."

"Did you see Barnes on Tuesday, 22nd?"

"No I did not."

"Did you take him down to order a bicycle?"

"No, I was in company with another man ordering the bicycle."

In answering the question so, McCormack had deliberately implicated himself, and knowingly so. In realizing that he was going to be found guilty, he sought to ensure that the others would be found innocent. He would take full blame. He could expect to be sent to prison for ten to twenty years. What had not sunk in was that if found guilty, he would face the death penalty.

"Did you see Barnes on the Thursday?" Jenkins continued.

"Yes, it would be sometime about seven o'clock, I think. He came to the door again at 25, Clara Street and Mrs. O'Hara let him in and he says that he was back again for to see that man that he had mentioned on the Monday before. So I told him that that man was not there, that somebody was making a fool of him. He was only about half an hour in the house altogether; it would be nearly eight o'clock when he left the house."

"Did he bring anything with him?"

"Yes, he had a small suitcase."

"Did he bring you anything?"

"No, he had nothing, only the suitcase and he left that standing in the hall."

"To your knowledge, was that suitcase opened?"

"No, it was not opened at 25, Clara Street."

"Beyond that, do you know anything about Barnes?"

"No, he is a complete stranger to me. I never met him before, only on them two occasions."

Jenkins then asked McCormack about his arrival in Coventry and his taking up lodgings with the Hewitts. Then a direct question: "Did you ever tell Mrs. Hewitt you were an operating man from Dublin, or words to that effect?"

"No," McCormack responded, "I never mentioned I was operating from Dublin, at least I never told her what I was, because it was nothing to do with her what I was as long as I paid her for my week's digs."

Jenkins asked about the purchase of the bicycle. McCormack, far from denying it, agreed that he and another man had purchased it. What he then said was damning. He literally confessed to his part in the murders.

"On Tuesday, 22 August, you and somebody else went to order a bicycle?"

"Yes," McCormack answered.

"Who was that?"

"I refuse to give his name, but it was not Peter Barnes."

"What sort of clothing was he wearing?"

"He was wearing a sports coat and flannel pants and a grey pullover, and he was wearing spectacles."

This description tied in with the description given by the shop assistants. The authorities so badly wanted this to be the clothing worn by Barnes, but no similar clothing was found at his flat in London. The implication was that a third man was involved, but had escaped the net.

"To your knowledge," Jenkins asked, "is that man in this country now?"

"He is not."

"Who bought the bicycle?"

"He bought the bicycle. I was standing outside while he was buying it."

"Was the bicycle collected on Friday, 25th?"

"Yes, I collected it."

"What was it to be used for?"

"I do not know. The orders I got was to collect the bicycle and give it to a man in 25, Clara Street."

The prosecution now became aware, if they were not aware of it before, that there were two more men involved, and that McCormack was not in charge of the team.

"Who took it away?"

"It was a man that was in the house, came to 25, Clara Street on Thursday with a parcel."

"Was that the man who bought the bicycle?"

"No, it was another man."

"Did you see a bomb?"

"Yes, I did."

6. The Arrest and Trial of the Coventry Bombers 119

"Did you make a bomb?"

"No, I do not know how to make a bomb."

"When did you see the bomb or the parts of the bomb?"

"On the Friday."

"Did anybody fit it together?"

"Yes, this man that called on the Thursday called on the Friday and fitted it together. The man that made the bomb took it away. He is not the man that ordered the bike."

"Is that man in this country now?"

"I do not think so; I've never seen him since."

"Did you see him take the bomb away?"

"Yes."

"What time was that?"

"On the Friday about ten after one."

"Did you know where he was going to take it?"

"No."

"Would you have been a willing party to the bomb being let off in Broadgate in the middle of the day?"

"No, I would not, not to Broadgate, not in the middle of the day."

"Or anywhere in the middle of the day?"

"No."

"Would you have been a willing party to anybody's life being endangered?"

"No, sir, I would not, because it is the instructions from the Irish Republican Army that no lives are to be endangered."

"Are you a member of what is known as the IRA?"

"I am, yes."

So there it was: McCormack had convicted himself by his testimony. Little heed would be paid to his statement that he would not have been part of setting bombs off in broad daylight with the risk to life of innocent people. The Coventry bombing was an atrocity. People wanted revenge, and the police and the judiciary wanted a quick end to the case. McCormack was guilty by his own testimony, but of what?

Mr. T.H. Winning, counsel for Mrs. O'Hara and her daughter, now cross-examined McCormack. It was brief and concerned the intended purchase of the two flour sacks. It was now Mr. O'Sullivan's turn. He began with a direct question to the accused: "Richards, do you approve of the murder of Elsie Ansell?"

The answer was clear and adamant: "I do not."

"Do you condemn the action of the man who murdered her?"

"Yes."

"If she was killed by a bomb which came from 25, Clara Street, did you do anything to prevent it?"

"No, I had nothing to do with it, but I think it was a mistake for that bomb to have gone off in the middle of the day. I do not think it was to be placed in Broadgate during the day."

"If the bicycle was necessary to the perpetration of the crime, you did something to assist it?"

"I called for the bicycle."

"You went with the man who ordered it on the Tuesday, and you collected it on the Friday?"

"Yes."

"Was the man who purchased the bicycle Peter Barnes?"

"No."

"Will you give my lord and the jury his name?"

"I will not."

After further questions concerning the bicycle, O'Sullivan asked, "Is it right that Barnes left a parcel behind?"

"No," McCormack answered.

The barrister asked further questions about the "white powder," as he described it. McCormack confirmed that the explosive chemicals had been in the suitcase found by the police in the outhouse.

"Was the white powder used in the making of the bomb?"

"Yes."

O'Sullivan, as was his job as prosecutor, now sought to link the two women to the crime.

"Was a white sack used also?"

"No, I could not get the white sacks and I gave it to him in a paper bag."

"When you were sending for the sacks, was that for this purpose?" Judge Singleton asked.

"Yes."

"For the purpose of making the bomb?" he queried.

"No, for the purpose of holding the powder."

Mr. O'Sullivan then continued his cross-examination concerning the use of the suitcase and the sacks. An interesting point came up when McCormack offered the following: "Well, it was my job for to keep the powder and distribute it to any man that called for me for some."

"Is that the purpose for which you came to England?"

"Yes."

Further questioning followed, then O'Sullivan asked, "Had you already begun to distribute white powder to men who called for it?"

"Not up to that time."

"You began about the beginning of August?"

"About the middle of August I distributed white powder."

"Did men frequently come and call at the premises?"

"Yes, Irishmen frequently came to see me at 25, Clara Street."

"Did the men who called bring suitcases with them?"

"No."

"Is it wrong to say they sometimes brought suitcases with them?"

"There was only one man who brought a suitcase."

"Was that a man bringing supplies?"

"No."

"How did supplies come?"

"I cannot answer that question."

"I must ask you to answer that."

"I will not."

After some further questioning to which McCormack refused to answer, Mr. Justice Singleton again interrupted. "Listen to me," he addressed McCormack. "You appreciate this, do you not? The jury are charged with the duty of trying you. You appreciate, do you not, if you are asked a question and you say every now and again, 'I refuse to answer,' it will not help you much. You appreciate that?"

"I do."

"Very well," said Singleton, "I will say no more."

Mr. O'Sullivan continued with his questioning. The question came around to the pit that McCormack dug in the house. If Hewitt was complicit in its construction, then that would implicate him. O'Sullivan wanted to know if McCormack had been ordered to construct it. McCormack said it was his own idea.

"Did you have the permission of Mr. Hewitt to make the pit?"

"No."

Hewitt knew of the pit and its intended use, but was not happy about the situation. In the end, after the considerable unease of his wife, he confronted his lodger.

"When Joe Hewitt came home in the evening from his work and saw the pit opened and some concrete in, he got on to me and asked me what right had I to open a pit in his house. He had a few hot words with me, and I told him I would close up the pit. The pit was never closed," McCormack revealed.

O'Sullivan now progressed to the night before the explosion and the visit of the "strange man."

"Was he there against your will, that man?"

"No."

"Was he there at your invitation?"

"No, he was sent to me and I admitted him."

"Who was the strange man?"

"I cannot give you his name."

"You know his name?"

"Yes, I know his name."

It was ascertained that the tools used in the construction of the bomb were not Hewitt's.

"You knew then he was making a bomb?" O'Sullivan suggested to the Irishman.

"I saw him with parts of a bomb there in the house. He had a clock and battery."

"Did he ever tell you what the clock was for?"

"Well, I knew it was used in a bomb."

"Was the setter of the clock found on you?"

"Yes."

Then O'Sullivan asked a very blunt question. "Did you say when you were charged with murder, 'I know nothing about it?'"

"That is right, and I still say I do not know anything about the murder concerned," McCormack defended.

The word "murder" concentrated the minds of all. The people accused had not been charged with being in possession of explosive substances, or being accessories, but with murder. A guilty verdict would see them all hang.

"How much powder did you supply to the man making the bomb?" O'Sullivan asked.

"It would be about 5 lbs."

"When you brought the bicycle back and saw this young man did you say to him, 'The bicycle is at the back door, I have got the bike.'"

"Yes."

"Did he then go out carrying a parcel?"

"Yes."

"Did you help him to pack up the clock bomb in a brown paper parcel?"

"No, he did that himself."

"So that the bomb must at that time have been set and ready to put on the carrier?"

"I could not tell you about the setting of the bomb."

"When you came back with the bicycle did you find him in an agitated condition?"

"No. He just said, 'You were a long time away,' and that was all."

"We know now that the bomb was set for 2:30 and you returned some time just after 1?"

"I returned ten minutes after 1."

"If somebody says he did seem agitated, would you dispute it?"

"No, because he could be agitated and I might not have noticed it."

O'Sullivan then went on to ask about McCormack's reaction when he heard that the bomb had gone off, not at night, but in the afternoon.

"I was very much surprised," McCormack said, "because I did not think it was made for to go off in the middle of the day."

"Had you discussed where it was to go off?" O'Sullivan asked.

"No, I did not know where it was to go off."

"Did Mrs. O'Hara say when you read the paper, 'My God, it is terrible to have all these people killed and wounded! That is the bomb you made'?"

"No, she said, 'My God, it is terrible that all these people have been killed!' She did not mention anything about the bomb that was made."

"Was there any other distributor in Coventry known to you?"

"Not in Coventry."

"Having supplied the powder for this bomb and seeing it made, did it never occur to you to ask where it was going to be exploded?"

"No, it was no business of mine whatsoever."

"Or when it was to be exploded?"

"No."

"Did you expect it to be exploded in Coventry?"

"No."

O'Sullivan questioned McCormack as to the morality of his actions, then turned to one of the co-accused, Joseph Hewitt. He asked McCormack how he had met Hewitt, and then as to their activities. They played darts and Ludo as an evening pastime, McCormack revealed. Then the prosecutor moved on to the other members of the family, and their comments after the explosion.

"Did you say 'We were saying what a terrible thing it was?'"

"Yes, Mrs. Hewitt and Mrs. O'Hara and Joe Hewitt were condemning the explosion."

"Were you condemning it?"

"Yes, I did condemn it."

"Are you sorry now for the part you played in the manufacture of this bomb?"

"I did not manufacture," McCormack insisted.

"In the preparation of the bomb?"

"No, I did not make it. I did no preparation of the bomb. All I was to do was to give out the chlorate."

"Were you distributing or supplying the potassium chlorate with the consciousness that it was to be used to make a bomb?"

"No."

"Are you sorry for that?"

"No."

Mr. Jenkins for McCormack, re-examined his client for clarification over certain points, then closed his cross-examination.

The next witness was Joseph Hewitt. O'Sullivan waited as the defense began their cross-questioning. He felt sure that Richards would be found guilty, and most probably Barnes; could he get Hewitt convicted too?

Hewitt was questioned by his barrister, Mr. A.M. Lyons, K.C., M.P., a formidable defense lawyer.

Hewitt gave his age and marital status, and the length of his stay in England. Preliminaries out of the way Lyons asked, "Are you yourself a member, or have you ever been a member of the IRA?"

Hewitt answered with an emphatic "No." There was no hint of equivocation.

"Have you any sympathy with that organization?"

"No."

"Have you ever supported or said a word to help the policy which they try to propound?"

"No."

"Did you know nothing at all about this incident in Coventry upon which these charges are today founded?"

"No."

Lyons then enquired about his early life and his arrival in Coventry. From the questioning Hewitt was revealed to be a model hard-working citizen. His only mistake, it could be shown, was that he had taken in as a lodger a man who, unknown to him, was a member of the IRA. Richards had visitors from time to time, Hewitt revealed, but he did not consider that to be suspicious. "Would you knowingly have been a party to any bomb making or bomb exploding or damage by bombs?"

"No, I would not have had it made in my house if I had known."

"So far as you knew up to the time of this case, was anything being done in your house towards the manufacture of a bomb?"

"Not to my knowledge."

"Did you get knowledge that there had been a hole dug in your house?"
"I did."
"Did you assist in digging it?"
"No."

Hewitt explained that his wife had complained about it and he spoke to his lodger. Then Lyons moved on to the day of the explosion. Hewitt had been at work all day. He had left the house at 7:30 a.m., and walked down to catch the bus. He returned home at a quarter past seven that evening. He had not left the factory at any time during his shift. Lyons had established that his client could have had no part in the carrying out of this terrible crime. Now he dealt with the question of cross-contamination.

"Had you at this time any reason whatever to suspect there would be anything at all on anybody's clothing that would come off on yours?"
"I could not say."
"Have you had on your clothes, or on your person, or in your pockets at any time to your knowledge, any of this potassium powder?"
"No."

Lyons then moved on to the construction of the bomb, anxious to show that Hewitt had played no part in its making.
"Have you taken any clock ever to pieces?"
"No."
"Had you any knowledge whatever of the part played by a clock in making a bomb, until this case?"
"No."
"Have you been concerned alone or with anybody in this bomb manufacture, or bomb explosion in Coventry, that day?"
"No."
"You swear it?"
"I swear it."

With that Lyons completed his examination of his client. Perhaps with a hint towards the theatrical, he had got Hewitt to swear that he was not involved in the bombing. In the course of his questioning he had also established that his client had been at work when the bomb went off. This was irrefutable; his work colleagues could testify to that. The only thing that could be said of him was that he lacked judgment in letting a room to McCormack.

Mr. O'Sullivan now stood up and began the cross-examination for the prosecution. His questioning was not going to be so benign. After a brief preliminary question, O'Sullivan asked Hewitt about McCormack: "Do you believe him now to be an officer of the IRA?"

"I could not say. I do not know anything about it."

"You repudiated the IRA?"

"I do not believe in it; I have nothing to do with it."

"Do you denounce it?"

"Yes."

O'Sullivan now set out to show that Hewitt, far from denouncing the IRA, was a sympathizer at least. Items found at Clara Street were then produced. There was an Easter Lily card which read at the top, "Break connection with England."

"Does that indicate membership of the IRA or sympathy with it?" O'Sullivan asked.

"I could not say."

Then there was a card which had been attached to a wedding present. It read, "From Officers and members of Betsy Grey branch. Cumann-na-mBan."

"What is Cuman-na-mBan?" O'Sullivan asked, knowing full well the answer. As an Irishman himself, O'Sullivan knew what the organization was.

"Well, this card here my wife had before I got married. My wife went to dances, Irish dancing and English dancing mixed, so these people gave her a present when we got married, and this was on the present when we received it."

"Can you tell my lord and members of the jury what is the Cumann-na-mBan?"

"Well, Cumann-na-mBan, as far as I know, is the Ladies Auxiliary of the IRA or something."

O'Sullivan then referred to another piece of evidence found in the Hewitt's home. It was the words to a Republican song.

"Is that one of the songs of the IRA?" O'Sullivan asked.

"I could not say."

Having such a song in the house displayed a sympathy towards a united Ireland, but there was nothing wrong in that. It did not display a sympathy towards the IRA's way of achieving that goal. But O'Sullivan had planted the seed in the mind of the jury that Hewitt was sympathetic to the cause. He now turned to the pit that McCormack had dug, the suggestion being that Hewitt had helped him. This line of enquiry proved ineffective. O'Sullivan turned to the tools found at 25, Clara Street. He manufactured a case to show that the tools and other bits and pieces about the house could have been used to make a bomb. In truth these tools and bits and pieces could have been found in any number of houses. O'Sullivan then asked, and it was loaded the way the question was framed, whether Hewitt was aware of the existence of explosive substances in the house: "Did you know that you were taking a grave responsibility in keeping explosives in the house?"

"No, I never knew I had explosives in the house; I never possessed any," Hewitt protested.

"Did you ever ask Richards whether this white powder was explosives?"

"No."

"Why not?"

"Well, it did not concern me."

The answer was weak. O'Sullivan latched on to it.

"Did you not ask the question because you were afraid of the answer?"

"No."

"What did you think the white powder was?"

"I had no idea."

"Did your wife plead with you more than once to have nothing to do with Richards?"

"Yes."

The examination reverted back to the hole McCormack had dug, and Hewitt told the court that he had spoken to his lodger, who then filled it back in. Hewitt admitted that he had made a cover to the filled-in hole. Then O'Sullivan moved on to the visitors to the house in the days leading up to the explosion. There was the unknown man, but Hewitt was unable to give any details. Then there was Barnes, who turned up on Thursday looking for "Norman." In the written statements of Mrs. Hewitt and her mother, there was an account that they believed that McCormack and one of the visitors were involved in bomb making, and as a consequence they had gone out and wandered the street until 11 p.m. before their return home, by which time the visitors had gone. Hewitt claimed that they were both confused when they had made the statements. Perhaps undue police pressure had been brought to bear. Hewitt was asked whether he had seen any white powder on Wednesday or Thursday. He replied, "No."

"Is the trench coat exhibited yours?" O'Sullivan asked.

"Yes."

"Can you explain how some potassium chlorate was found in the pocket of the coat?"

"No."

"Have you any explanation to give how it came to be there?"

"I might have picked them up off the floor and put them in my pocket, but I could not say how they got there."

"I suggest you were aware throughout the last fortnight before this explosion of the nature of the work that Richards was doing."

"No."

"I suggest you were aware that explosives were being stored in your house."

"No."

"I suggest you were aware and cooperating on the night of 24 August when the preparations were being made."

"No," Hewitt said, claiming, "There was never no bomb made at my house to my knowledge, and I have never had anything to do with the making of a bomb."

Hewitt was stood down. The next witness called was his mother-in-law, Mrs. O'Hara. In her account of the case, barrister Letia Fairfield was to write: "The two women prisoners gained immediate sympathy, only deepened by their testimonies in the witness box—so evident was it that both had been unwillingly caught up in a current of events too strong for them. Poor flustered Mrs. O'Hara was a "bad witness," in the technical sense of the term, if ever there was one, creating as she did all sorts of unnecessary mystifications by her failure to understand simple questions. She had lived almost wholly among Irish folk during her three years in Coventry and was, one gathers, still puzzled by English accents and turns of speech. Her daughter, Mary Hewitt, gave the impression of a more stable, simpler character, wholly taken up with the interests of her husband and baby, from whom she had now been separated for three months."[4]

Thursday, 14 December, the fourth day of the trial, saw the summing ups. Mr. O'Sullivan began for the prosecution. His speech betrayed that sympathy towards the two women as outlined by Fairfield. Surprisingly he asked for "a measure of charity in judgment" on the part of the jury. For he must have been aware that a guilty verdict would mean execution, and the two, possibly the three men, were not directly responsible for the outrage. O'Sullivan spoke of McCormack's misguided courage; he told of the tenderness displayed by Barnes towards a child in the letter he had written; and he described Hewitt as "an unfortunate man."

Mr. Douglas Jenkins spoke for the defense. The person responsible for the explosion was not in the dock, he said, a point not disputed by the prosecution. Richards had confessed to his part in the case, but he had claimed that his instructions were that human life was not to be endangered. Barnes's coming to Coventry was purely accidental, Jenkins claimed. He was looking for a man he thought could help him to find work. It might be that the bomb was not properly made and was not intended to go off at the time it did. Jenkins was followed by Mr. Winning, defense barrister for Mrs. Hewitt and her mother. His submission was that it was impossible to imagine a jury saying that the two women, one with a small child, had any part in what had happened.

Mr. Justice Singleton summed up in his charge to the jury. He outlined the evidence presented. It was long and considered. He summed up, "You will please now consider your verdict and tell me with regard to each one of these prisoners do you find him or her guilty or not guilty." The jury retired at 4:10 p.m. They returned into court at 4:41.

7

Sentence and Appeal

The jury returned into the court and took their seats. The Clerk of the Assize addressed them.

"Members of the jury, are you agreed upon your verdict?"

The foreman of the jury rose. "Yes sir."

"Do you find the prisoner Peter Barnes guilty or not guilty of murder?"

"Guilty of murder," the foreman recorded.

"You say he is guilty and that is the verdict of you all?"

"That is the verdict of us all."

The Clerk then asked, "Do you find the prisoner James Richards guilty or not guilty of murder?"

"Guilty of murder."

"You say he is guilty of murder and that is the verdict of you all?"

"That is the verdict of us all."

So far the verdicts were as expected. Now came the verdict on Joseph Hewitt. "Do you find the prisoner Joseph Hewitt guilty or not guilty of murder?"

"Not guilty of murder."

There was an audible sigh at this verdict. The Clerk continued, "Do you find the prisoner Brigid O'Hara guilty or not guilty of murder?" In the light of Joseph Hewitt's being found not guilty, it was to be expected that this would be the same verdict on the two women, and thus it proved to be. Brigid O'Hara and her daughter Mary were found not guilty.

Mr. Justice Singleton ordered, "Let Joseph Hewitt, Brigid O'Hara and Mary Hewitt go down." They were free for the moment.

The Clerk of Assize then addressed to two convicted men, "Prisoners at the bar, Peter Barnes and James Richards, you stand convicted of murder;

have you anything to say why judgment of death should not be pronounced upon you according to law?"

Peter Barnes spoke first. "I would like to say as I am going before my God, as I am condemned to death, I am innocent, and later I am sure it will all come out that I had neither hand, act or part in it." He paused momentarily, then added, "That is all I have to say."

McCormack, though he had not played any part in the actual explosion, accepted his fate. "My lord, before you pass sentence I have something to say. I wish to state, my lord, before you pass sentence of death on me, I wish to thank sincerely the gentlemen who have defended me during my trial and I wish to state that the part I took in these explosions since I came England I have done for a just cause. As a soldier of the Irish Republican Army I am not afraid to die, as I am doing it for a just cause. I say in conclusion, God bless Ireland and God bless the men who have fought and died for her. Thank you."

James McCormack (left) and Peter Barnes (right) were both found guilty of the murder of five people in the Coventry bombing, and were subsequently hanged. The verdict was controversial in that neither man was directly involved. Barnes was in London at the time.

The "black cap," a square of black cloth, was placed on Mr. Justice Singleton's head, a symbol that he was going to pronounce a death sentence.

"Peter Barnes and James Richards," he began, " the jury have returned a true verdict according to the evidence. The sentence of the Court upon each of you is that you be taken from this place to a lawful prison and thence to a place of execution and that you be there hanged by the neck until you are dead; and that your body be afterwards buried within the precincts of the prison in which you shall have been confined before your execution, and may the Lord have mercy on your souls."

The chaplain in the court responded with, "Amen."

Chief Inspector William Parker, who had gathered the evidence against the prisoners, was recalled. The judge thanked him and the other police officers involved. Mr. Justice Singleton then addressed the chief prosecutor. "Mr. O'Sullivan, with regard to three of the accused, the two Hewitts and Mrs. O'Hara, there are other indictments for consideration, are there not?"

"Yes," O'Sullivan agreed.

On 15 December 1939, the Hewitts and Mrs. O'Hara again appeared before Mr. Justice Singleton, charged with the murder of four other persons killed in the Coventry explosion. They all pleaded not guilty. Mr. Richard O'Sullivan for the prosecution informed the judge that he had been instructed to offer no evidence against the three accused. The judge then directed the jury to return a verdict of not guilty. The three were then charged on five counts under the Explosive Substances Act. All three again pleaded not guilty. Addressing the court, the judge said that it would not be in Joseph Hewitt's interest to try him at that Assize. He was remanded in custody. The judge then addressed the jury and instructed them to bring in a case of not guilty regarding the two women. As a consequence, they were released.

On 6 February 1940, Joseph Hewitt appeared at the Central Criminal Court in London, or the Old Bailey as it was more familiarly known. He was charged with maliciously causing an explosion, and having explosive substances in his possession. No evidence was offered by the prosecution. Again the judge instructed the jury, who brought in a verdict of not guilty. Joseph Hewitt was freed.

In Ireland news of the guilty verdicts on Barnes and McCormack were met with dismay, a view reflected across the broad spectrum of Irish life, from politicians of whatever persuasion to the man in the pub. Neither of the two convicted men had been directly responsible for the explosion; Barnes had actually been in London when it occurred. Both had been involved in the early stages of the operation, and thereby could, or should, have been charged with possession of explosive substances and conspiracy to cause explosions, but murder? No. That was the belief of the majority, not only in Ireland, but across the world. For Barnes in particular there was disbelief that he could in any way be held responsible for the actions of the man who had left the bomb.

The legitimacy for the conviction for murder in British law was twofold. The guilty men had engaged in activities known to be dangerous to life, and life had been lost accordingly. One might perhaps have argued a case for manslaughter, in that the true target was believed to have been a power station, not personnel. But the other principle of law was that of common purpose. Where two or more people agree to commit a crime that results in death, all the persons involved are guilty of murder, not only the person who did the actual killing. This law was often applied to Irish prisoners involved in what might be termed political crime. It was also used in industrial disputes, and other crimes involving lust or financial gain. So it was not specifically applied to subdue political unrest. To Irish eyes, though, it did seem to be a case of the British establishment extracting its pound of flesh from the unwitting accomplices in the absence of the man responsible.

As was to be expected, an appeal against the conviction of Barnes and McCormack was begun almost immediately. There was a new team, headed by Messrs. Lehane and Hogan, solicitors of Dublin, paid for, it is generally accepted, by the IRA itself, with money donated by certain influential people in Ireland. Mr. Albert Wood of the Eire Bar was appointed to put the case, ably assisted by their former barrister, Mr. Douglas Jenkins, who was all too familiar with the case. The grounds for appeal in both cases were the trial judge's refusal to grant a separate trial for Barnes and McCormack from that of the other three. This, it was alleged, gravely prejudiced the men's trial, and prevented justice from being done. The judge had also failed to inform the jury that the evidence of the two women required corroboration. In the case of Barnes in particular, the judge had failed to point out to the jury that in his statement to the police, he had claimed that he was not and never had been a member of the IRA. This point had not been brought forward. Barnes's visit to Coventry, it was contended, had no connection with the IRA, and he had no knowledge of any proposed explosion. In the case of McCormack, the judge had failed to point out to the jury that the evidence of Mrs. O'Hara on oath, differed in many respects to important particulars from the written statement she had made to the police that McCormack had no knowledge that any bomb was to be placed in any position where life might be endangered, or injury likely to be caused to anyone, and that he would not have been a party to such proceedings. In fact he would have taken steps to prevent such an atrocity.

The appeal was heard on 22–23 January 1940 at the Court of Criminal Appeal, before the Lord Chief Justice (Lord Hewart), Mr. Justice Hilbery and Mr. Justice Hallett. Opening the appeal, Mr. Wood submitted that the refusal of the judge to allow Barnes and McCormack to be tried separately had resulted in a miscarriage of justice. The statements of the two women had incriminated the men in the making of the bomb. Yet their statements were full of grave discrepancies. Mr. Justice Hallett, in response, pointed out that on three separate occasions the trial judge had warned the jury that the statements and evidence of the women witnesses contained discrepancies which should be taken into account.

Mr. Wood pointed out that when one accused person in his defense sought to incriminate another, that was a good reason for not trying them together. Hallett's response was that it was not part of the two women's defense that there was a bomb plot in which Barnes and McCormack were involved. Their evidence was that they did not know there was a bomb plot.

Wood submitted that no warning that he could see had been given to the jury in regard to the evidence of accomplices. The judge had also failed to direct the jury that they should not be prejudicial against the other people charged, because one of the prisoners, McCormack, had admitted that he was a member of the IRA. Mr. Justice Hilbery asked, "Since when has it been the law that a direction is defective because the judge did not remind the jury that it must act without prejudice?"

The court concluded for the day.

The following morning the court reconvened. Mr. O'Sullivan, chief prosecutor in the original trial, was summoned to deal with the matter of the women's corroboration. He quoted previous authorities that showed that the judge had acted correctly. He was able to show that the evidence of the women apart, the case against the two, Barnes and McCormack, was overwhelming. At the end of the appeal the Lord Chief Justice delivered his judgment. He cited previous cases so that Wood and his team would know how he had come to his decision. The grounds for appeal were dismissed. Barnes and McCormack were to hang.

On 29 January, President de Valera made a personal appeal to the British Prime Minister to intervene, as did the Protestant Archbishop of Dublin. The Vatican interceded, as did a number of prominent people in Britain. Tom Barry, who had opposed the bombing campaign, addressed a mass meeting in Cork in support of a reprieve for the two men. He even proposed that he should go to England and go to prison in their place until a "fair trial" could be held. The only thing that might have appeased Britain was the handing over of the two principal perpetrators: Dominic Adams, who had been in charge; and Joby Sullivan, the unidentified man who had committed the murders. By this time Barry must have known that his friend Joby O'Sullivan was the real murderer. Would he have named him? It is unlikely.

On the Monday evening following the dismissal of the appeal, the Home Secretary announced that he could not justify recommending any interference in the due process of the law. Earlier in the day the Attorney General had refused an appeal to the House of Lords against the dismissal of the men's appeal by the Court of Criminal Appeal. The date for the execution of the two IRA men was set for Ash Wednesday, 7 February 1940.

On the night before his death, Peter Barnes wrote a letter to his brother, still protesting his innocence: "If some news does not come in the next few hours all is over. The priest is not long gone, so I am reconciled to what God thinks best. There will be a Mass said for each of us that morning before we go to our death. Thank God I have nothing to be afraid of. I am an innocent man and as I have said before, it will be known yet that I am. The only thing that worries me now is the thought of my poor father and mother, but I know God will comfort them. I will write my last few lines to my mother tomorrow [Tuesday]. I will know more by then. Say a prayer for me. God be with you."

On the same night, James McCormack wrote to his sister in Mullingar. Both his parents were dead. "This is my farewell letter, as I have been just told that I have to die in the morning. I know that I would have to die, so the news did not come as a great shock to me, but thank God that I am prepared, as I shall be thinking of God and of the good men who went before me for the same cause."

At 8:50 a.m. the two men received the last blessing. In their individual cells their arms were bound behind them. The two men walked together to the scaffold. Accompanying them was Father J. Collins, Roman Catholic chaplain to the prison, and the warden, Mr. H. Colinson. The gallows had been erected side by side. There were four executioners: Thomas W. Pierrepoint (chief executioner), Mr. T.M. Phillips, Mr. S.W. Cross, and Albert Pierrepoint (nephew of the chief executioner). The two men died simultaneously at 9 o'clock that morning at Winson Green Prison in Birmingham.

There were no incidents outside the prison, around which the police had kept watch throughout the preceding night, and only a small crowd had gathered on the day itself. They had been kept back some 100 yards from the prison. People waiting for buses and trams nearby were closely scrutinized by the police. All night through there had been a police presence. At dawn small groups of people gathered nearby, and plainclothes detectives from Birmingham CID kept a close watch for any scenes of suspicious behavior. Precautions were put in place to prevent any demonstration or outrage following telephone calls the previous evening received at police headquarters in Steelhouse Lane, threatening bombing reprisals if the two Irishmen were hanged. In charge of the whole operation, and present from the early morning, was the Chief Constable, Mr. C.C.H. Moriarty, himself an Irishman of old Protestant stock. As the clock approached 9 a.m., police officers in uniform and in plainclothes, were stationed in all the streets surrounding the prison at intervals of about ten yards, and at street junctions there were little groups of policemen. As was the custom at the time, curtains in houses around the prison were drawn. As the time approached, the crowds were quiet and orderly, and made no attempt to press forward. All traffic passing the front of the prison was stopped for about a quarter of an hour before the execution. At the inquests at the prison, verdicts of "Judicial hanging" were returned in each case. Dr. John Humphrey, the prison surgeon, said that death was instantaneous in each case. At six minutes past nine, a warder passed through the wicket gate and posted two white notices stating that sentence of death had been duly administered. The notice concerning McCormack, his real identity still a secret, read:

> I John Humphrey, the surgeon of H.M. Prison, Birmingham, hereby certify that I this day, examined the body of James Richards, on whom judgment of death was this day executed in the said prison, and that, on examination, I found that the same James Richards was dead.
>
> Dated this 7th day of February 1940.
> (Signed) John Humphrey.[1]

As a preventive measure against possible IRA demonstrations in Coventry, the police visited the homes of all known sympathizers. In truth there were few of them now left in the city. Deportation under the Prevention of Violence Act had seen to that. Several men recently arrived from Ireland were required to produce evidence of identity. They were also closely questioned about their associates and movements. A general warning was issued. As it was, the day passed off quietly. On the following day Ireland went into national mourning: flags were flown at half mast, cinemas and theaters closed, sports meetings were canceled and masses were offered for the repose of their souls.

There was bitterness in Republican circles towards the Irish government in that it had not done more. On the evening of 21 February, 104 former officers of the old IRA held a meeting. The outcome was a proposal to form a new Irish Republican movement on 2 March 1940. Former Dublin Brigade leader Simon Donnelly was elected as president of a committee of fifteen members. The newspaper reporters present were informed that the new party would be ready to take over the reins of government on either a corporate or fascist basis. De Valera was not having any of that sort of nonsense. At a meeting of the new party held at the Meath Hotel in Dublin, the building was surrounded and 13 prominent members were arrested and imprisoned under the new powers.

With the outbreak of war, the Republican prisoners were moved to Dartmoor, Britain's most feared prison, where they were located as a group on D Wing. Peter Walsh was appointed O.C., and Mick Ferguson was quartermaster. They maintained their own discipline, and worked hard at their appointed tasks. They even agreed to paint their own wing if paint was supplied. In short, they were no trouble to their warders, and the arrangement suited the prison authorities. Previously in August, at the time of the Coventry outrage, the eleven Republican prisoners then incarcerated at Dartmoor were severely beaten up by both warders and prisoners alike, so badly that they had to be hospitalized, but as time passed things settled down once more to some degree of normality.

Then things changed. At Easter 1940, with the conviction and detention of more IRA prisoners, news reached the Republican prisoners in Dartmoor of the executions of Barnes and McCormack. Enraged at the execution of perceived innocent men, they staged a rooftop protest, and using the paint provided, a combination of green, white and orange, they painted Irish tricolors out of their bed sheets, which they then flew over Dartmoor's rooftops. The protest escalated when they set fire to the wing. The authorities now had no option but to react with force to put down the riot. With a free use of batons, the prison guards, with police back-up, soon regained control of the Republican wing. The prisoners were then isolated. Some of them were dispersed to other jails, but those remaining now refused to wear prison uniforms. They were put into punishment cells on E Wing for their part in the riot, completely naked during the day. Everything was removed except a Bible and a cardboard chamber pot. As the war progressed, alternative "uniforms" were adopted by the Republicans and a degree of normality was resumed.

8

The End of the Campaign

On the early morning of the Coventry explosion, bombs went off in Liverpool city center at Lloyd's Bank in Victoria Street and on Stanley Street. The day after, there were explosions in Lancashire, Liverpool and Blackpool. One of the three Liverpool explosions occurred near a first aid post in Dovecot. In Blackpool an explosive device was discovered in the forecourt of the central police station. It was rendered harmless. Two bombs, however, did go off in Blackpool, one outside the Town Hall, and the other at nearby business premises. On the same night, Christopher Kenneally was arrested when a bomb he was carrying went off prematurely. The acid in the balloon had eaten through the rubber more quickly than anticipated. After throwing away a parcel of thirteen sticks of gelignite, he was fumbling through his coat pocket to retrieve the fuse; smoke and flames were coming from his clothing. Seeing what was happening, some more astute members of the public pounced upon him, while others summoned the police. He was arrested and taken away for questioning.

That same night, 28 August, two cast iron Royal Mail pillar boxes were blown up in Liverpool. Thankfully no one was about at the time.

Kenneally's lodgings in Upper Parliament Street were placed under observation by Special Branch. Any visitors were followed. There were four of them. For the moment, the police stayed their hand in the hope of rounding up all the bombing team. The police followed two visitors in particular back to a house in Prescott Road, Rainhill. Enquiries with the neighbors revealed that they were a Mr. and Mrs. James Smith. For the moment the police waited. Mrs. Smith was one of the aliases of 19-year-old Margaret McDonnell. Hearing of the arrest of Kenneally, she panicked. On the night of 29 August she booked a passage to Ireland by way of Holyhead. Unfortunately she caught the wrong train and ended up in the middle of the night at Wigan. Here she was approached by two members of the Railway

Police. She gave her name as Dobson, and her address as Prescott Road, Rainhill. The police telephoned the police in Liverpool to corroborate her story. With the address flagged up as a possible IRA house, Special Branch ordered her arrest. In Liverpool the police went to the house, but Mr. Smith gave a seemingly convincing explanation. The police, still interested in bagging the complete team, did nothing for the moment. Smith, the alias of 36-year-old Vincent Crompton, realized that McDonnell had abandoned him. He now made plans for his own departure the following day. Before he left, though, he primed a bomb to go off. The bomb exploded on the night of 30 August. Despite the explosion, there was still a considerable amount of forensic evidence for the police and fire brigade to sift through. The Smiths' house proved to be an IRA bomb factory.

The police now pounced. They raided the homes of Kenneally's visitors. John Carney, George Whittaker and Margaret McDonnell were subsequently arrested in connection with the Liverpool bombings. Vincent Crompton, who briefly eluded them, was subsequently arrested. All five members of the gang were sent for trial at Liverpool Assize in October 1939. Crompton was sentenced to 20 years' penal servitude for conspiracy to cause explosions, and causing explosions. Carney and Whittaker got 7 years for possession. Christopher Kenneally, still a minor, was given three years Borstal, and Margaret McDonnell, who was considered to be peripheral, was bound over to keep the peace for 2 years.

Now the IRA campaign was eclipsed by events in Europe. On 1 September 1939, Germany invaded Poland from the west; the Soviet Union invaded from the east, ostensively to prevent the eastern advance of the German army. World War II had begun. On 3 September, Britain and France declared war on Nazi Germany. Holland and Belgium proclaimed their neutrality. British Prime Minister Neville Chamberlain was replaced by Winston Churchill. He offered de Valera the Six Counties if he would join the Allies. De Valera refused. He did not trust Churchill, and perhaps rightly so. The Protestants would not have meekly gone into a unified, and as they saw it, a Catholic Ireland.

The IRA continued with its futile campaign, but the national newspapers gave little coverage to the outrages after the outbreak of what was to become World War II. No more lives were lost in the IRA's campaign, perhaps more due to luck than judgment. Most of the later incidents would have been classified as secondary in the original "S-Plan," as was witnessed in London, where wiring was severed in two telephone kiosks on 29 October. On 4 November the wires were cut in four telephone kiosks in the capital. Incendiary devices were dropped into sixteen pillar boxes, destroying the mail, and mail trains working out of Euston suffered incendiary attacks. More telephone wiring was cut on 5 November. It was no more than vandalism, hardly the sort of thing that would force the British to the negotiating table over the Six Counties. A close guard by the British authorities on seaports ensured that fresh supplies and fresh recruits were prevented from arriving. There was a mass arrest and deportation of suspects. Those who were not arrested, now devoid of direction, began drifting homewards. The remaining teams in England then went to ground, and bided their time.

On 18 November the bombs started going off once more. There were four explosions at business premises in London. Two bombs were discovered in time and rendered helpless. On 24 November two police boxes and two public telephone kiosks were damaged by explosives. That same night there were explosions at telephone kiosks in both Birmingham and Coventry. At Southampton on the night of 28 November, there was an explosion in a lavatory at the central railway station, and a second in the grounds of a former library. Wiring was cut at three telephone kiosks in London, and a further one was cut the following night, 29 November. A warning from the police in Birmingham was telephoned through to Coventry that there had been explosions in telephone kiosks and police boxes. The chief constable initiated a detailed search within the city. A constable discovered an unexploded bomb behind a police box near the central fire station in Hales Street at 12:30 a.m. on Saturday morning. It was a homemade bomb enclosed in a coffee tin. Gingerly the policeman picked it up, then rushed with it into the fire station, where it was placed in a bucket of water and made safe. On 7 December there were seven cases of incendiarism in Birmingham.

As the trial of the Coventry bombers got underway, the IRA's response was a pathetic spate of incendiary devices. On 12 December there were two attempted cases in an Oxford Street store in London. On the 14 there were firebomb attempts at a cinema in London and one in Birmingham. There were six incendiary devices discovered in the mail at Andover in Hampshire. On 19 December there was an explosion at a business premise in Birmingham, but then it was a return to incendiary devices. There were no more bombers coming over from Ireland. Those suspected of being IRA sympathizers were refused entry to Britain, under the Prevention of Violence Act passed in July.

On 31 December 1939, the chief constable of Coventry presented his annual report to the city council. It was a measured report:

> Of the six cases of murder, five were the result of the violent explosion which occurred in Broadgate on the afternoon of the 25th August, and for which terrible crime three men and two women were arrested after the most exhaustive

8. The End of the Campaign

enquiries and untiring efforts of the police officers charged with the task, several of whom did not pause for rest for two days and nights and continued their investigations for long hours without refreshments. Such is the devotion to duty of members of the Police Force, and this applies to all ranks. The year has been marked by a series of explosions to cause malicious damage commencing from the month of February and the police were faced with considerable difficulties until wider powers were given under the Prevention of Violence (Temporary Provisions) Act, 1939, which came into force on the 28th July last. Under this Act, up to the close of the year, 9 persons from Coventry have been expelled to Ireland, and Prohibition Orders granted against 2 persons who had left the country. The enormous task of examining and checking information of suspects and searches of houses continue, and will continue until this cowardly type of crime is stamped out.

Throughout the remainder of December and into 1940 there were incendiary attacks on the postal system in Birmingham, Wolverhampton, Crewe and London. Buses also came under attack in what amounted to no more than vandalism. The bombing team that had attacked Birmingham on 19 December 1939 struck again in the city on 14 February 1940. Two shops were bombed, and three bombs were discovered and rendered harmless.

The police were closing in on the remaining bombers. Information was coming in from the public regarding suspicious characters. Dan Keating, OC in London, escaped just prior to a police raid on his place of work, Mooney's Bar in the Strand. He had worked in London back in 1937, charged by the IRA with establishing safe houses. He got to know the city well. He was there until the end of November 1939, when, following a number of close shaves, he returned to Dublin. In January 1940 he was asked to go back. There were hardly any active members remaining. Keating was tasked with reviving the campaign. The sole remaining active unit comprised Bill McAllister, Jimmy O'Neill and Maggie Nolan. Things were getting hot for them. They decided temporarily to leave London. They moved to Rollinton Road in Bristol. Keating went down to see them. When he got there he saw a policeman standing outside the premises. It was a case of closing the stable doors after the horse had bolted. The unit, probably aware of police interest, had fled. Keating kept walking, passed the house, and made his way back to the station, where he caught the next train back to London.

Keating established another active service unit comprising himself, Terence Perry and Jackie Daly. Their campaign began on 22 February. There was an explosion in a public lavatory, and more dangerously a bomb exploded in Oxford Street, one of the busiest streets in the capital. Luckily it went off late at night, but all the same seven people were seriously injured. This was reckless abandon and hinted at desperation. They started a blaze at the Grosvenor Hotel in Park Lane, and on 1 March set a number of fires at a big department store in Queen's Road, Bayswater. On the 6th they set off a bomb outside a Park Lane bank, and another in King's Inn Road, London. Then Perry was caught, leaving just two of them. They set off an explosion near Paddington Town Hall on 17 March. An unexploded bomb they had left was discovered on the following day in a litter bin at Grosvenor Place, and rendered harmless. The last bomb they left exploded on 18 March at a refuse depot in Westminster as workers were dealing with street litter. No one was injured. To continue, Keating realized, was pointless. He sent Daly back to Dublin, then began destroying all incriminating evidence prior to his own departure. The final total for the campaign was 300 explosions, 10 deaths and 96 injuries.

The increase in security surrounding infrastructure targets in England had a major effect on the IRA's ability to conduct operations. The seizure of bomb-making materials and the difficulty in acquiring new materials meant increased improvisation, which in turn led to increased exposure to discovery. In an interview for BBC Radio Ulster, recorded just before his death in 2007, Keating told how he had gone back to his lodgings for lunch one day, when he received a warning telephone call from a fellow barman, Paddy Coffey. "The police are looking for you," he said. Keating quickly packed a bag, but on his way downstairs he was met by a number of policemen. "Is Dan Keating here?" they demanded. "He is just after getting on a bus back to work," Keating told them. Perhaps naively, they did not question him further, but set off back to Mooney's Bar. As they went off in one direction, Keating took off in the opposite. He decided to get out of England as soon as possible. Realizing that the police would question every Irishman arriving at an Irish-bound port, aboard a London train, he made alternative transport arrangements. He caught a bus to Leeds, and from there caught another bus to Liverpool. Here he met up with a Republican supporter, Con Connor, a night security man at the port of Liverpool, who smuggled him aboard a ferry boat to Dun Laoghaire.

As abruptly as it had begun, it was over. In the whole campaign since January 1939, two men had been sentenced to death, 23 men and women to penal servitude for 20 years, 34 for periods of 10 to 20 years, 23 for 5 to 10 years, and 14 for terms of under 5 years. The last IRA men to be convicted were the three sentenced at the July 1940 Assize in Birmingham; James Hasty received 10 years, Thomas O'Hanlon received 8 years, and Terence Perry, Keating's ASU member, 6 years. Within two years Terence Perry, a

8. The End of the Campaign

native of Belfast, had died of tuberculosis in Parkhurst Prison on the Isle of Wight. His death followed that of Joseph Malone, another Belfast man imprisoned in Parkhurst, who died 21 January 1942. William Gaughran, imprisoned under a pseudonym, was released from prison in 1947, suffering with the later stages of TB. Within two months he was dead. Conditions for IRA prisoners in English jails were never going to be easy.

Even the most diehard Republican realized that the English campaign had failed. Most of the senior officers had been arrested or were recalled. Skilled men were no longer available. The IRA was forced into sending boys and girls, including the 16-year-old Brendan Behan, who had scarcely settled into his Liverpool digs when he was arrested. GHQ barely had enough funds, and with a lack of personnel, called a halt to the campaign. Those who returned to Ireland found it a country greatly changed. There was to be no toleration of the IRA by de Valera's government, which had announced a policy of strict neutrality. Hundreds were arrested just upon suspicion, and interned at the Curragh military camp in Kildare. Caught up in the arrests were both Dominic Adams and Joby O'Sullivan. The IRA had been effectively neutered, but where was the IRA's chief of staff, Sean Russell?

Russell was in Nazi Germany. The IRA's connection with Nazi Germany appears to have originated when former IRA chief of staff Andy Cooney visited the country with his wife in 1936. He proposed a collaboration against Britain. In the following year Tom Barry visited Germany accompanied by Jupp Hoven, a German intelligence agent. His aim was to gain German support in a military campaign against Northern Ireland. Though there was interest, the belief in German intelligence circles was that the IRA in Ireland did not have enough strike power to achieve success. It was not until the bombing campaign opened that German intelligence took any real interest in the IRA. In February 1939 the Abwehr sent an agent, Oscar Carl Pfaus, over to Dublin to make contact. He first approached Eoin O'Duffy, former Blueshirt commander, and avowed enemy of the IRA. Nonetheless, through his secretary O'Duffy put Pfaus in touch with IRA chief of staff Maurice Twomey. As a result, James O'Donovan, author of the S-Plan, made four visits to Germany to discuss the possibility of acquiring German arms and wireless equipment for the IRA. What the Germans wanted was for the IRA to adopt Tom Barry's plan of an all-out assault on the North, thus diverting British troops from France to defend the Province. What they failed to do, though, was to offer practical aid to the IRA. Negotiations stalled.

Then, through its consulate in Genoa, the Germans learnt that the

IRA chief of staff, Sean Russell, who was in New York, was preparing to sail to Italy, with a view of continuing on to Germany for further talks. Russell duly arrived in Genoa on 1 May 1940, and was taken to Germany, where he was installed in a very fashionable house at the expense of the German Foreign Ministry. Helmut Kilssmann, Russell's contact in Berlin, expressed the opinion that the IRA leader made an excellent impression in Berlin. "He was a munitions man and he knew what he was about," he said. On 5 August, Russell held talks with Hitler's foreign minister, Joachim von Ribbentrop. As a gesture of their confidence in him, the Abwehr brought about a reunion between Russell and Frank Ryan. Ryan, who had fought in the International Brigade in Spain's civil war, had been captured by Franco's forces and had spent more than a year under sentence of death in the notorious Burgos Prison. Admiral Wilhelm Canaris, the head of the Abwehr, secured Ryan's release and his transfer to Germany. It was a curious renewal; Ryan the socialist, who had fought against fascism, and Russell, who had embraced it. Both were Irish Republicans, though, and their struggle for Irish unification overcame all past differences. Russell is alleged to have said to Ryan, "I'm going to Ireland tomorrow, Frank. Will you come with me?" Ryan readily agreed.

On the night of 7–8 August, Russell and Ryan sailed from Wilhelmshaven aboard a U-boat commanded by Korvetten-Kapitan Hans-Jerrit von Stockhausen, bound for Ireland. The two men, along with a powerful radio transmitter, were to be landed at Smerwick Bay on the Dingle peninsula on 15 August. On the voyage, Russell began to suffer bouts of vomiting and stomach pains. There was no doctor aboard. Russell was given laxatives but the pain grew worse. On 14 August, the day before the two men were due to land, Russell died in Ryan's arms. The probable cause of death was a perforated duodenal ulcer. The IRA chief of staff was buried at sea a hundred miles west of Galway. Ryan had no idea of Russell's mission, and perhaps curiously, declined to be landed in Ireland. The U-boat eventually returned to Germany via the French port of L'Orient. Ryan saw out the rest of the war in Germany.

The principal German agent sent to Ireland was Hermann Goertz. Following Russell's arrival in Germany, he had been dropped by parachute in May 1940, to prepare the ground. His radio transmitter was lost during the drop. Attempts to replace it proved futile. The following year Goertz was arrested and interned before anything had been established between him and his IRA contacts. As a result neither the IRA or Nazi Germany benefited from their association with each other. The whole collaboration proved futile. In a series of articles published in the *Irish Times* after his death, Goertz described the IRA dismissively: "The IRA had become an underground movement in its own national sphere, heavily suppressed by men who knew all their methods. Inside the IRA, nobody knew what game was really played, not even their leader. Their internal means of communication were as primitive as boys playing police and brigands. They got no further than the open message in the sock of a girl. And what messages! There was no code—they did not want to learn the most simple code, they preferred to sacrifice their men and women. They had not a single wireless operator; they made no attempt to learn message discipline, their military training was nil. I once said to one of them whom I admired for his personal qualities: 'You know how to die for Ireland, but of how to fight for it you have not the slightest idea.' In spite of the fine qualities of individual IRA men, as a body I considered them worthless."[1] That somehow seemed to sum up the bombing campaign. In the fullness of time even Jim O'Donovan, author of the "S" Plan, admitted that the campaign had no hope of succeeding.

By the end of World War II, the IRA was in a moribund state. Most of its members were imprisoned or interned. On 10 March 1945, Paddy Fleming, as chief of staff of the Army Council of the IRA, ordered a ceasefire to the bombing operations. The campaign had been a failure. Its stated aim was to bring terror to England, forcing the British authorities to the negotiating table with a view to their withdrawal from Northern Ireland, thus bringing about a united Ireland. The very idea was ludicrous. Even if the British had withdrawn, the Protestant people of Northern Ireland would have fought against being forced into a united Ireland against their wishes.

9

The Irish Response to the Campaign

When the sabotage campaign opened in England in January 1939, President de Valera introduced the Offenses Against the State bill. He was determined to prevent the Republican movement from drawing the Irish people into confrontation with the British government. Although there had been no military operations by the IRA in Eire for several years, and the announced policy of the Army Council had guaranteed no hostilities within the 26 counties, de Valera's Fianna Fail Government nonetheless decided to act. On Monday morning, 14 August, a series of raids was carried out by the Irish Special Branch based at Dublin Castle, on Republican homes throughout the city. Among those arrested was George Plunkett, signatory to the Ultimatum to the British Government issued in the previous January, and brother to 1916 Proclamation signatory, Joseph Mary Plunkett. Others arrested included veteran Republican Joe Clarke, publisher of the *Wolfe Tone Weekly*, official journal of the movement, and Myles Heffernan, adjutant of the Dublin Brigade of the IRA. The following day, 15 August, armed detectives surrounded a training session being conducted in County Offaly by Harry White of Belfast. They moved in and arrested all the participants. White was sentenced to three years' imprisonment, while the trainees each got eighteen months.

On 22 August the Irish government passed the Offenses Against the State Act, giving powers to the police to arrest without warrant, detain without charge, and search and interrogate suspects. On 25 August the Military Tribunal was reintroduced, having been phased out two years earlier. It was commissioned to sit in Collins' Barracks, Dublin, before senior army officers. It had the power to issue the death sentence. World War II began on 3 September. While Britain went to war, Ireland remained neutral.

9. The Irish Response to the Campaign 147

Nevertheless on the previous day a "State of Emergency" was declared in the Irish parliament, putting Ireland on a war footing. On the 3rd an Emergency Powers bill was introduced in the Dail, which included measures to be taken against the Republican movement. The Irish Special Branch was reorganized, and Gerry Boland, noted for his anti-IRA stance, was appointed minister for justice. The crackdown under Boland began on 9 September. A house in Rathmines Park, in south central Dublin, was raided, and four members of IRA Headquarters staff were arrested. They were Larry Grogan, Peader O'Flaherty, Willie McGuinness and Paddy McGrath. From evidence gathered, follow-up raids then took place on Republican homes and places of work throughout the Free State. A total of sixty-four prisoners were taken into custody and lodged in Arbour Hill Military Prison, Dublin, and interned without trial under section four of the new Offenses Against the State Act. Others, considered to be more dangerous, appeared before the Military Tribunal in Collins' Barracks, and were later transferred to Mountjoy Prison. To silence any Republican protest, the Irish government banned the *Wolfe Tone Weekly*.

In Northern Ireland since the previous December, Republicans had already been interned without trial in Crumlin Road Jail, Belfast. A pre–Christmas RUC raid had captured thirty-two prisoners, mostly Belfast men and women. Internment in Northern Ireland, or the Six Counties as they were known in Republican circles, was to last until December 1945.

With so many loose tongues in Republican circles, it was inevitable that Dublin Special Branch would hear of the whereabouts of James O'Donovan's training camp for bombers. In October, Killiney Castle was raided by a team led by Inspector Mansfield. All they found were some mattresses and blankets and a few old alarm clocks. On 14 October 1939, an explosion at the outer wall of Mountjoy Prison failed to breach it, in an attempt to secure the release of Grogan, McGuinness, O'Flaherty and McGrath. McGrath was director of operations on the IRA GHQ staff, the man who was overseeing the English campaign. The four men then went on a hunger strike against their detention. The government responded on 31 October by issuing a statement that the hunger strikers would not be released.

In November 1939, the Sheriff Street Postal Sorting Office in Dublin was raided, and £5,000 was stolen. Later in the month the National Bank at Cloncliffe Road was held up and £200 was taken. By their successful expertise in carrying out the robberies, the government knew that the IRA was behind both robberies. As the hunger strikers grew weaker, some of them were removed to Jervis Street Hospital, Dublin, for greater medical attention. On 5 December, with the assistance of a Republican sympathizer on the staff of the hospital, Paddy McGrath escaped from custody and went on the run.

On 23 December, in what was surely the height of folly, the IRA raided the Magazine Fort in Phoenix Park, Dublin, and using thirteen trucks, escaped with 1,084,000 rounds of ammunition, almost the whole of the Irish Army's reserve stock. The government reacted strongly by pushing through an Emergency Powers Act on 9 February 1940, to strengthen the Offenses Against the State Act, in record time. The Act allowed the internment without trial of citizens, closing the gap in the application of habeas corpus. The police could arrest people merely on the "opinion" rather than as formerly "being satisfied" that they were a danger to the state. Over the next two weeks most of the stolen ammunition was recovered. Senior IRA officers were arrested in the roundup that followed. Sylvestor Fitzsimons and Bertie McCormack were among the first two. Fitzsimons refused to answer any questions and was sentenced to three months' imprisonment in Mounjoy. McCormack was able to account for his movements, and these were verified from other sources. Nonetheless he was an IRA man, and was accordingly interned.

With its members being arrested, those senior members of the IRA still at liberty called a meeting on 17 February 1940 at the Meath Hotel, Parnell Square, Dublin. Of course the IRA was by now heavily infiltrated by Irish Special Branch informers. News of the meeting filtered back to Dublin Castle. Armed Special Branch men, backed up by Free State troops, raided the hotel and arrested sixteen people. They each got three months in Mountjoy Prison for refusing to answer questions, then indefinite internment in the Curragh, following their release. Conditions on "D" wing, the political wing of Mountjoy, were particularly harsh. Political status was denied to the prisoners. Their diet was poor, and they were ill-treated by the warders. Talking was not allowed. In addition, the IRA men were locked in their cells from 4 p.m. until 7:30 a.m. the next day. A number of them went on a hunger strike. Then word spread through "D" wing that two of their number were to be taken before a Military Tribunal with a strong probability that they would be shot. On 14 March the prisoners seized control of the wing and barricaded it off in order to prevent the removal of the two men. The warders, with police support, stormed the barricade and retook the wing. The prisoners were beaten back into their cells, and then the warders turned high-pressure hoses on them. The mutiny was over.

The hunger strike was the prisoners' only means of fighting back. Minister for Justice Gerry Boland had announced that the hunger strikers would not be released, as on previous occasions. Nevertheless the hunger strike continued. Tony Darcy died in St. Bricin's Military Hospital, Arbour Hill, on 16 April 1940. He had been fasting for fifty-three days. Sean McNeela died three days later on 19 April, after fasting for fifty-six days. Still the government would not give way. Carmelite priest the Rev. John O'Hare, pastor to the prisoners, pleaded with the remaining members of the IRA GHQ still at liberty to intercede. They did so, and the prisoners were ordered to cease their hunger strike. At the inquest of the two men, the jury requested that the men on "D" wing should be granted political status. At Easter 1940, two black coffins were carried in the Easter Rising commemoration in Dublin in memory of Barnes and McCormack, who had been hanged in England earlier that year. In the Dail the following week, Jerry Boland, referring to the coffins, issued the dark threat, "If the IRA want coffins, I will fill plenty of them. They need not carry empty ones."

On 25 April the IRA struck back at their enemy. A bomb exploded in the Dublin headquarters of Special Branch, injuring sixteen people. The police struck back with a vengeance. Republican homes were raided. The inhabitants, men and women, were roughly treated. Then Special Branch got lucky. In the home of one of the bombers a plan of the headquarters was discovered, drawn on the back of an envelope. Turning it over, the policemen discovered the name and address of Geroid MacCarthaigh. As a consequence he too was arrested and interned in the Curragh. For the IRA it was the same old problem, dating back to the Irish-American dynamite campaign of the 1880s. Written records were left lying about, when really, if there was a need for them at all, they should have been destroyed after reading. It was a lesson they had failed to learn.

President de Valera went on the radio, declaring that the state was under internal attack. This was a preliminary announcement, for on 3 June there was a massive roundup of Republicans in early morning raids. Some six hundred and forty people from every one of the 26 counties were seized. They were taken by the truckload to the Curragh, or Cork Jail. The women were interred in Mountjoy Prison. This combined police and military action was designed to uproot the entire Republican movement. Wartime censorship concealed the true scale, and brutality, of the operation from the Irish people.

About the middle of June, Tomas MacCurtain, son of a famous Cork Republican from an earlier generation, was brought before a Military Tribunal on a capital charge. He was still recovering from the earlier hunger strike. MacCurtain was found guilty and sentenced to death by hanging for the death of Detective Roche, who had died during the scuffle to arrest him. There was an immediate response to the sentence. Petitions were started, and influential people from around the world urged de Valera to commute the sentence. After some agonizing time, de Valera agreed to mercy. MacCurtain was transferred to the horror that was Portlaoise Prison. Portlaoise showed that when it came to brutality the Irish had learnt well from the British.

By August 1940, just prior to the outbreak of World War II, there were between 1,000 and 1,500 men and women in prison or in internment camps in England and in Ireland, on both sides of the border. A new internment camp at the Curragh had been built to accommodate more arrivals. As the prisoners in Cork Jail were being prepared for the move, volunteers of the 1st Cork Brigade began to dig an escape tunnel into the prison from the grounds of the mental asylum next door in a bid to free them. Cork Special Branch became aware of what was going on, and launched an armed raid on the asylum. They discovered the shaft. Looking down, they saw two men, and rather recklessly opened fire upon them. John Joe Kavanagh was severely wounded, and later died of his injuries in an ambulance on his way to hospital. Roger Ryan was also seriously wounded, but later recovered. There were two other men just inside the tunnel. They refused to come out until they had assurances that they would not be killed. Once these were given, the two men, one of whom was Joseph B. O'Sullivan—"Joby" Sullivan, the Coventry bomber—emerged from the earthworks, their hands raised in surrender. Because they had surrendered, they were sent not to prison, but were interred in the Curragh.

Previously on 15 August, a house at 98a, Rathgar Road, Dublin, was surrounded by armed police from Dublin Castle. Inside were Tom Hunte, Tom Harte and Paddy McGrath, recently escaped from police custody. They were called upon to surrender, but decided to fight their way out. A brief but fierce fire-fight developed. Two policemen, Sergeant McKeown and Detective Constable Hyland, were killed, and IRA man Tom Harte was seriously wounded. Escape was now impossible. As the man in charge, McGrath decided to surrender. The three men were charged with murder and brought before a special military tribunal. They were found guilty, and sentenced to death by shooting within seventy-two hours. There was no right of appeal. Dramatically, Hunte was reprieved, and interred at the Curragh, but at 6:45 a.m. on 6 September, the other two, Paddy McGrath and Tom Harte, were taken out and stood up against the boundary wall with the women's prison in Mountjoy, and shot dead. Harte had taken part in the earlier 1939 bombing campaign in England.

9. The Irish Response to the Campaign   151

September 1940 saw the completion of the construction of a new internment camp at the Curragh military base in County Kildare. All male internees from Cork Jail and other prisons were now sent there. Some 700 Republicans were held without charge. Most of them had been held since the massive sweep over the 26 counties way back on 3 June. The original internment camp was a cordoned-off area of near-derelict huts dating back to the time when it had been a British Army barracks, and was surrounded by barbed wire. Sanitary and kitchen facilities had been primitive at best. Heating in the huts was provided by small turf stoves which gave off little heat. When it rained, the water seeped through the roofs, soaking bedding and personal belongings.

In the new camp there were 18 newly built huts, with a separate dining hut and kitchen. There was also a "glass house" or punishment block, where prisoners who had committed offenses were temporarily incarcerated. There was a latrine block, named by the prisoners as "Bolands" after the justice minister. Beyond the barbed wire were guard huts. The new wooden huts had been constructed upon the concrete foundations of the pre–1922 British cavalry stables. Conditions in the new camp proved to be equally harsh. Food was adequate, but hardly nourishing. Discipline was strict. The main problem amongst the prisoners was boredom.

In December matters came to a head. The prisoners presented five demands for improvement to the camp commandant. Days passed, there was no response. Saturday, 14 December, was picked as a day of protest. Six huts were to be set ablaze. The day was chosen because there was a horse-racing meeting at the course nearby. Normally that part of Kildare was more or less devoid of people. The prisoners knew that the racegoers would see the smoke from their burning huts, thus preventing the matter from being hushed up under wartime censorship. The fires were begun and soon the huts were blazing away, smoke billowing across the open plains.

The camp authorities sent word of the riot to Dublin, and armed soldiers and the fire brigade were rushed to the Curragh. As the fire brigade worked to put out the flames, the soldiers entered the camp and pushed the prisoners back. The prisoners responded to the violence, defending themselves with whatever came to hand. The soldiers responded with live rounds, wounding a number of the prisoners. The riot was eventually subdued, and the prisoners were locked in the remaining huts until Monday morning without food. Released, they were lined up and marched towards the dining hall, as was the usual custom. Fourteen soldiers from outside, not realizing the procedure, believed that the prisoners were going to try to rush them, so opened fire. Two men were wounded before the soldiers were ordered to cease fire. Later that day the alleged ringleaders of the riot were forced to run the gauntlet to the glasshouse, the guards beating them with clubs and rifle butts. They were put into solitary confinement for ten weeks before being brought before military courts, where they were sentenced to between two and five years' imprisonment. From then on discipline within the camp became even more brutal. The authorities were determined to break the prisoners.

In one of the periodical roundups that followed, James O'Donovan, author of the "S" Plan that led to the bombings in England, was arrested at 8 a.m. on 26 September 1941, at his County Dublin home, and interred at the Curragh. There he remained for two years until released through ill health. Among the papers seized at his home were names and contacts. Of special interest to the police were his Nazi connections, which were seen as a threat to Irish neutrality.

In 1942, Coventry bomber Joby O'Sullivan, who had arrived with the prisoners from Cork Jail, and interned at the Curragh, temporarily escaped when taken for treatment at the dental hospital in Lincoln Place, a medical institute next to Trinity College in Dublin. He was later recaptured, taken before a military tribunal, and sentenced to imprisonment in Portlaoise Prison. The prison at Portlaoise is some fifty miles from Dublin. It was known as "Ireland's Bastille." Justice Minister Boland had decided that any Republicans who offered armed resistance, or who had their death sentences commuted, should be sent there. Escapees were also to be sent there, and that included O'Sullivan. From July 1940 until June 1943, the regime was unrelentlessly harsh. The system was designed to break the Republican prisoners. They were not allowed to talk, unless addressed by a prison warden. Certainly they could not talk to their fellow prisoners. There was no reading matter other than a Bible. Any infringement of the rules was punished by beatings and bread and water diets. The IRA men refused to be treated as criminals. They refused to wear prison uniform; they refused to accept a prison number. The authorities insisted that any letters addressed to them must have the prisoner's number. Any letter going out must have their prison number. The prisoners refused to accept this, as a result of which they never received, nor sent out, any mail in all the years they were imprisoned. Refusing to wear a uniform, they were left naked. As protection against the cold, each cut a hole in his blanket, and wore it like a poncho. They became known as the "blanket men." This form of covering was considered immodest by the prison authorities, so prisoners were confined to their cells. They could not receive visitors; they could not attend Sunday Mass. This was particularly hard, for the majority of the prisoners held strong Catholic beliefs. Refusing to wear a uniform, they were never allowed outside their cells except for a weekly bath in cold water. Many of the Republican prisoners never saw daylight in all their many years of incarceration. As an added torment, lights were turned on in the cells at erratic times in the night as a security check. When this happened the prisoners had to stand by their cell door and call out to the guard that they were there. If they did not, they were beaten.

The system was particularly harder for some, such as men like Jim Crofton, a former Special Branch man who was looked upon as a turncoat, a betrayer. He had helped Republicans by passing on information. Then there were men like Joby O'Sullivan who had escaped from custody. Retribution had to be dealt out to them as an example to the others. They were singled out for special cruelty. Some broke under the physical strain; some, like O'Sullivan, were driven mad. He was later sent to Dundrum Mental Asylum, where he remained for several years, completely institutionalized. De Valera had achieved what he had set out to do. He had broken the IRA.

By the end of war in 1945, de Valera had been in continual power for thirteen years. In that time he had transformed the twenty-six-county Irish state into a sovereign independent country through the democratic process of the 1937 Constitution Act. Eire, as it had become, was a republic in all but name. The British Crown was now recognized by the Irish as merely "the symbol of co-operation" between Ireland, Canada, Australia, New Zealand, South Africa and Great Britain—countries who were combined in an "association." No mention was made of empire or commonwealth. The new Irish constitution was a renunciation of almost all the points that Britain had insisted upon in the treaty signed in London in December 1921. The new constitution laid claim to all thirty-two counties of Ireland, but curiously the word Republic was not used in the Act. To have done so, it was felt at the time, would have made it more difficult to resolve an eventual solution of the Northern Ireland "problem." Eleven years later, however, on Easter Monday, 18 April 1949, John Costello's weakened coalition government declared a republic, in order to boost their popularity. Britain responded with the Ireland Act that declared "that in no event will Northern Ireland, or any part thereof, cease to be part of his Majesty's dominions and of the United Kingdom without the consent of the Parliament of Northern Ireland." Partition had been legalized.

10

Release, Repatriation and Reflection

The Curragh closed a good year and a half after the end of World War II, in December 1946, and the prisoners who had never been charged were released to pick up their lives once more. Most upon release severed their connections with the IRA. From the Irish government's perspective, internment and imprisonment had been successful in breaking the IRA threat to Irish neutrality. By Christmas 1946, just eight Republicans were still imprisoned in Portlaoise. Recently released prisoner Eddie Gallagher made a sworn affidavit about the terrible conditions in the prison. Up until then details had been concealed by wartime censorship. His statement made for grim reading. The case of the remaining prisoners was taken up in the Irish Parliament by Senator Luke Duffy. Minister for Justice Boland obstinately refused to grant any concessions to these enemies of the state, as he saw them. Matters came to the boil regarding ill treatment when hunger striker Sean McCaughey, one of the remaining seven, died on 11 May. While state censorship might conceal what was going on in the prison, the state could not control a public inquest. Sean McBride, former head of the IRA, but now a constitutionalist, was appointed by the family to represent them in court. Dr. Duane, for twenty years a prison doctor, was called to the stand. McBride questioned him regarding McCaughey:

> McBRIDE: "Are you aware that during the four and a half years he was there he was never out in the fresh air or sunlight?"
> DUANE: "As far as I am aware he was not."
> McBRIDE: "Would I be right in saying that up to twelve or eighteen months ago he was kept in solitary confinement and not allowed to speak or associate with any other persons?"
> DUANE: "That is right."

10. Release, Repatriation and Reflection 155

McBride: "Would you treat a dog in that fashion?"
Duane (after a pause): "No."

The pause and the simple word "no," by a prison official, showed that even those who worked within the system were appalled by the treatment. McBride sought to question the man who was held to be responsible, Portlaoise's warden, Major Barrows. His request was refused. The minister for justice was undoubtedly behind this refusal. Later Major Barrows was to relate that he did not have independent control of the prison. He was closely watched by senior prison warders for any signs of concessions towards the prisoners. If he had made any concessions, hardline members of his staff would have reported it to Boland, the IRA's bitterest enemy.

The jury, having heard the evidence at the inquest, gave the verdict, as directed by the coroner. But then by way of a caveat, the foreman of the jury outspokenly condemned the conditions in the prison. The press took up the story, now no longer restricted by wartime censorship. In the Dail, Duffy once again demanded an enquiry, but Boland, intransigent as ever, refused. Others took up the cause in the Irish Parliament. De Valera responded by seeking to impose restrictions on free speech and criticism of the government on the floor of the Dail. Fine Gael, the party in opposition, and the Labour Party too, very naturally refused to support de Valera, and condemned him in his bid to stifle free speech.

The Labour Party conducted its own enquiry into the treatment of political prisoners in Portlaoise, and published its findings. The findings were indeed horrifying. Following a re-examination of the evidence against them, three of the prisoners interviewed in the Labour enquiry were released at Christmas 1946. Pressure also came from the Irish lobby in the United States. This brought about change. In the new year, 1947, political prisoners were allowed to wear civilian clothes. This permitted them to leave their cells, to enjoy the sunshine, to practice their religion, and finally to receive visits from their families.

In December, having lost two by-elections,[1] de Valera looked for a vote of confidence in his government, and called a general election for February 1948. In the resulting election his party lost seats, their majority cut to sixty-eight. Fine Gael won thirty-one, and a new Republican party, Clann na Poblachta, won ten. Labour won fourteen and the other smaller combined parties won twenty-four. After some horse-trading, a new "inter-party," as it was called, its components unified in a shared distaste for de Valera and his pursuit of power, and led by Fine Gael's John A. Costello, came together to form a new government. In early March 1948, barely three weeks after the election, the new government released the last remaining five Republicans from the torment that was Portlaoise Prison.

At the end of 1948 and the beginning of 1949, the last Republican prisoners in English jails for their part in the bombing campaign were also released. These final releases were of five men serving twenty years each: Jack McCabe of Cavan, Vincent Crompton of Liverpool, Joseph Collins of Cork, Laurence Dunlea of Cork, James O'Regan, also of Cork, and Leo Duigan of Leitrim, who had been serving ten years. The last releases of all were Jack McCabe and Joe Collins, who had used the alias of Connor McNessa. There had been a widespread campaign for their releases following the end of World War II by the Republican Prisoners Release Association. Its headquarters were at 9, North Frederick Street, right in the heart of Georgian Dublin. The Association's secretary for many years was Peter Campbell of Tyrone. He had himself received ten years on the same charges with Leo Duigan at the Old Bailey in 1939. Campbell was released from Parkhurst Prison on the Isle of Wight in May 1947, after serving eight years of his sentence. Campbell, born in New York of Irish parents, was deported to the U.S. but then returned to Ireland. Dan McCafferty, who had been sentenced to four and a half years in prison, was also released. Upon his arrival in Dublin in 1943, McCafferty had been immediately arrested and interned in the Curragh, before transfer to Portlaoise. He was finally released in 1948.

With the release of the prisoners sentenced in connection with the bombing campaign in England, attention now turned to the remaining prisoners in Belfast Jail. By February 1949 there were eight internees in number: Frank Morris of Tyrone, Bob McMillan of Belfast, Liam Burke of Belfast, Alfie White of Belfast, Jimmy Steele of Belfast, Hugh McAteer of Derry, Jack McCaffrey of Antrim, and John Graham of Belfast. There were also five men sentenced to death, but reprieved: Belfast men Harry Cordner, Joe Cahill, Jimmy Perry, John Oliver and Paddy Simpson. By November 1949 the prisoners had been reduced to five, but it was not until the beginning of October 1950 that the last prisoner, Jimmy Steele, was released. He died in 1970, having spent the greater part of his life in prison for his political beliefs.

So it was ended, the bombing campaign against England. Seven innocent people had been killed, along with three IRA men who were altering the timing on a pre-set bomb in order to avoid casualties. Sean Russell, who had instigated the campaign, a man still vilified by certain elements within the Republican movement for his Nazi connections, was also dead, his body cast overboard from a German U–boat. James O'Donovan, author

10. Release, Repatriation and Reflection

of the "S" Plan, had sunk into obscurity, and a number of misguided young men were dead, either shot by the state, or having starved themselves to death in prison in the search for political status. The Northern Ireland state remained, even more determined to maintain its connection with Britain. It is difficult to see how precisely the IRA campaign could have produced the desired result of a united Ireland. The campaign has been generously described as inept; it was certainly not influential enough to determine a change in England's policy towards Ireland. In the aftermath of the Second World War, the IRA seemed to offer little. The movement had been broken, if not destroyed. Morale was low amongst its surviving members. The public were indifferent; and that perhaps was the worst of it—the public were indifferent.

The one positive thing that came out of the campaign was the emergence of author and playwright Brendan Behan. Born in 1923, he joined the IRA at the age of fifteen, and was admitted to the city's 2nd Battalion. Judged, and rightly so, to be too young to take part in the bombing campaign against England, he sailed to Liverpool on his own initiative with some harebrained scheme of attacking Liverpool Docks. In November 1939, barely ten hours after his arrival, he was arrested in possession of explosive chemicals. It turned out that Behan, after a few drinks, could not hold his tongue, boasting of what he was going to do, and that led to his arrest. He was imprisoned in Walton Gaol while awaiting trial, and in February 1940 was sentenced to three years' Borstal training at Hollesley Bay on the bleak east coast of England. In 1941 he was deported to Ireland under the Prevention of Violence Act, 1939.

Following the annual Easter Commemoration at Glasnevin Cemetery, on 5 April 1942, Behan was involved in a shooting incident with a member of the Irish Special Branch, Detective Kirwin. He managed to escape, and evaded arrest until 10 April, when he was arrested and charged with attempted murder. Behan was tried on 25 April 1942, and sentenced to fourteen years' imprisonment. He served time in Mountjoy and Arbour Hill Jails until September 1943, when he was transferred to the Curragh Internment Camp. Here he shared a hut with Dominic Adams, Mick Traynor, Paddy McNeela, Kevin O'Sullivan, Sean O'Neil and others. He was released in the general amnesty at the end of December 1946.

Behan turned to writing, producing an autobiography of his early exploits, the very colorful *Borstal Boy*, published in 1958. He followed this up with *Confessions of an Irish Rebel*, published posthumously in 1965. Behan also commemorated the men who had died during the campaign and its aftermath in his poem, "The Dead March Past." He refers to Sean Russell, and to McGrath, who was executed by the Free State; the explosion at Castlefin; and the deaths of Barnes and McCormack, whom he refers to in the lines:

> The two that swung in Birmingham, with ordered step,
> From off the gallows floor.

Following the end of World War II and the gradual release of the convicted Irish bombers, a committee was got together to secure the repatriation of the bodies of Barnes and McCormack. The *Cork Examiner* (22 January 1983) revealed that in June 1949 a request was made to 10, Downing Street, the office of the British Prime Minister Clement Atlee, for the return of the remains of the two men. At that time the request was turned down. The reorganized IRA's futile Border Campaign of 1957–62 stalled any further correspondence over the issue for the next few years. In 1967, some five years after the ending of the campaign, people within the Republican movement began once more canvassing opinions over petitioning for the return of the bodies of Barnes and McCormack. Tomas MacGiolla, president of Sinn Fein at its ard comhairle meeting of that year, was of the opinion that the bodies of the two men should be brought home.

The cause was taken up in the *United Irishman*, the Sinn Fein newspaper founded in May 1948, and a committee was formed known as Runai Cumann Athdhuichiu Barnes agus MacCormaic. Public opinion was swayed that the bodies should be returned to Ireland for reburial. The Irish government took up the cause and approached the British. They, it appeared, were not adverse to returning the bodies. What the Irish government did not want, however, was for the repatriation to be used as a recruitment vehicle for the IRA. They took over the organization for the return of the bodies, to the annoyance of the Republican movement.

There was a flurry of letters to the newspapers in Ireland over the delay, prompting Caithlin Ui Mhuimheachain to respond in the *United Irishman* (June 1969):

> A Chara,
>
> As Secretary of the Barnes and McCormack Repatriation Committee I have had many queries from all parts of Ireland regarding the lengthy delay in the bringing home from England of the remains of these two brave Irishmen. Lest any should think that it is due to inactivity of the above committee, I wish to assure them all that this is not so.

Miss Ui Mhuimheachain then went on to blame the delay on the "Twenty-six Counties" government, as the Irish Republic was known to diehard Republicans.

10. Release, Repatriation and Reflection

Eventually, at the end of June 1969, all details were ironed out. The date set for the disinterment was 3 July. Fr. Farrell, priest at St. Patrick's Church, Dudley Road, and Roman Catholic chaplain to Winson Green prison, was in attendance when the bodies were disinterred in the little cemetery in the prison yard. The bodies were put into new coffins, and driven down to Birmingham Airport, where they were loaded aboard an Aer Lingus flight to Dublin the following morning. The *Birmingham Post*, in a low-key article, noted in its edition for 5 July that upon arrival at Dublin airport, "A lone piper, three plain clothes detectives, a sixteen man guard of honour in black berets and a hundred elderly men and women welcomed back the bodies of the two IRA men at Dublin." The two bodies lay in state at the Franciscan church in Dublin. Hundreds of people filed past the coffins, each draped in the Irish tricolor. Then the two coffins were taken to Mullingar, County West Meath, for burial the next day.

On the morning of Sunday, 6 July 1969, the day of the funeral, the London-based *Sunday Times* dropped its bombshell. On its front page it ran with the story, "Wrong man hanged...." The two *Sunday Times* reporters had gained access to the Scotland Yard police files on the case, and tracked down the man who the British police now knew had planted the bomb that had killed five innocent people in Coventry. The newspapermen did not reveal his name, but promised that they would, if an impartial commission of enquiry into the circumstances of the conviction and execution of Barnes was instituted. The "nervous soldier in the IRA," as O'Sullivan was known in the article, had over the thirty intervening years time to revise his version of events to show himself in a better light.

The "official" version of events, as claimed in senior IRA circles, was that the Coventry target was an electrical power plant, in accordance with the "S" Plan directive of attacks on economic targets. The bomber, not knowing the time, the IRA claimed, had panicked and abandoned the bicycle bomb. This version does not stand up to examination, however. Coventry had a plethora of public clocks, and no more so than in the street where the bomb went off. There was a large clock suspended across the road, and a second, two doors up from the scene of the explosion above the shop of H. Samuels, jewelers. So Sullivan had no excuse in that respect. He would have known the time precisely. What O'Sullivan revealed to the two reporters was altogether alarmingly different from what was believed to have happened. He told the reporters he had previously met his director of training [Adams, who likewise was not named], outside of Coventry Central Post Office. The two of them strolled down the street smoking cigarettes as if they had not a care in the world, he revealed in his interview.

The IRA Bombing Campaign Against Britain, 1939–1940

Coventry, August 1939. Joby O'Sullivan's excuse for leaving the bicycle with its bomb in busy Broadgate was that he was unaware of the time. Notice the two public clocks.

Outside of Montague Burton's tailoring shop in Broadgate they stopped. "This is where you will place the bomb," Adams allegedly said. "It will be in the carrier of a messenger boy's bicycle and you'll put the bike against the kerb at 2:30." O'Sullivan, according to his account, protested that he would not have much chance of getting away unseen at that time in the morning. The town center was regularly patrolled by the police. His director of training explained to him that it was to be 2:30 in the afternoon. O'Sullivan alleged that he protested that innocent people would be killed, but his director threatened, "You'll do it because if you don't you'll be court martialled and shot the minute you set foot in Ireland again."

In an interview with David O'Donaghue in 2006, then researching his book *The Devil's Deal*, former Provisional Sinn Fein president Ruairi O'Bradaigh dismissed the conversation between O'Sullivan and Adams. "For the record," he informed O'Donaghue, "the penalty for refusing to obey an order is dismissal from the ranks of the IRA. The threat to shoot is nonsense. Members of the IRA are volunteers. Any of them can resign at any time." O'Sullivan, a member of Fianna Eireann, the youth wing of the IRA, from the age of thirteen, and later a volunteer member of the

IRA, would have known this. O'Sullivan was laying the blame at Adam's door. When the *Sunday Times*' reporters met him in 1969, O'Sullivan was a broken man, old before his time, a product of the brutal system practiced in Portlaoise. In his day, though, O'Sullivan had been a hardcore IRA man. He had first come to the attention of the Irish authorities as early as March 1935 when he and another man, Jeremiah Canty, were arrested for the possession of firearms and membership in an illegal organization. After the Coventry bombing O'Sullivan had returned to Ireland and taken part in an attempt to break men out of Cork Prison. Later he was interned by the Free State government, but managed to escape and go on the run. Sullivan was a reckless man. What he did, he did willingly.

Regardless of O'Sullivan's account of what had happened on 25 August 1939, the truth is that the daylight bombing in Coventry appears to have been part of an unsanctioned coordinated "spectacular." On the day before the Coventry bombing, a team of Special Branch officers from New Scotland Yard had raided an IRA safe house at 32, Leinster Gardens in London. There they discovered three bombs destined for the Bank of England, Westminster Abbey and New Scotland Yard. These bombs were timed to go off at half past two in the afternoon, exactly the same time as the Coventry bomb. All of the three London targets would have been crowded with people. Their means of transport to the targets, just as at Coventry, were carrier bicycles. What was planned was coordinated mass murder.

In his story to the newspaper, O'Sullivan, while not revealing to McCormack the time that the bomb was going to go off, attempted to talk him into leaving Coventry straightaway. He knew that the police would not rest until they had discovered the perpetrators. He, O'Sullivan, and Adams had all planned their escapes. O'Sullivan revealed to the *Sunday Times*' reporters, "I had to get to Broadgate, plant the bomb and then get to Coventry railway station before 2:20 p.m. to catch the train to Nuneaton, where I would change for Leicester." He had previously worked out his escape route right down to the times of the trains. After planting the bomb, he related, "I walked off down the street as if I had a message to deliver, looking neither right nor left. It was 2:15 when I got to the station The train was due to leave at 2:20 p.m." At this point he could have telephoned the police, by simply dialing 999, and warning them that a bomb was due to go off at 2:30 p.m.–but he did not. "I went to the booking office and bought a single ticket to Leicester," he continued. "Then I got my suitcase and small bag from the left-luggage office. The bag held a complete change of clothing. In the toilet I stripped to the skin and left the clothes I'd been wearing, lying on the floor. I washed my hair and scrubbed my hands to remove any traces of potassium chlorate. I put on my new clothes and walked back to my compartment. I slipped all of the old clothing out of the window at intervals along the line." Arriving in Leicester at 3:50 p.m. O'Sullivan shaved, darkened his hair with hair oil and combed it into a new style. As a curious twist to his story, he revealed to the two reporters that he bought a pipe, and went to the cinema to fill in the time until his train departed. By 5:30 p.m. he was on his way to Dublin by way of Crewe and Holyhead. At Holyhead as the crowds boarded the ferry, all Irishmen with tickets from either Coventry or Birmingham were stopped and questioned. With a ticket from Leicester, he boarded the ferry untroubled by the police.

The Republican movement was quick to counter the *Sunday Times* story that the bomb was deliberately placed in the busy daytime Coventry street. The *Irish Press* (7 July 1969) quoted a high-ranking member of the Republican movement (generally considered to be Cathal Goulding, then head of the IRA.) He gave the "official" Republican version that the bomb was to be used against a military installation, but the bomber, unaware of the time, panicked and ran away. To emphasize this, the source also pointed out a number of minor discrepancies in the story. Ruari O'Bradaigh, one-time president of Sinn Fein, was later to comment that "the explosion in the city center was certainly not IRA policy and was unintentional and accidental with horrific results. People of that period told me that an electrical power plant was the target." Goulding at the time of the explosion was but a teenager, only recently admitted to the IRA. O'Bradaigh, as he himself admitted in his version, was not then at the center of things. Neither of them had participated in the bombing campaign; neither of them knew the mindset of the men taking part in the campaign in England. Up until the Coventry bombing, the campaign had proved futile. The afternoon timing for the Coventry and London bombs, 2:30 p.m., and their locations, indicates a new phase: a shift away from economic targets to out-and-out terrorism. The bombers had become desperate men.

Having fled England, Adams returned to Dublin, where he was appointed onto the Headquarters staff. In December 1939, the younger members of the staff, including Michael Traynor of Belfast (later to become adjutant general), Jack McNeela, Tony Darcy of Galway, and Adams, put forward proposals to launch guerrilla raids from the Free State across the border into Northern Ireland. This was in essence the later border campaign carried out between 1957 and 1962. At the time the IRA possessed between three and five hundred Thompson submachine guns. They were an ideal guerrilla weapon for close quarters fighting. What they lacked, however,

10. Release, Repatriation and Reflection

was a supply of .45 caliber American ammunition for this weapon. The Irish Free State Army was well supplied with such ammunition. In what was surely the height of folly, the IRA raided the Irish government magazine in Phoenix Park, and got away, temporarily, with the desired ammunition. Within a fortnight most of the ammunition had been recovered, and as a consequence of the raid, internment was introduced. No government could possibly tolerate such a flouting of its authority.

Upon his release from internment at the end of World War II, Adams and fellow Belfast man James P. Trainor were arrested in November 1945 and charged with armed robbery. The charge dated back to 23 June 1936, when the two men allegedly held up bank messenger John Madden in Upper O'Connell Street, Dublin, and using violence, stole £1,931 from him for the Republican cause. After nine years, memories were vague. At their trial both men were found not guilty, and walked away. In 1950, Adams, Leo Duigan and Paddy McNeela, formerly appointed by Willie McGuinness, were dropped from GHQ staff, when Tony Magan, new chief of staff, brought in his own men as replacements. Adams, no doubt bitter at his treatment, returned to Northern Ireland and apparent obscurity.

Joby O'Sullivan, whom Irish writer Tim Pat Coogan (though not identifying him) later described as a "psychopath," having fled England on the day of the Coventry atrocity, returned to Ireland. By January 1940 he was in Cork. Tensions there were running high. On 3 January a small group of IRA men were pounced upon by Irish Special Branch. In the melee, police officer John Roche was mortally wounded when a handgun in the coat of Tomas MacCurtain went off. MacCurtain was arrested and charged with murder. As he awaited trial, Special Branch launched a round up of known IRA men. Among those arrested was Denis Griffin, Battalion O.C. in Dunmanway. Joby O'Sullivan, who had evaded the trawl, was appointed O.C. in his place. Derry Kelleher, Battalion Adjutant, referring to the arrest of Griffin, was to say, "His successor did not have the same competence." O'Sullivan was looked upon as a bit of an adventurer, a chancer, a man who took unnecessary risks.

O'Sullivan came up with a plan to rescue MacCurtain. It was to be at the end of the remand hearing, on 2 February at the Courthouse in Cork, when MacCurtain was expected to be led away from the rear door of the building. On the night before, O'Sullivan, "Skipper" Mahoney and Bill Hayes entered the building armed with a Tommy gun. They found their way down to the basement to wait. The following day, other armed IRA men surreptitiously surrounded the building. Their job was to cover the flight of the IRA men inside. The business of the day was expected to conclude at 3 p.m., when all the prisoners would then be transferred back to Cork Jail together. The proceedings went quicker than expected, and all the cases were concluded by 2 p.m. The IRA men inside were caught unawares. The men outside could only watch as the prisoners were transferred safely back to the prison.

With the imminent hanging of Peter Barnes and James McCormack at Winson Green Prison on 7 February, O'Sullivan placed the full facts of the case before Tom Barry, that both men were innocent. Barry, for his part, offered to travel to England, but his offer was rejected by the British authorities. Thereafter the identity of the Coventry bomber was to remain hidden for over 30 years.

On the evening of 12 April 1940, armed IRA men took over the Cork radio station, which was then located in a part of the women's prison in Sunday Well Road. Their purpose was to highlight the plight of 5 men on hunger strike in St. Brican's Hospital in Dublin, then nearing their final days. The news in Irish was interrupted, and Joby O'Sullivan spoke for five minutes. Outside other IRA men lay in ambush, with instructions from O'Sullivan to fire on any police cars that might arrive—but none did. The IRA men, their mission complete, got safely away.

By July 1940 there were around 170 IRA men interned in Cork Prison. With the opening of an extension to the Curragh internment camp, it was decided to move all the prisoners there. The date set was early August. As local O.C, O'Sullivan came up with the idea of breaking into the prison to rescue them before they could be transferred. Entrance was to be made via a tunnel dug from the grounds of the La Retraite Convent next door. Work got underway. A shaft was sunk, then the tunnel leading off was begun. It would appear, though it was never ascertained, that a nun, spying groups of strange men in the grounds, informed the police. For a time the police watched, identifying the men as IRA. On 3 August they pounced. There were four men in the works, Joby O'Sullivan, Roger Ryan, Joe Kavanagh and Connie Byrd. They were unarmed. It should have been possible to have arrested the men, but instead the police opened fire with Tommy guns. John Joe Kavanagh was killed outright. Roger Ryan was seriously wounded, but later recovered. O'Sullivan and Byrd were at the tunnel face, and after reassurances that they would not be killed, they came to the surface and surrendered. Minister for Justice Gerald Boland suppressed the coroner's report on Kavanagh. O'Sullivan and Byrd were sent to Arbour Hill Prison but were later transferred to the Curragh. Some little time later O'Sullivan escaped. Under guard he had been taken to the dental hospital in Lincoln Place, Dublin, for treatment. Seizing the opportunity, he escaped through a small toilet window, and was away. He remained on the run for over a year. In July 1941 he gave evidence, or partook in some way, in the detainment and trial of senior IRA man, and Russell's deputy, Stephen Hayes, who had been charged with being a spy for the Irish government. Whether he was or not, Hayes escaped his IRA captors and sought refuge with the Irish police. Soon after, O'Sullivan was recaptured and imprisoned in Portlaoise Prison, the most feared of Irish jails. The regime was brutal, designed to break the prisoners. They broke O'Sullivan, and he was sent to Dundrum Criminal Lunatic Asylum, where he spent a number of years in restricted care.[2]

On Sunday, 6 July 1969, despite heavy rain, thousands of people followed the coffins of Barnes and McCormack the two-mile distance from Christ the King Cathedral in Mullingar to the town's cemetery. At the graveside the last salute was sounded by Fianna Eireannn. Then four young men of Oglaigh na h'Eireann, dressed in black rolled necked shirts, dark trousers and wearing berets and dark sunglasses to protect their identities, stepped out from the crowd and assembled before the coffins. In unison they fired three volleys of revolver shots into the air in salute. There was a dramatic hush in the crowd, then the four men holstered their guns and walked away to be lost amongst the vast crowd, evading the watchful state police. At the graveside, eulogies were delivered by Sinn Fein President Tomas MacGiolla; followed by Jim O'Regan of Cork, a socialist and former Brigadista, who had fought in Spain for the Republican cause under Frank Ryan; and finally Jimmy Steele of Belfast. During his graveside oration, MacGiolla was surprisingly heckled by dissidents, representatives, he later discovered, of the emerging Provisional movement. O'Regan delivered his speech, then Jimmy Steele stepped forward. He was a lifelong IRA man, a man with considerable influence. He had been arrested in his home city in July 1936 for IRA activities. Released after his sentence was complete, he was immediately interned in Crumlin Road Jail, from where he escaped on 15 January 1943. In March 1943 he was involved in the escape of twenty-one IRA prisoners from Derry Jail, taking them over the border to Donegal. He was later recaptured and interned once more. By 1966 with the Republican movement's shift to the left, Steele, an old-fashioned IRA man, found himself sidelined by the mainly Southern-controlled Army Council. Now here at the gravesides he had his say. He attacked the movement's turn to the left, adding, "One is now expected to be more conversant with the thoughts of Chairman Mao than those of our dead patriots." The Provisionals had arrived, and with them began a war that lasted over a quarter of a century.

Even as the IRA were denying the *Sunday Times* account, that evening RTE, the Irish broadcasting station, in its popular *This Week* program, broadcast an anonymous interview with the Coventry bomber.

By an extraordinary coincidence, interviewer Mike Burns and colleague Sean Duignan had also traced Joby O'Sullivan through a file in the Scotland Yard archive. The file showed that Special Branch in England had pursued the case. Their most recent address for him was a flat above a greengrocer's shop in Werburgh Street in Cork. It was noted that O'Sullivan was working as a swimming instructor. The newsmen eventually met up with O'Sullivan at the old Embassy Hotel on the corner of Fitzwilliam Street and Baggot Street in Dublin. His appearance was disheveled. He was badly dressed, elderly and nervous. O'Sullivan admitted that he was down on his luck. He was staying in the Iveagh hostel, an institute for homeless men. After a few drinks he was persuaded to visit the RTE studios to record an interview.

O'Sullivan admitted, in what was to be broadcast as an anonymous interview, that he was the Coventry bomber. He lied, claiming that the bomb-laden bike had got stuck in the tram tracks, and fearing that it would explode prematurely, he abandoned it. The story was at odds with what was reported by witnesses at the trial of Barnes and McCormack. They claimed that he had cycled down the road, then parked the bicycle at the curb. With a name, and the admittance that he was the bomber, the two reporters went to see the head of news at RTE, Jim McGuinness, a senior figure in the IRA during the 1940s and 1950s. He confirmed that Joby O'Sullivan was indeed the bomber who had killed five innocent people. The interview was broadcast, but O'Sullivan's name was not revealed.

As the present "Troubles," as they are euphemistically called, came to an end with the signing of the Good Friday Agreement in 1998, so also in that decade came reports of the deaths of many of the men and women who had participated in the earlier 1939–40 bombing campaign in England. They were old now, many in their eighties and nineties. They had survived English jails, internment in Northern Ireland and the Free State, and worse still the harsh conditions of Portlaoise. There was a peace, but Ireland was still divided, and that would have been one of their last regrets, one feels. News of their deaths appeared in the weekly Republican newspapers the *United Irishman* and later *Saorise*. With their obituaries we also discover the names of those who took part, and who were never captured. In something akin to a throwaway comment *Saorise* (December 1989) refers to "Richard Goss of Dundalk who had been active on the English campaign." Goss had formerly been O.C. in Manchester. Upon his return to Eire he was arrested and executed in July 1941 for shooting and wounding a soldier in a bank raid in County Longford. At the commencement of the bombing campaign Paddy McNeela was living in England, having migrated there from Ballycroy, County Mayo. He lived for a time in London, before moving to a village in the Home Counties. He was asked to take part in the bombing campaign and was summoned to Dublin for training. He carried out attacks in London. McNeela was never captured. There was Harry White, who was sent to London in 1938 to prepare the campaign. He took part in incendiary attacks. He too was never captured. Returning home, though, he was later interned at the Curragh. Shea Murphy recalled his career as a bomber in an article, "Parnell upon the wall," published in the *Bell* in July 1947. Terry McLaughlin, who also evaded the police, had an incendiary bomb go off in his hand, leaving acid burns all over his clothes. He discarded his coat before anyone else in the street noticed it. His main concern was not about arrest, but rather what a girl he was intending to meet that Sunday morning might say if he turned up without a coat. There was Eoin McNamee from County Tyrone, who was also sent to London in December 1938. He was a keen supporter of the of the later Provisional IRA, when they emerged in 1969. Seamus Burke died after a long illness on 13 February 1989, in his 81st year. He was never arrested for his part in the campaign, but came under police suspicion. In the end he was deported from England. He was arrested in the Republic upon his return and interned in the Curragh.

Uinseann MacEoin, himself interned in the Curragh in the 1940s, in his book *The IRA in the Twilight Years*, records a number of participants of the campaign who likewise in some cases were never arrested. There was Denis Griffin, "Skinner" Griffin as he was known, because he was tall and thin. Fellow IRA man Jim Savage, speaking in 1996, refers to him as being held in high esteem. After his escape from England, Griffin was arrested in the general roundup of IRA men by the Free State police, and interned in the Curragh. There was his brother, Tommy Griffin, "escaping back to Ireland, only barely in front of the posse, by the skin of his teeth." There was Jim O'Regan of Cork. He had gone off to Spain with Frank Ryan and joined the International Brigades in their fight against fascism. Being wounded, he returned to Ireland and took up once more with the IRA. He was persuaded to join the bombing campaign in England, but was caught and sentenced to 20 years for conspiracy to cause explosions. Likewise there was Nicky Cleary from Wexford, who under an alias was caught and served 10 years' imprisonment in England. Survivor "Pickier" Connolly we know of because of his arrest and trial in England. He was born in 1915.

His grandfather had been killed by Black and Tans in 1920. His uncle, a diehard Republican, was killed by Free State forces in 1922. In 1931 Connolly joined the IRA, and in 1936 emigrated to England. Arrested for possession of explosive substances, he was sentenced to 6 1/2 years and served his time in Brixton, Maidstone and Albany Prisons.

For many, though, there were no obituaries. After internment they drifted back to their former lives if they could, severing links with the IRA. For others, with no family ties, they became drifters, finishing their lives in doss houses and inner-city digs. They found it difficult to cope with everyday life. It was a form of post-traumatic stress. Basic things, like having to make decisions, was sometimes beyond them. For the last four or five years, everything had been decided for them by the prison authorities. They felt awkward around women and children. They got angry in their frustration. Even simple things like crossing the road produced anxiety. Some turned to drink, others suffered nervous breakdowns, and in death they took their secrets to the grave. Joby O'Sullivan appears to have been such a man. Uinseann MacEoin, for whatever reason, did not interview O'Sullivan. There was no obituary for him in the Republican newspapers, either. His date of death is unsure, but he appears to be that Joseph O'Sullivan who died on 11 October 1982, aged 72, in Our Lady of Lourdes Hospital, Midleton, County Cork. He died of natural causes. His occupation on his death certificate is given as "labourer."

Nor did MacEoin interview Dominic Adams. There is a curious silence about the man who ordered the Coventry bombings. At the Army Convention of September 1949, the first called in in ten years, Tony Magan, who had been involved in the English campaign, was appointed chief of staff. Tomas MacCurtain, son of the murdered Sinn Fein Lord Mayor of Cork, Tomas senior, was also elected onto the Army Council, as was Armagh-born Paddy McLogan, who had opposed the bombing campaign in England. Other, younger men, such as law graduate Joe Christle and the charismatic Cathal Goulding, were appointed to junior positions on the GHQ staff. There was seemingly no place for Dominic Adams, who had once been so prominent in the IRA. He was sidelined, and drifted into obscurity. Dominic's nephew, Gerry Adams Jr., President of Sinn Fein, in response to an enquiry from the author of *The Devil's Deal*, David O'Donaghue, claimed that he had no knowledge of his uncle Dominic's IRA career. This seems highly unlikely, as Tim Pat Coogan suggested to the present author that Gerry Adams was very close to his uncle. Enquiries to Sinn Fein headquarters in Belfast concerning Dominic's death have also proved unrewarding.

10. Release, Repatriation and Reflection

This family amnesia would seem to be hiding a dark secret. This secret was revealed by the Dublin-based newspaper, the *Irish Observer* (4 December 2011):

> A senior member of Sinn Fein/IRA in Belfast has told the *Irish Observer* that the Sinn Fein/IRA leadership in Belfast knew that Gerry Adams Snr [Gerry Adams' father] was a child rapist and shortly before he died Gerry Adams Snr admitted that he had been working for the British security services for almost 30 years.
>
> However while the Sinn Fein/IRA leadership knew that Gerry Adams Snr was both a prolific child rapist and RUC agent, the Sinn Fein/IRA leadership afforded Gerry Adams Snr a full IRA funeral. Gerry Adams TD has been forced to admit publicly that he knew his father and brother Liam were child rapists, however Gerry Adams TD has failed to admit that he knew that his father Gerry Adams Snr was an RUC agent and responsible for the deaths and imprisonment of dozens of Irish Catholics.

If Gerry Adams Sr. had been arrested over his pedophilia, it would have been easy enough for the Northern Ireland Special Branch to turn him—and they obviously did, if the *Irish Observer* is to be believed. The choice was clearly exposure and imprisonment, or work for them; and that is what he apparently did. In the 1950s, IRA personnel began being picked up by the police, and IRA raids were thwarted. The leadership in the south became concerned, rightly suspecting an informer. All further intelligence with the North was stopped as a consequence.

All this raises the question: was Dominic turned too? The day after the Coventry bombing, the police in England named him as their prime suspect. He was named not under his pseudonym of "Norman," but under his real name, Dominic Adams. His name appeared in the local newspapers with the question–Where is Dominic Adams? The police had discovered that he was in charge of the Coventry IRA cell that was responsible for the Coventry bombing. An arrest warrant on a charge of murder was issued. Notification would have been sent all over the United Kingdom, including Northern Ireland. After his return to Northern Ireland following his dismissal from IRA GHQ in 1950, the RUC must have become aware of his presence in Belfast, and they would have known that he was wanted for murder. Others within the Republican movement recognized him in and about Belfast in the late 1960s—and yet seemingly he was not arrested and sent for trial in England, as one might have expected. The only possible explanation would appear to be that he too was turned in exchange for his liberty, and he too became a police informer. This is speculation, of course, until the records of the Police Service of Northern Ireland (PSNI) become available, but if true, and if Dominic Adams was also discovered to have been a police spy, this would no doubt have prompted Gerry Adams to feign ignorance of his uncle's later IRA career in order to protect his own position. One informer in the family is bad enough, but two?[3]

For James O'Donovan, author of the "S" Plan, his demise made the national dailies. His obituary appeared in the *Irish Times*, perhaps the most influential of Irish newspapers. He died in Dublin's Meath Hospital on 4 June 1979. O'Donovan had been taken there from Our Lady's Manor nursing home in Dalkey, County Dublin, suffering from kidney failure. Born in 1896, he was eighty-two years old at the time of his death.

Paddy Fleming, who had initially started the bombing campaign back in January 1939 by putting his name to the declaration sent to the British authorities, died in the Mater Hospital, Dublin, in 1983, aged 83. In later life, no longer an active member of the IRA, he was appointed chief steward of the Bord na gCon, the controlling body of the Irish greyhound racing industry. He and his wife Eileen, née Tubbert, a member of Cumann na mBan (the women's branch of the IRA), had settled down, and saw out their days in Sandymount, a pleasant suburb of south Dublin.

Mairtin Standuin's obituary appeared in *Saoirse*. He was born in Liverpool, England, and was chosen to take part in the bombing campaign because of his non-Irish accent. He operated a successful explosive chemical distribution center from Liverpool, and as the police closed in he successfully escaped to Ireland. Here he was not so fortunate. He was picked up in a Special Branch raid and interred in the Curragh until the end of World War II. Standuin died in December 1994.

Paddy O'Connell died on 27 August 1995. He had joined the IRA in 1933 in Tipperary. After Christmas 1938 he went to England in preparation for the beginning of the bombing campaign. He was arrested and tried at the Manchester Assizes of March 1939, and sentenced to twenty years' imprisonment. He served his time in nine jails, much of it in solitary confinement.

Mossie Higgins, who was involved in the 1939–40 campaign, escaped detection, and returned to Ireland, evading internment in the process. He died in February 1996, and it is only through his short obituary that we know of his involvement. There were other evaders too. Ulster man Albert Price died in July 1996, aged 81. He was involved in the campaign until its end, and managed to avoid detection. He returned home to Belfast, where he was interned. While in Derry Jail in 1943, he and twenty other prisoners tunneled their way to freedom. He crossed the border into Donegal, in the Irish Free State, but was interned in the Curragh. He was the father of the Provisional IRA Price sisters, Dolours and Marian.

10. Release, Repatriation and Reflection

The obituary of Charles Casey, tried at the Central Criminal Court in London in March 1939, appeared in *An Phoblact*, the IRA newspaper, on 8 January 1997. Casey was born in Ireland 1915, and in the 1930s moved to London. He joined the Gaelic League, and was recruited into the IRA. By now he had a London accent. He took part in the subsequent bombing campaign, was arrested and sentenced to 14 years' imprisonment. Upon his release he returned to Ireland. He died on 28 December 1996, in his eighty-first year. Michael Cafferty took part in the bombing campaign, and again he was never caught. He was interned in Ireland during World War II. Cafferty was later involved in planning the border campaign in Northern Ireland of 1957–62. He died on 25 March 1977, aged 86.

Josephine Murray, who was suspected of involvement in the bombing campaign up in Liverpool, but against whom nothing could be proven, was deported from England. She died in May 1997. Sean Griffin died in the following month of June 1997. He and his friend, John Foley of Glencar, took part in the 1939 bombings. They both escaped detection and returned to Ireland. Michael "Micksey" Conway, together with Sean Fuller of Kerry (operations officer in Birmingham at the start of the campaign) and Paddy McGrath of Dublin, trained volunteers in Killiney Castle, Dublin, for the sabotage campaign in England. McGrath was later executed in the Free State by a firing squad. In 1950 Conway became a brother in the Cistercian Order. He died in December 1997, aged 87. Leo Duignan, sentenced to ten years' imprisonment at the Central Criminal Court in London, died in Dublin in March 1998. He was buried in Shanganagh Cemetery, Shankhill, County Dublin.

Rita McSweeney, sentenced to five years' imprisonment for her part in the bombing campaign, died on 31 January 1999. She was 82 years old. She was born in County Waterford in 1916. Ten years later the family moved to Liverpool, where her father had found work as a tailor. She joined Cumann na mBan, and with her now Liverpool accent, was ideal for recruitment into the bombing campaign. She acted as a supplier and courier. Arrested under the alias of Barbara Jones along with Dick Timmons, alias Richard Cohen, following the discovery of another IRA unit, she was tried at Carmarthen Assize in Wales. She served her term of imprisonment in Aylesbury Jail, in Buckinghamshire. McSweeney was released in 1943 and deported to Ireland. She married Paddy McGlynn in 1951 and the family settled down at Phibsboro, north Dublin.

Paddy McNeela, quartermaster general in the 1939 English campaign, and participant in the raid on the magazine fort in Phoenix Park, died in February 1999. In July 1940 he was shot and wounded by Free State Special

Branch policemen. Upon his recovery he was interned in the Curragh, remaining there until May 1945.

Though the bombing campaign was directed against England only, the IRA in Glasgow, Scotland, was very much involved. It was from here that the chemicals that made the bombs were distributed. The police in England got onto the suppliers in Scotland when packaging was found that gave a Glasgow address. Timothy Daley and Cormac McGarrigle were arrested and put on trial at the subsequent Glasgow High Court in May 1939, and John Carson, Edward Gill and Michael James O'Hara were tried in August of that year. One of the survivors of the roundups was Frank McGowan. He was appointed quartermaster when Joe Kerr was brought in from Belfast as the new O.C. The new setup included 21 new men who acted as distributors. McGowan's obituary appeared in *An Phoblacht*. He died in Glasgow in January 2002, aged 82.

Dan Keating, who operated out of London during the bombing campaign, died in October 2007. Born in 1902, at Kiltallagh, County Kerry, he joined the 1st Kerry Brigade of the IRA in 1920. He took part in two flying-column ambushes in 1921 that left at least 5 police officers, 4 British soldiers and 5 IRA men dead. Keating remained true to his Republican ideals and in the civil war that followed he was interned by the Free State government. Upon his release he remained a volunteer in the IRA and in 1939 took part in the bombing campaign in England. Returning to Ireland in 1940, he was again interned in the Curragh. Upon his release he married, and left the IRA. He found work as a barman in the Comet Bar in North Dublin. Keating continued to support the Republican movement and was actively involved in fundraising. Upon his retirement and the death of his wife in the late 1970s, he returned to Kiltallagh. Stubborn, if you like, he refused his state pension on the grounds that the government was not the legitimate government, and he refused to meet Irish President Mary McAleese on his 100th birthday, because he felt she had compromised her Republican beliefs by inviting the British Queen, Elizabeth II, to Ireland. No man to compromise himself, he attacked the Sinn Fein leadership of Gerry Adams for entering into power-sharing in Stormont. Dan Keating lived to be the oldest man in Ireland, dying at the age of 105. He was the last survivor of those who participated in the War of Independence and the bombing campaign against England.

Appendix I:
The "S" Plan

1. TIME

(a) In order to exercise maximum world effect, the diversion must be carried out at a time when no major war or world crisis is on.

(b) If it is carried out at a time when trouble is anticipated, the jumpiness and nervous expectation of the government as well as the potential panic of the people can be exploited to the full.

If it is carried out at a time of recovery from crisis or relief after a serious war-scare, a certain amount of demoralization and general relaxation of vigilance and precautionary measures can be relied upon. This will assist operations.

(c) Since for ordinary guerrilla, winter conditions and darkness are advantageous, zero hour should be about the beginning of winter. Since further for reasons which will be discussed later, the campaign should open with the more major operations and these will both be facilitated by darkness and at the same time cause greater havoc or disorganization by being carried out when hours of darkness follow, the campaign should begin at a moonless period.

(d) All indications point to either October 20th or November 18th.

2. PROCLAMATION

(a) Republic to be proclaimed and the allegiance of all Irish subjects demanded, special reliance being placed on the response of the young, virile element of the nation and also those who, however subsequently divided by the rivalries and chicanery of leaders, showed that they had the true interests of Ireland at heart by fighting the enemy at a time when that enemy was unequivocally defined, i.e., when the struggle was a straight, direct issue (for this purpose 1000 facsimile reproductions of the original Proclamation should be in readiness).

(b) Ultimatum to be issued to England demanding her complete evacuation of all Irish territory and territorial waters, demanding her absolute registered renunciation of all claim to suzerainty over the whole territory of Ireland as bounded by the seas and channels, demanding her complete withholding of all subsidy or financial influence from subordinate legislatures or agents within the territory of Ireland who might be partial to the continuance of English interference in Irish affairs, abrogating unilaterally all and any pacts or agreements entered into by usurping legislatures; imposing time limits for the fulfillment of these demands and declaring that failure to express immediate willingness to negotiate under For-Power guarantee of safety to negotiators will be followed by effort on our part when opportunity arises and by every means at our disposal, to ensure that the repeatedly expressed national will of Ireland to own absolutely her own soil and to control it independent of any outside influence shall be supreme.

(c) Copies of the Ultimatum together with Proclamation shall be sent, *so as to arrive* simultaneously, to the British Premier, (?) the Prime Minister of Northern Ireland, (?) the Prime Minister of Southern Ireland, the Vatican, the French President, the American President, the Ambassadors of Germany, Italy, etc., for transmission to Chancellor Hitler, Il Duce Mussolini etc.

(d) Copies shall be transmitted to the following with the intimation that originals have been sent to the British Government:

> Scottish Nationalist Party
> Welsh Nationalist Party
> British Labour Party
> Independent Labour Party
> (English) Council of Civil Liberties
> (American) Council of Civil Liberties
> (Belfast) Council of Civil Liberties

(i) The Scottish and Welsh Nationalist Parties will be assured of the sympathetic interest of Ireland in their aspirations and of the abiding affection of the Irish people for them as kindred of a common race. Assurance will be given also that there can be no enmity between these peoples and ours and that no conflict of opinion or loyalty can eventuate unless in these countries their own best national interests are subordinated to alien imperialistic interests. [The above and the "every means at our disposal" at the end of para. 2(b) are as far as hint can be given of the nature of the measures contemplated.]

(ii) The two Labour parties will be assured of the sympathy of the democratic Irish people with their efforts for the betterment of the conditions of the English people, with whom the people of Ireland have no quarrel except in so far as by acquiescence in the actions of their government, they assume—admittedly wholly undesired—a degree of responsibility for its conduct. They are in a position of great strength to demand immediately a cessation of interference in Irish affairs and a complete withdrawal and evacuation, which can be the only possible prelude to the much desired and lasting amity of two neighbors, whose propinquity places each in a position of interdependence. The Labour Parties must however bring every pressure to bear to secure the instant concession of the whole and historic Irish demand. Their failure to do so will indicate that they are prepared to subordinate morality and justice to their superficial material interests and thus that they are content to share equally with the imperialist and undemocratic oligarchy in control, the responsibility for the continued repression of Ireland.

3. THE GENERAL PLAN

The main plan divides into two Departments—Propaganda and Action. It is difficult to say which is the more urgent and important—the release of the Propaganda campaign or the pushing ahead of the preparations, military and otherwise, for Action.

It is vitally necessary that a start be made immediately on the wide diffusion of the case for Ireland and the justification of the adoption of any and every means at our disposal to subjugate the obdurate will of our inveterate and powerful opponent to the still indomitable but weakly effective will of Ireland. It must be shown that this is the time to strike, that England has never been in so critical a condition, barred as she is by political tradition from adopting the only measures that would ensure her strength, namely, totalitarian methods. The efforts of the principal organizers may be over-exclusively concentrated on the Action side of the conflict—hence it is essential immediately to take into at least partial confidence as many of the reliable active workers and sympathizers as can be of assistance in the neglected Propaganda department. It holds there even more than in the case of the military preparations that the job cannot be done overnight. It is already much too late to be making an organized start in this direction—every day from now will count vitally. Numbers of energetic workers must be pressed and recruited into this service immediately. The misinterpretation, the ridicule, the false propaganda that will be broadcast a thousand fold more effectively than we can possibly aspire to, may have a shattering effect on otherwise moderately effective military action. It may make all the difference between sympathy and hostility at home. The need for instant concentration on this side, the plenty of expenditure on printed matter, booklets, maps, leaflets, etc., is again stressed. It will be reverted to again. (Germany's insistent success is due to the people's comprehension of their aims through radio and the printed word. People will think—and on right lines—if they get enough reading matter, etc.)

The General Plan, already described as consisting of two departments, Propaganda and Action, can be further developed as roughly shown in the following schematic diagram.

4. PROPAGANDA

5. ACTION

As shown in 3 above, Action is divided into two main branches, Direct and Political. No attempt is made at this stage to subdivide Direct Action into Tactical or Strategical considerations. The Political Division will be dealt with later. (See 5(b) below.)

A. Direct Action

1. This may concern itself with Military, Air or Naval Opposition or movements, should these arms be called actively into service in suppressing our sabotage and other activities. Our weakness would reduce this form of action to a minimum.

2. The second legitimate but probably very inaccessible aim could be the destruction or sabotage of aeroplane factories and stores, munition factories and stores, etc. These would probably be so well guarded that success would be chancy.

3. The third target, and this will probably be the most important, because the most effective, the most unequivocal and the most justifiable—is the Public Services.

Appendix I

4. The fourth group could be such key industries as were at all accessible.

5. The fifth group could be commerce, banking and shipping; ordinary industries, cotton mills, etc.; grain, tobacco and spirit stores, motor tyre stores, timber yards, etc., etc.

6. The last group to be considered might prove to be an important one, especially if adopted as punitive action for incitement to repressive violence against our campaign or merely for the spreading of injurious propaganda about the revolutionaries and Ireland generally. This is the large-circulation English Press.

We come now to the consideration of each of these groups in detail:

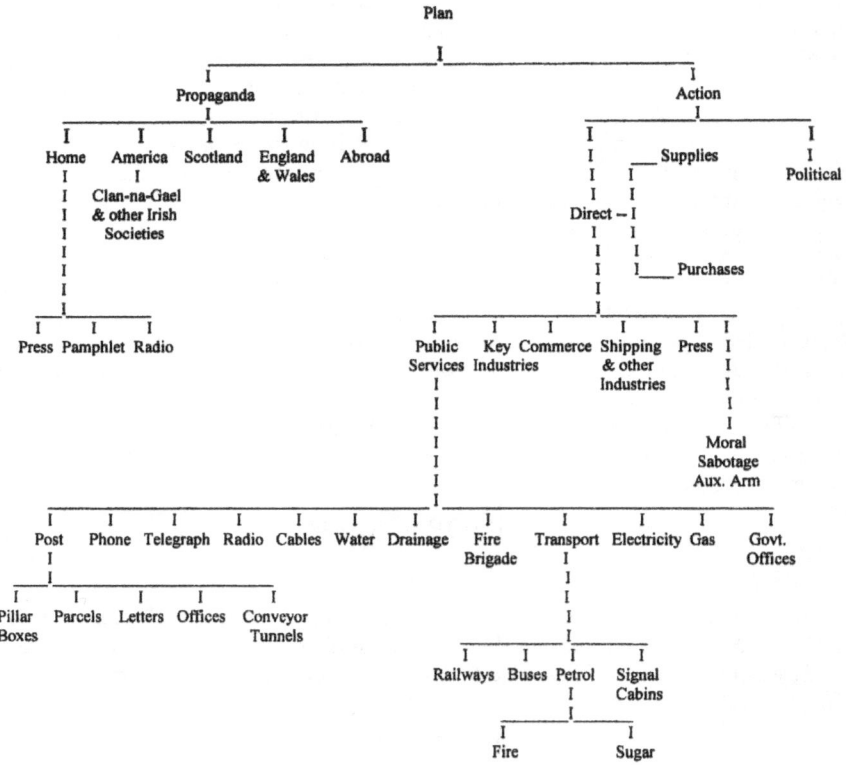

1. PUBLIC SERVICES

Most of the Public Services considered below will be found to offer two types of target, one where it is centralized or concentrated, the other where it is scattered or widespread—the latter will be referred to as diffused outposts.

(i) The Postal Service

This lends itself to a wide range of destructive activity, which will be hard to localize or trace and easy to have repeated. In this case, the diffused outposts would be pillar boxes and smaller post offices.

(a) As a last stage operation, the dropping of incendiary material into letter boxes and its ignition by the familiar methods could be fallen back on with virtual impunity.

(b) As an intermediate stage operation there could be the dispatch at G.P.O.s of letter packages made up containing incendiary unit No. 1 (See Manual of Instructions) just in time for collection, so as to permit of their transit such distance as to make it possible that this would form part of a large bulk of similar packages.

(c) As an intermediate stage operation also, there could be the similar dispatch of the same Incendiary Unit No. 1 made up into parcel post packages. This would have the great advantage of allowing very much more combustible and flame-spreading material to be included, but again this as compared with letters there probably would not be the same volume of parcels in sufficient close proximity.

(d) There are special cases in which a major operation might be possible if Intelligence is capable of organizing it. Such operation on the theory accepted in this Plan should be arranged for the earliest possible stages of activities, as otherwise, in the general alarm and precautionary atmosphere brought about by the commencement of the campaign, it would be too well guarded subsequently.

As an example of the type meant would be an attack by incendiary explosive, or mechanical blockage on the 6½ mile long postal tunnel between Paddington and Whitechapel. The assumption is that at various points along this unattended route, there would be manholes or access of some sort.

(ii) The Telephone System
Most action here is suggested as later stage type.

(a) Tapping and other forms of interference.

(b) Destruction of instruments.

(c) Disconnection of police-boxes and any other important and clearly defined lines.

(d) Cutting of wires and cables in quantity.

(Note—In Britain the figures show Birmingham has fewest phones per population. The towns with the largest proportion of 'phones are London, Eastbourne, Bournemouth, Worthing, Southport, Brighton, Cambridge, Edinburgh, Chester, Blackpool, and Oxford.)

(iii) The Telegraph System
Similar throughout to (ii) (a-d) above.

(iv) Radio and Broadcasting
Since other stations can always carry on, this would be a doubtful type of operation.

(a) Interfering or sending conflicting and disturbing items.

(b) Destruction of instruments or stations.

(c) Demolition of aerials might in certain cases be possible.

(v) Cables
These are usually clearly indicated and are often in very isolated places. A delay-action land-mine might possibly be employed. The disorganization would

probably not be very great unless simultaneously planned at various points. The operation is essentially one that might be left to intermediate or later stage in programme.

(vi) Water

As water is essential to life, any ideas such as pollution, etc., must be rigorously ruled out and *this principal applies generally* apart altogether from ethical considerations, the Hague Convention representing civilized international opinion and agreement condemns all such actions and we should be doing Ireland and our cause infinite harm by adopting any such means.

(a) Scarcity and rationing would however prove a warrantable dislocation and often viaduct pipe-lines are exposed not buried and, in isolated districts, would lend themselves to delay-action landmine treatment, flooding being caused at the same time as shortage.

(b) The only exposed pipe-lines connected with a hydro-electric scheme (?) are those serving the Galloway scheme. But this is in Scotland and therefore probably outside the Plan.

There are however, subject to confirmation, exposed pipe-line connected with a now no doubt very important aluminium factory in Scotland ? (Argyll) which is probably engaged on shadow aeroplane parts, etc., production.

(vii) Drainage

This important service in large towns might be made the object of an early stage attack. The method proposed would demand considerable self-possession and possibly (in the event of questioning which however is unlikely) some resourcefulness. It is to hire a lorry, load up one or two tons of quick setting cement, also a manhole guard rail and a tarpaulin. Stop at a main sewage conduit manhole. Erect manhole guardrail and cover over with tarpaulin, dump in bag by bag the whole load. A "Repair Work" street notice might heighten the illusion and help render the activity unremarkable. The whole operation could be completed in 15–20 minutes at most with two men.

(viii) Fire Brigade

No effort should be made to make a major operation out of this service (for humanitarian reasons).

(a) The method adopted by the Black and Tans in Cork and elsewhere however should be borne in mind—they cut fire-hoses, which rendered them ineffective for the extinction of fires already caused and were not readily replaceable.

(b) As a late stage operation of diffused type, false alarms could be raised in many quarters simultaneously. Without active intervention this in large centres would be equivalent to setting fire to certain buildings, for a real fire that coincided with the false alarms would stand a smaller chance of timely aid.

(ix) Electricity

As a brief indication of the tremendous importance of this service the following figures might be considered. It might first be said that apart altogether from dislocation of industry business and transport, the moral and panic effects of extensive black-outs, i.e., from the viewpoint of lighting only, can be very great.

There are 112 generating stations directly controlled from the Central Electricity

Board's control rooms at Newcastle, Manchester, Leeds, Birmingham and London. (This is the largest number ever operated in parallel anywhere.)

The length of the transmission in the "Grid" is 4125 miles of which 2898 miles are 132,000 volts.

There are 300 switching and transformer stations. The total capital invested in overhead transmission lines is £9,700,000, in underground cables is £5,800,000 and in switching and transformer stations is over £14,000,000. (Note.—Supplementary details of a more practical nature will be found in the Manual of Instructions.)

If destruction is contemplated it can be carried out at many points. Study of the "Grid" map of its transmission lines would indicate towns which could be isolated by simultaneous attack on the two or more alternative feeds afforded by its position in the "rings" or "loops." Also towns, to which only one major supply is available, thus confining the necessity of attack to only one point.

The stations and numerous small sub-stations in towns and cities are all open to attack, but probably the remote, isolated lines passing through open country are the easiest targets.

In selecting these consideration should be given to the size of towns and the degree of dependence for industry on electricity. (See Appendix I.) Of all towns Coventry would seem to be the most dependent in relation to its population. (But see para. (b) below.) It is not wholly dependent on the Grid as it has its own generating station.

Delay-action land-mine attention is indicated, and should be simple to organize, but obviously must be practically the first job, as, consequent upon the opening of the campaign, the defensive measures adopted would almost certainly include patrolling of the major transmission lines. Even if no operation of this nature were carried out, yet if as a precautionary measure, patrols were established, this would be a very successful result owing to the sense of insecurity created and the actual immobilization of so many men (on patrol, guard, and watchman duties). This applies generally and must be borne in mind when gauging the effect of operations in other spheres.

(a) The numerous London generating stations are almost entirely if not entirely interconnected by very high voltage (oil-fitted) underground cables. As these will be inaccessible unless Intelligence has localized them carefully and shown attack to be practicable, London from this viewpoint must be overlooked.

(b) The second most important centre is that centred around Birmingham, within a fifty miles radius. Besides Birmingham itself, which is the second biggest city in England (greater in population than either Liverpool or Manchester) there are small towns and important industrial centres as Coventry, Wolverhampton, Northampton, Rugby, Leicester, Warwick, etc. (see Map in rough notes). These all have their own generating stations, but it is legitimate to assume that forcible rupture of the "Grid" feeds into any of them will either leave them inadequately supplied or deprive the Grid of their surplus production on which the system would be partially dependent.

(c) The double-circuit line of towers (i.e., with six wires) running south out of Birmingham for some miles would obviously give twice the return in dislocation for the same effect as compared with the more common single-circuit (with three wires) lines. This line also in the event of simultaneous attack on the other alternative feeders out of Birmingham (two more only) and accompanied by possible disturbance in London, would have added importance, since via Warwick and—it is one of the standby feeds into London.

(d) The third most important area which will repay examination is the Liverpool, Manchester, Leeds area. The same principles as previously indicated should hold here.

(x) Gas

This does not lend itself to favourable consideration for two reasons, first, damage could hardly be inflicted without loss of life and secondly, the ever-present dangers of fire insure that the maximum precautions against have already been taken and success would be doubtful. The latter principle as explained elsewhere is generally applicable in all such cases, e.g., petrol stores, explosive factories, etc., where there is a great and ever present risk from fire and explosion.

(xi) Government Offices

Under the circumstances these are a legitimate target. Where collusion is possible, i.e., where a sympathetic or active government employee is available, nothing could be simpler than the depositing in suitable form Incendiary Unit No. 2 preferably or alternatively I.U. No. 1 in cupboards or such places prior to locking up or closing hour. Owing to the wider scattering of staffs, especially senior officers, on a Saturday afternoon, the dislocation would be probably be greater if the job were timed for 1 p.m. on Saturday rather than 5 p.m. or 6 p.m. on a weekday. Moreover, the likelihood of any of the staff working late on a Saturday is very much less than on a workday. This lessens the possibility of a too-early alarm being given. Again, flames or smoke would be much longer in attracting attention during the daylight hours than at night-time.

(a) The only sub-divisions necessary at this stage are the centre targets such as Admiralty, War Office, Foreign Office, etc. as contrasted with diffused outposts. The older buildings, although no doubt brought moderately up to date with automatic fire-extinguishing equipment, are probably a better mark than such new buildings (the example, given though not governmental, would no doubt otherwise be a fair mark as the London County Council building).

An operation against any of the above would have to be one of the early jobs, depending on the facilities available to the particular member of the staff or person otherwise gaining legitimate entry, and the general tightening-up brought about by the opening of the campaign.

(b) Diffused outposts, e.g., post offices, inland revenue offices (Custom and Excise), Coastguard stations, etc., could be regarded as intermediate or late jobs.

(xii) Transport

This section of the public services is probably the most important of all, because, even more than interference with electricity, which is a comparatively small factor in industry and social life, serious dislocation would have a paralyzing effect on every branch of industrial and commercial life. Even to produce partial or local dislocation simultaneously would have a completely unsettling effect on the country's economic life, because the sense of insecurity would slow down the whole stream of commerce and cause tremendous dissipation of energy by necessitating a policy of protection or watchfulness for every movement. (See also 5(b)(2) on Key Industries.)

(a) Sea. Stores in shipping sheds. Ship's cargoes. I.U. No. 2? Interference with navigational lights or warnings not to be considered.

(b) Air. Military aviation at all times a legitimate target. No delay-action to be contemplated which could happen during flight. Any operation which would have the effect of delaying the start of Air Mails, etc. for the Continent would occasion world-wide comment and interest.

(c) Rail. This sub-divides into steam and electric, the latter including Tubes etc. Both are highly accessible at sidings, junctions and in loco sheds and this forms a desirable, justifiable, and fairly easy objective, the electric being easier to put out of action. This form of attack is most desirable since it can inflict no personal injury. Trains, coaches, and their laden cargoes should all be easy to arrange for.

As parts of ordinary cargo, IU 2 should be suitably arranged. Electric signal cabins as nerve centres of big lines would also be a target. It should first be established that wrecking would not involve wholesale collisions. This possibility is extremely unlikely as in that case an electrical blackout, which is normal contingency to be guarded against, would have the same effect. (In this connection, from a technical work, is taken the instance of an electric line falling on railway, telephone and signaling lines: A big North Sea storm caused the insulators on the 33 kv. Line to be covered in salt, resulting in almost constant flashing over. It had the effect of rendering the signaling instruments almost inoperative and this, in turn, had the effect of slowing down all the trains.)

Railway cloakrooms, luggage stores and merchandise sheds constitute a first class objective for the application of I.U. 2. Since the certainty of grip of the initial flames would be largely conditioned by time, the success of such jobs depends on delay action arrangements prior to definite locking up time.

(d) Trams, trolley-buses and buses can all be tackled during garaging periods. It would be necessary to find out at what hour cleaners commenced their duties—probably midnight or 1 a.m. to 5 or 6 a.m. I.U. 2 could here be employed or smallest possible units of I.U. 1 dropped into many petrol tanks simultaneously.

A minor degree of dislocation could be secured at a late period in the campaign by the addition of sugar (molasses or golden syrup, etc., better if in suitable capsules with loose lid) to the petrol.

(e) Private and commercial transport. Open to attack at intermediate or late stages in ways similar to those described above, when major operations for any reason could not be safely carried out.

The above concludes what may be regarded as the system of Public Service.

2. KEY INDUSTRIES

These, especially in so far as armaments or aeroplane factories, etc. are concerned, constitute a very important target, though naturally less diffused or widespread than the Public Services.

In fact, from the viewpoint of damaging the military strength of the nation, a well organized or fortunately timed and circumstanced attack on a particular key industry might have a crippling effect on the country's re-armament programme.

Analysing various such industries, there could hardly be found one which would have a more crippling effect on the military aviation and mechanization programme than the destruction or dislocation of magneto factories. A glance through aeroplane or automobile magazine advertisements will show where these are mostly manufactured. Precision instruments of all kinds, including lathes, etc., all form a similar target.

Generally it might be hazarded that heavy chemical industries are mostly in Glasgow or Lancashire, coal mining, etc., in Newcastle and northern areas and South Wales, cotton in Manchester, etc.—all above a line north of the Birmingham area. South of the Birmingham area, and in the London area, heavy chemical industries again and the lighter engineering and other industries. But in the Birmingham area itself, many vital key industries. This is largely a guess and should be confirmed.

3. COMMERCE, SHIPPING, BANKING, OTHER INDUSTRIES

There is no need to elaborate this section, which is too wide in its scope to commit to detail. Generally, attack on any of these would come at intermediate or later stages of the campaign.

4. PRESS-NEWSPAPERS

This section also requires no examination. If certain newspapers habitually behave in a hostile fashion towards Ireland or if in connection with this particular campaign they have incited to fiercest reprisal or have distorted the obvious aims and suppressed the truth as furnished to them by our Propaganda Bureau, then they have left themselves in for legitimate punitive action. The time and the weapon employed are of our own choosing. Here it is unlikely that incendiary methods would avail, although if the most delicate and vital parts of the huge machines can be located, and if suitable access can be had at the idle hours, this also might be possible. Sledgehammer methods would serve but would almost certainly be impracticable. What is desired therefore, is to ascertain the number and types of the machines, study these in an up-to-date text book or Printing Machinery catalogue or get expert's information and devise some type of sand or spanner [i.e., wrench] in the works which will have the effect of permitting the usual trial run through of the machine but will ensure their progressively increasing gumming-up or disintegration (e.g., crown wheel in a motor car can be "chewed up" very rapidly once one chip off a cog is present).

5. MORAL SABOTAGE. AUXILIARY ARM

(a) The most essential preparation for this form from the viewpoint of Direct Action is to secure from every possible source, class stocks of stationery (i.e., letterheads and official envelopes, rubber stamps, etc.) from Government and other Departments.

Such a store of notepaper, etc. laid in previously to the opening of our campaign, in the possession of our Intelligence or Headquarters, would be an invaluable asset. Instructions and documents of all kinds could be successfully counterfeited as emanating from Admiralty, War Office, Air Ministry, Foreign Office, Dominions Office, Department of Education, etc., and also the various Railways, Companies, Electricity Commissioners, etc.

These could be availed of in thousands of ways as the imagination dictates and could be used to play into or co-operate with direct attack on certain objectives.

Numerous letters could be dispatched at the same time causing simultaneous action, perhaps of a secret nature, such as troop or A.R.P. mobilizations, etc., using some such safe and express method of delivery as the District Messenger Service.

(b) For two reasons it might be desirable to have our men join various of the precautionary units such as A.R.P. Given men well suited to "Carry this off," they should join at once or on the wave of the first popular organizing appeal that may be made. First, it would give them an insight into the kind of precautions that are being actually taken against outbreaks of fire, etc. Secondly, it would make them "respectable" in the eyes of neighbors and might serve to cloak various activities of theirs, e.g., carrying packages, etc., which might ultimately arouse suspicions. Further, if equipped with badge, armlet or gasmask, etc., and able to produce their certificates as to unit and rank etc., it might come in useful when in a tight corner by nearly being caught in the act or in the neighbourhood just after a job.

(c) A National Register of England will probably soon be decided on. She cannot organize efficiently for war without it. The prevention of its being taken should be easy by burning depots where returns go to, etc.

This concludes the details of Section A of ACTION as distinct from PROPAGANDA. It might be well to add certain general principles that emerge from consideration of Section A (i.e., DIRECT ACTION).

ADDENDUM TO SECTION A

(1) For every man we have, the enemy has ten thousand men. Operations must therefore be so foolproof and so certain in action as to afford 10,000:1 margin of safety, i.e., freedom from detection or capture.

(2) Included in the very first series of operations should be those major operations at centres where the favorable population available is very small and where at a later date such major operations would be difficult. This would incidentally put off the scent those whose duty it would be to try to locate the headquarters of the organizers of the campaign.

(3) The most major and "centralized" operations should come first. This, because at the first spot of bother, all precautionary measures, special patrolling corps, watch guards, etc., will be put on a war-time basis. These will probably be sufficient to render operations of this type impossible or much more chancy at a subsequent date.

(4) The discovery of dud Incendiary Unit or delay–Action mine would give away the focal points of action, the probable scope of activities, and, still more vital, the materials on which our weapons are based. The procuring of even the most innocent of these materials at a subsequent date might conceivably arouse dangerous suspicions. Supplies (adequate to the campaign) of all materials down to the last item, must therefore be laid in and suitably divided into at least three dumps in each area, so that capture of one would inflict only 33.3% blow at the area's organization.

(5) Since the avoidance of the discovery of a dud is important two units should be incorporated in every case where feasible instead of only one.

Appendix II: Persons Convicted in Great Britain in Connection with the IRA Campaign During 1939–1940

(Many of these persons were charged under false names)

Name	Date & Place of Conviction	Offense	Sentence
Barnes, Peter	December 1939, Birmingham Assizes	Murder	Death
Behan, Brendan	February 1940, Liverpool Assizes	Possessing explosive substances	3 years' Borstal
Bradford, Gerard	June 1939, Central Criminal Court	Conspiracy to cause explosions	20 years' Penal Servitude
Bradley, William	December 1939, Birmingham Assizes	(1) Conspiracy to cause explosions (2) Possessing explosive substances	10 years' Penal Servitude
Broderick, Joseph P.	July 1939, Manchester Assize	Possessing explosive substances	10 years' Penal Servitude
Brown, William	April 1939, Central Criminal Court	Causing an explosion	10 years' Penal Servitude
Burns, Francis James	March 1939, Central Criminal Court	(1) Conspiracy to cause explosions (2) Possessing explosive substances	3 years' Borstal

Persons Convicted in Great Britain

Name	Date & Place of Conviction	Offense	Sentence
Campbell, Michael Rory	March 1939, Manchester Assizes	(1) Conspiracy to cause explosions (2) Possessing explosive substances	20 years' Penal Servitude
Campbell, Peter	May 1939, Central Criminal Court	Possessing explosive substances	10 years' Penal Servitude
Carney, John	October 1939, Liverpool Assizes	(1) Conspiracy to cause explosions (2) Causing explosions	7 years' Penal Servitude
Carson, John	August 1939, Glasgow High Court	Possessing explosive substances	10 years' Penal Servitude
Casey, Charles James	March 1939, Central Criminal Court	(1) Conspiracy to cause explosions (2) Possessing explosive substances	14 years' Penal Servitude
Clarke, Martin Patrick	July 1939, Birmingham Assizes	(1) Conspiracy to cause explosions (2) Possessing explosive substances	20 years' Penal Servitude
Cohen, Richard	November 1939, Carmarthen Assizes	Possessing explosive substances	14 years' Penal Servitude
Collins, Joseph	March 1939, Manchester Assizes	Possessing explosive substances	20 years' Penal Servitude
Connell, Edward John	April 1939, Central Criminal Court	Causing an explosion	20 years' Penal Servitude
Connolly, James P.	March 1939, Central Criminal Court	Possessing explosive substances	6½ years' Penal Servitude
Conway, Ann	September 1939, Central Criminal Court	(1) Conspiracy to cause explosions (2) Possessing explosive substances	10 years' Penal Servitude
Conway, Rose	September 1939, Central Criminal Court	(1) Conspiracy to cause explosions (2) Possessing explosive substances	10 years' Penal Servitude
Crompton, Vincent	October 1939, Liverpool Assizes	(1) Conspiracy to cause explosions (2) Causing explosions	20 years' Penal Servitude
Crotty, Daniel	January 1940, Central Criminal Court	Conspiracy to cause explosions	10 years' Penal Servitude
Dacey, Timothy	March 1939, Glamorgan Assizes	Possessing explosive substances	7 years' Penal Servitude
Deviney, Patrick	March 1939, Manchester Assizes	(1) Conspiracy to cause explosions (2) Possessing explosive substances	14 years' Penal Servitude

Appendix II

Name	Date & Place of Conviction	Offense	Sentence
Donaghy, Patrick	September 1939, Central Criminal Court	Conspiracy to cause explosions	20 years' Penal Servitude
Dower, Patrick	June 1939, Central Criminal Court	Conspiracy to cause explosions	20 years' Penal Servitude
Duggan, Dennis	March 1939, Central Criminal Court	(1) Possessing explosive substances (2) Conspiracy to cause explosions	20 years' Penal Servitude
Duggan, John	July 1939, Manchester Assizes	Causing an explosion	20 years' Penal Servitude
Duignan, John Leo	May 1939, Central Criminal Court	Possessing explosive substances	10 years' Penal Servitude
Dunlea, Lawrence	July 1939, Birmingham Assizes	Conspiracy to cause explosions	20 years' Penal Servitude
Dunlop, Gerard Anthony	June 1939, Central Criminal Court	Conspiracy to cause explosions	20 years' Penal Servitude
Evans, James John	October 1939, Central Criminal Court	(1) Conspiracy to cause explosions (2) Possessing explosive substances	20 years' Penal Servitude
Fitzpatrick, Daniel	March 1939, Central Criminal Court	(1) Conspiracy to cause explosions (2) Possessing explosive substances	8 years' Penal Servitude
Foley, John	May 1939, Central Criminal Court	Possessing explosive substances	5 years' Penal Servitude
Furlong, Emily Mary	July 1939, Birmingham Assizes	Conspiracy to cause explosions	5 years' Penal Servitude
Furlong, Evelyn Mary	July 1939, Birmingham Assizes	Conspiracy to cause explosions	3 years' imprisonment
Furlong, Mary Ann	July 1939, Birmingham Assizes	Conspiracy to cause explosions	3 years' Penal Servitude
Gallagher, Molly	March 1939, Central Criminal Court	Possessing explosive substances	3 years' Borstal
Gavahan, John	March 1939, Manchester Assizes	(1) Conspiracy to cause explosions (2) Possession explosive substances	20 years' Penal Servitude
Gibson, John	October 1939, Central Criminal Court	(1) Conspiracy to cause explosions (2) Possessing explosive substances	20 years' Penal Servitude

Persons Convicted in Great Britain

Name	Date & Place of Conviction	Offense	Sentence
Gill, Edward	August 1939, Glasgow High Court	Possessing explosive substances	10 years' Penal Servitude
Glenn, Jack	March 1939, Manchester Assizes	(1) Conspiracy to cause explosions (2) Possessing explosive substances	20 years' Penal Servitude
Glenn, Mary	March 1939, Manchester Assizes	(1) Conspiracy to cause explosions (2) Possessing explosive substances	7 years' Penal Servitude
Gray, Gary	September 1939, Central Criminal Court	(1) Conspiracy to cause explosions (2) Possessing explosive substances	10 years' Penal Servitude
Griffin, Michael	May 1939, Central Criminal Court	Possessing explosive substances	10 years' Penal Servitude
Hannan, John Joseph	March 1939, Manchester Assizes	(1) Conspiracy to cause explosions (2) Possessing explosive substances	7 years' Penal Servitude
Hasty, James	July 1940, Birmingham Assize	(1) Possessing explosive substances (2) Possessing firearm with intent to endanger life	10 years' Penal Servitude
Healy, John	March 1939, Central Criminal Court	(1) Conspiracy to cause explosions (2) Possessing explosive substances	10 years' Penal Servitude
Jones, Barbara	November 1939, Carmarthen Assizes	Possessing explosive substances	5 years' Penal Servitude
Jordan, Daniel	October 1939, Central Criminal Court	(1) Conspiracy to cause explosions (2) Possessing explosive substances	20 years Penal Servitude
Kane, George Brendan	March 1939, Central Criminal Court	Conspiracy to cause explosions	7 years' Penal Servitude
Keane, John Joseph	June 1939, Central Criminal Court	Possessing explosive substances	10 years' Penal Servitude
Kenneally, Christopher	October 1939, Liverpool Assizes	(1) Conspiracy to cause explosions (2) Causing explosions	3 years' Borstal
Kennedy, Samuel	February 1939, Falkirk	Conspiracy to steal explosives	5 years' Penal Servitude
Logue, Jack	March 1939, Central Criminal Court	(1) Conspiracy to cause explosions (2) Possessing explosive substances	3 years' Borstal
Lyons, James Michael	March 1939, Central Criminal Court	(1) Conspiracy to cause explosions (2) Possessing explosive substances	10 years' Penal Servitude

Appendix II

Name	Date & Place of Conviction	Offense	Sentence
Magill, Thomas	March 1939, Birmingham Assizes	Possessing explosive substances	7 years' Penal Servitude
Malone, Joseph	June 1939, Central Criminal Court	Possessing explosive substances	5 years' Penal Servitude
Martin, John Percy	April 1939, Central Criminal Court	Possessing explosive substances	10 years' Penal Servitude
Mason, Michael Joseph	March 1939, Central Criminal Court	(1) Conspiracy to cause explosions (2) Possessing explosive substances	17 years' Penal Servitude
McAleer, Patrick	June 1939, Central Criminal Court	Conspiracy to cause explosions	20 years' Penal Servitude
McBrine, Patrick	December 1939, Birmingham Assizes	Conspiracy to cause explosions	15 years' Penal Servitude
McCabe, Jack	November 1939, Manchester Assizes	(1) Causing an explosion (2) Attempt to cause an explosion (3) Possessing explosive substances	20 years' Penal Servitude
McCafferty, Daniel	March 1939, Central Criminal Court	Possessing explosive substances	4½ years' Penal Servitude
McCafferty, James	March 1939, Central Criminal Court	Possessing explosive substances	5 years' Penal Servitude
McCann, Robert	March 1939, Birmingham Assizes	Possessing explosive substances	10 years' Penal Servitude
McCarthy, Daniel	March 1939, Central Criminal Court	(1) Conspiracy to cause explosions (2) Possessing explosive substances	4 years' Penal Servitude
McCluskey, Hugh	March 1939, Birmingham Assizes	Possessing explosive substances	10 years' Penal Servitude
McDonnell, Margaret	October 1939, Liverpool Assizes	Conspiracy to cause explosions	Bound over for 2 years
McGarrigle, Cormac	May 1939, Glasgow High Court	Possessing explosive substances	15 months imprisonment
McGeough, John	May 1939, Birmingham Assizes	Possessing ammunition with intent to endanger life	10 years' Penal Servitude
McGillycuddy, Denis	May 1939, Central Criminal Court	Possessing explosive substances	10 years' Penal Servitude

Persons Convicted in Great Britain

Name	Date & Place of Conviction	Offense	Sentence
McGillycuddy, Joseph	May 1939, Central Criminal Court	Possessing explosive substances	10 years' Penal Servitude
McGillycuddy, Paul	May 1939, Central Criminal Court	Possessing explosive substances	10 years' Penal Servitude
McGowan, Francis	March 1939, Central Criminal Court	Possessing explosive substances	7 years' Penal Servitude
McNeece, Francis	February 1939, Falkirk	(1) Possessing explosive substances (2) Conspiracy to steal explosive substance	7 years' Penal Servitude
McNessa, Connor	July 1939, Manchester Assizes	Causing an explosion	20 years' Penal Servitude
McSherry, Terence	February 1939, Falkirk	(1) Conspiracy to steal explosive substances (2) Possessing explosive substances	10 years' Penal Servitude
Mitchell, John	March 1939, Central Criminal Court	(1) Conspiracy to cause explosions (2) Possessing explosive substances	5 years' Penal Servitude
Moore, Herbert	September 1939, Central Criminal Court	(1) Conspiracy to cause explosions (2) Possessing explosive substances	10 years' Penal Servitude
Morgan, James	November 1939, Leeds Assizes	Possessing explosive substances	12 years' Penal Servitude
Murray, Timothy	June 1939, Central Criminal Court	Conspiracy to cause explosions	20 years' Penal Servitude
Murrihy, John	May 1939, Central Criminal Court	Possessing explosive substances	5 years' Penal Servitude
Nelson, Thomas	September 1939, Central Criminal Court	(1) Conspiracy to cause explosions (2) Causing an explosion	20 years' Penal Servitude
O'Connell, Patrick	March 1939, Manchester Assizes	(1) Conspiracy to possess explosive substances (2) Possessing explosive substances	20 years' Penal Servitude
O'Hanlon, Thomas	July 1940, Birmingham Assizes	Possessing explosive substances, a firearm and ammunition	8 years' Penal Servitude
O'Hara, Michael James	August 1939, Glasgow High Court	Possessing explosive substances	10 years' Penal Servitude
O'Regan, James Francis	October 1939, Central Criminal Court	(1) Conspiracy to cause explosions (2) Possessing explosive substances	20 years' Penal Servitude

Appendix II

Name	Date & Place of Conviction	Offense	Sentence
O'Regan, John Joseph	October 1939, Central Criminal Court	(1) Conspiracy to cause explosions (2) Possessing explosive substances	Bound over for 2 years
O'Shea, Michael	March 1939, Central Criminal Court	(1) Conspiracy to cause explosions (2) Possessing explosive substances (3) Possessing a firearm with intent to endanger life	5 years' Penal Servitude
Perry, Terence	July 1940, Birmingham Assizes	Possessing explosive substances, firearms and ammunition	6 years' Penal Servitude
Preston, Michael	March 1939, Central Criminal Court	(1) Conspiracy to cause explosions (2) Possessing explosive substances	12 years' Penal Servitude
Rice, Stanley Joseph	December 1939, Birmingham Assizes	Conspiracy to cause explosives	10 years' Penal Servitude
Richards, James	December 1939, Birmingham Assizes	Murder	Death
Ryan, John	April 1939, Central Criminal Court	(1) Conspiracy to cause explosions (2) Possessing explosive substances	18 months' imprisonment
Stapleton, Edward	September 1939, Central Criminal Court	(1) Conspiracy to cause explosions (2) Possessing explosive substances	10 years' Penal Servitude
Stuart, Peter	March 1939, Central Criminal Court	(1) Conspiring to cause explosions (2) Possessing explosive substances	15 years' Penal Servitude
Walker, Joseph	March 1939, Central Criminal Court	Conspiracy to cause explosions	18 months' imprisonment
Whittaker, George	October 1939, Liverpool Assizes	(1) Conspiracy to cause explosions (2) Possessing explosive substances	7 years' Penal Servitude
Woods, Ella May	September 1939, Central Criminal Court	(1) Conspiracy to cause explosions (2) Possessing explosive substances	10 years' Penal Servitude

A number of those convicted were convicted under aliases. Their real names, where known, are listed below:

Alias	Real Name	Alias	Real Name
Gerard Bradford	Gerard Kirk	John Martin	Pearse McLaughlin
Richard Cohen	Dick Timmons	Michael Mason	Michael Cleary
Gerard Dunlop	Gerard Lyons	Herbert Moore	Charlie Dineen
Gary Gray	Gary Jones	Michael Preston	Patrick Fleming
Barbara Jones	Rita McSweeney	James Richards	James McCormack
Connor McNessa	Joe Collins	Peter Stuart	Peter Walsh

Others convicted under aliases, their files still not available to the public, and sentenced to 10 years for possessing explosives include:

Mary McCarthy	George Stannard	Thomas Hunt
Winifred Walsh	Augustine P. Quigley	Nora Riley
James Murphy	Thomas J. Byrne	Mary Stanton
Patrick Kelly	John Sinnett	James Wynne

Appendix III: Expulsion Orders Under the Prevention of Violence Act 1939

These were people suspected of being members of the IRA or having IRA sympathies, and were deported.

Expulsion Order No.	Period of Expulsion	Name of Person
23174	1940	Bradley, Dympna Anne E.
22693	1939–46	Bradley, James
23173	1940	Bradley, Margaret Eileen
23100	1939–40	Brady, Patrick
23171	1940–47	Breheny, James alias O'Brien
23094	1939–53	Burke, Seamus
23141	1939–40	Callen, Margaret
23140	1939–40	Clarke, Joseph Patrick
23083	1939–53	Clarke, Sean
22675	1939–46	Collins, Patrick Joseph
23131	1939–53	Collins, Timothy, alias Murphy, John
23103	1939–54	Comer, Michael
23074	1939–53	Conway, Patrick
23136	1939–40	Cotter, Maurice
23130	1939–53	Coyne, Patrick
23098	1939–44	Curtin, Edward or Albert Edward alias Cronin, Bartholomew
23099	1939–44	Curtin, William Francis
23115	1939	Delahunty, James
23112	1939	Dolan, James Gerald
23072	1939–46	Duffy, Francis Joseph
23085	1939–53	Dunn, Maureen
23084	1939–53	Dunn, Sheila
22678	1939–46	Edmond, Hugh
22674	1939–46	Farrell, James
23116	1939	Farrell, John Joseph alias Sean O'Farrell

Expulsion Orders Under the Act of 1939

Expulsion Order No.	Period of Expulsion	Name of Person
23110	1939–40	Faughan, Harry alias Stephens, Harry, alias Collins
23070	1939–46	Ferrin, Patrick alias Fern
23150	1940	Fleming, William
23172	1940–53	Flynn, Aeneas
23111	1939	Flynn, James
23078	1939	Fogarty, Daniel
23194	1942	Foley, John
23142	1939–40	Folley, Robert
23196	1942	Furlong, Emily Mary
23075	1939–53	Gallagher, James
23101	1939–54	Gill, John
23202	1944	Glenn, Mary
23147	1939–40	Griffin, Thomas
23107	1939	Guiry, Nellie May
23123	1939–53	Hanily, Frank, Hanley
23200	1943–44	Hannon, John Joseph
23127	1939–54	Hannaway, Thomas Francis
23153	1940–53	Haughton, William Henry
23152	1940	Hogan, Robert
23086	1939–56	Hughes, Annie Veronica
23128	1939–53	Hughes, Patrick Joseph
23155	1940–53	Keane, James
23168	1940	Keane, John Austin, alias Kane, John alias Cain, J.
22694	1939–46	Kearns, Mary
23119	1939–53	Kelly, Michael or Michael Joseph
23181	1940	Kenny, John or Sean
23143	1940–53	Kerr, Joseph
23089	1939–45	Kinnie, Edward Joseph alias Kenny, Edward Joseph
23077	1939–53	Lavelle, Michael or Flannagan
23149	1940–45	Lennon, James
23073	1939–53	Long, Thomas Francis
23151	1940–53	McAlarney, Patrick alias McAlerney
23192	1939–42	McCafferty, Daniel
23197	1943	McCafferty, James
23139	1939–40	McCabe, Frank
23134	1939–43	McClean, Patrick or McLean; order suspended on appeal
23144	1939–40	McConville, Kathleen, née Price
23090	1939–40	McCormack, Hugh
23177	1939–41	McCormack, Michael
23120	1939–53	McCormick, Hugh Patrick
23076	1939–54	McDonnell, Patrick
23178	1940	McKenny, Patrick
23159	1940–53	McMulkin, Maurice
23093	1939–53	McNabb, Joseph John k/a Sandy
23204	1944–46	McNeece, Francis—order unenforceable due to period of residence
23121	1939–53	McNeil, William
23177	1940	Magill, William
23080	1939–53	Martin, Thomas
23193	1942–53	Mitchell, John
23118	1939–53	Moffit, Patrick
23138	1939–40	Molloy, Thomas James
23160	1940–53	Moss, James
23195	1942	Murphy, John, alias Murrihy

Appendix III

Expulsion Order No.	Period of Expulsion	Name of Person
23097	1939–53	Murray, Frank
23105	1939–53	Murray, Margaret
23108	1939	Nevin, Joseph
23145	1940–53	O'Connor, Martin Joseph
23091	1939–44	O'Connor, Joseph
23102	1939–54	O'Flanagan, Michael James or Flannagan
23103	1939–54	O'Flanagan, Margaret
23161	1940–45	O'Gorman, Kevin Joseph Gerard
22677	1939–46	O'Kane, Michael or Kane
23146	1940–53	O'Kelly, Thomas Conleth
23137	1939–45	O'Phelan, Eamon or Edward
23162	1940–53	O'Sullivan, Albert
23092	1939–53	O'Sullivan, Ghebert Albina
23069	1939–53	O'Toole, Daniel Patrick
23114	1939	Reidy, Thomas
23096	1939–53	Roche, Kathleen
23154	1940–53	Rooney, Peter
23106	1939	Ryan, Edmund
23176	1940–45	Ryan, John
23104	1939–54	Scurry, Norah
23158	1940–47	Shaw, Bernard
23125	1939–45	Skelton, Andrew
23088	1939–53	Smith, Thomas
23113	1939	Stapleton, Michael Joseph
23175	1940–45	Walker, Joseph
23135	1939–47	Walsh, James Joseph
23095	1939–53	Weaver, Frank or Francis
23133	1939–40	Whelton, Norah
23071	1939–53	Wiggins, William John
23132	1939–46	Winters, William

Chapter Notes

Introduction

1. Ironically, it is believed that Collins ordered the assassination of Sir Henry Wilson on 22 June 1922. His murderers were two London-based IRA men, Joseph Sullivan (alias John O'Brien) and Richard Dunne (alias James Connolly). Both men were caught, tried and hanged. Collins himself was assassinated, allegedly by Irish Republican volunteer Sonny O'Neil, on 22 August 1922.
2. Hansard, 12 March 1939.

Chapter 1

1. Though the S-Plan declared that there would be no attacks upon the Celtic countries of Great Britain—namely Northern Ireland, Scotland and Wales—the campaign nevertheless began with assaults on customs posts on the border of Northern Ireland and Eire, and on 3 September 1939, an unexploded bomb was discovered under the main LMS railway line of the Glasgow to Edinburgh express at Shotts in Lanarkshire.
2. Uinseann MacEoin, *The IRA in the Twilight Years* (Dublin: Argenta Publications, 1997), 828.
3. Ibid., 623.
4. David O'Donoghue, *The Devil's Deal* (Dublin: New Island, 2010), 99.
5. Ibid., 95.
6. Paxo, a homemade explosive prepared from chemicals widely available—chlorate of potash mixed with sugar or charcoal, or with a metallic substance such as oxide of iron or aluminum powder. It took its name from a popular turkey stuffing mix which it supposedly resembled; MacEoin, 821–2.
7. Ibid., 773. The statue of a mounted King George II blown up in St. Stephen's Green was later removed and repaired. The cast bronze statue is approximately 9.5 ft. tall. It now stands outside the Barber Institute of Fine Arts on the University of Birmingham campus, England.
8. James McCormack; there are a number of variations in the spelling of his surname, from MacCormic, to McCormic, to McCormick. But McCormack is the spelling that appears on his grave stone in Mullingar, and this is the spelling I have used.
9. Special Branch Review of IRA Activity, 13 April 1939. National Archives, Kew, HO 144/21357.
10. McEoin, 774.
11. A Letter From Michael Cleary OC IRA Britain, to Sean Russell, Chief of Staff, IRA: "A chara, Stephen [Hayes] will have informed you of the progress we are making and the amount of money we will require to carry on. I would be glad if you could send over £500 as Michael's work will require a large sum to be carried out effectively, see enclosed, and besides I would feel far more confident if I had more finance under my control. It is not necessary for me to tell you that none of the money shall be wasted. Cardiff sent a man over to you on Monday last but he used the name McDonagh instead of Walsh. I hope he made contact all right. In Bankside, two men attempted to get into this building, one being really a plumber, but were unable to get further than the front office as they were

informed that 'There must be a mistake as only our own workmen are allowed to carry out repairs in the building.' However, we will devise some means of attacking this place even if it has to be stuck up. Eoin [MacNamee] is getting himself into trouble. A bicycle of his was stolen some time ago and he happened to see it at a garage near where he lives. He had an argument with the proprietor and they both went to a policeman with the result that Eoin charged the man with theft of the bike. Later that night his landlady left a note saying if he had any papers in connection with the IRA to destroy them as she had heard the men talking in the garage and they intended to do him harm. We have a couple of very good girls working for us and it may be necessary for me to ask one of them to become whole time but I will not be wanting her just at the moment. I suppose I can use my own discretion in this matter. I am sending this communication by R. McCann and trust you will give him the once over as I think he will be useful for Intelligence. I would be very pleased if you could arrange to get some revolvers and ammunition over also some galvanometers." —Mise le Meas, OC Britain.

12. H. Montgomery Hyde, *United in Crime*, 104.

Chapter 2

1. Brendan Behan, *Borstal Boy* (New York: Knopf, 1959), 9.
2. McEoin, 623.
3. Uinseann MacEoin, *Harry* (Dublin: Argenta Publications, 1985), 74.
4. *Coventry Herald*, 25 March 1939.
5. O'Donoghue, 293. From an "anonymous source to the author," O'Donoghue puts forward a claim that the Hammersmith Bridge bombing "was carried out by two sisters from Belfast who were part of an IRA active service unit in London headed by a London-born IRA man with a Cockney accent." In reality the names of the four men involved have been confirmed. Women from Cumman na mBan were used as carriers, not bombers, and for the depositing of incendiary devices in cinemas, department stores and hotels, where they could pass virtually unseen.
6. O'Donoghue, 99.
7. Mary Furlong's son Jack married Kathleen Kearney, sister of Peadar Kearney, who wrote the words to "A Soldier's Song," adopted as the Irish National Anthem.
8. McEoin, 598.
9. Robert Fabian, *Fabian of the Yard* (New York: British Book Centre, 1953), 77–8.

Chapter 3

1. The explosion at Milverton railway station may have been the work of Eoin McNamee. At the time of the police trawl in London he had escaped to the West Midlands, basing himself in the Stratford-upon-Avon and Leamington Spa region. He and Sean Fuller, one of the Birmingham based operations officers, were then told to report to GHQ in Dublin. Here they met Mairtin O'Cadhain and discovered a growing disillusionment with the campaign. Provoked by Russell, Fuller resigned from the IRA. He was replaced by Dominic Adams. McNamee briefly returned to London to confer with the new OC, Leo Duigan, then returned safely to Ireland.
2. *Coventry Telegraph*, 4 July 1939.
3. Ibid.

Chapter 4

1. Hansard, 24 July 1939. The popular weekly magazine *Punch*, 2 August 1939, published a cartoon of an IRA bomber with an old-fashioned bomb in one hand and a bag marked "Foreign Subsidies" in the other, indicating Nazi involvement in the campaign.
2. O'Donoghue, 110.

Chapter 5

1. A plot of land rented out to an individual, usually by the local authority, for the cultivation of flowers or vegetables.
2. Dialogue is taken from the evidence given in the subsequent trial.
3. *Coventry Herald*, 14 August 1939.
4. 25 Parnell Square was an IRA safe house in Dublin.
5. Bernadette Devlin, *The Price of My Soul* (New York: Knopf, 1969), 20.

Chapter 6

1. Letitia Fairfield, *The Trial of Peter*

Barnes and Others (London: William Hodge, 1953), 17.
2. Fairfield, 113.
3. Fairfield, 111–2.
4. Fairfield, 21–2.

Chapter 7

1. *Birmingham Mail*, 7 February 1940.

Chapter 8

1. *Irish Times*, August 1947.

Chapter 10

1. An election held during the life of a Parliament to fill a vacant seat in the lower chamber.
2. Without naming him, Tim Pat Coogan, in his book *The IRA: A History* (p. 97), states that Sullivan was at the time of the bombing, "a psychopath, who later received extensive treatment."

3. IRA GHQ Dublin had compelling evidence that the Belfast brigade had been compromised by informers, and therefore details of the Border Campaign of 195/1–/22, were not imparted to that brigade. Joe Cahill recalled how his suspicions were aroused with the failure of a number of unspecified operations within the city. By this time Dominic Adams was back in Belfast. Dismissed from the IRA GHQ staff, would that have made him bitter enough to have betrayed the IRA? For further discussion see: Enda Staunton, *The Nationalists of Northern Ireland* (Dublin: Columba Press, 2001), 225; and John Maguire, *IRA Internments and the Irish Government* (Dublin; Portland, OR: Irish Academic Press, 2008), 91–2.

Bibliography

Manuscripts

National Archives, Kew, London:
ASSI 13/69
CAB 43 Series
CJ 1/62 deValera to Eden, 29 Jan. 1940
Crim. 1 Series
EF 5/38
HO 45 series
HO 144 Series
KV 2/769, KV4/232, IRA Outrages
MEPO 2 & 3 Series
P.Com 9
War Cabinet (1940) 147 & 173

National Archives, Dublin:
Dail Eireann, Vol. 74, 2 March 1939.
Documents on Irish Foreign Policy, Vol. VI, 1939–41(2008).

British Government Publications
Hansard—Report of Parliamentary Proceedings, 1939–40.

Books
Allason, R. *The Branch*. London: Secker & Warburg, 1983.
Behan, Brendan. *Borstal Boy*. London: Corgi Books, 1961.
_____. *Confessions of an Irish Rebel*. London: Hutchinson, 1965.
Bowyer Bell, J. *The Secret Army*. London: Sphere Books, 1972.
Coogan, Tim Pat. *The IRA*. London: Arrow Books, 1970.
_____. *Ireland in the Twentieth Century*. London: Arrow Books, 2004.
De Valera, Eamon. *Ireland's Stand: Being a Selection of the Speeches of Eamon de Valera during the War (1939–45)*. Dublin: M.H. Gill & Son, 1950.
Devlin, Bernadette. *The Price of my Soul*. London: Pan Books, 1969.
Fabian, Robert. *Fabian of the Yard*. London: Heirloom Modern World Library, 1955.
Fairfield, Letitia. *The Trial of Peter Barnes and Others*. London: William Hodge, 1953.
Fisk, Robert. *In Time of War*. London: Paladin Books, 1983.

Flynn, Barry. *Soldiers of Folly: The IRA Border Campaign, 1956–1962.* Cork: Collins Press, 2009.
Macardle, Dorothy. *The Irish Republic.* London: Corgi Books, 1968.
MacEoin, Uinseann. *Harry.* Dublin: Argenta Publications, 1985.
_____. *The IRA in the Twilight Years.* Dublin: Argenta Publications, 1997.
McMahon, Paul. *British Spies and Irish Rebels: British Intelligence and Ireland, 1916–45.* Woodbridge, UK: Boydell & Brewer, 2008.
McManus, Francis, ed. *The Years of the Great Test.* Cork: Mercier Press, 1967.
Maguire, James, and James Quinn. *Dictionary of Irish Biography from the Earliest Times to the Year 2002.* Cambridge University Press, 2009.
Montgomery Hyde, H. *United in Crime.* New York: Roy Publishers, 1955.
O'Donoghue, David. *The Devil's Deal.* Dublin: New Island, 2010.
Ryan, Meda. *Tom Barry.* Cork: Mercier Press, 2005.
Sillitoe, Sir Percy. *Cloak without Dagger.* UK: Pan Books, 1956.
Stephan, Enno. *Spies in Ireland.* London: Four Square Books, 1965.

Newspapers and Periodicals

The Bell, 1947
Birmingham Mail
Birmingham Post
Daily Herald
Daily Telegraph
History Studies: History Society Journal 9, 2008.
Illustrated London News
Intelligence & National Security 25, No. 3, 2010.
Irish Freedom
Irish Press
Irish Times
Liverpool Echo
The Observer
Saorise
Sunday Times
Time, 19 Feb. 1940.
Times
United Irishman

Index

Adams, Dominic 18, 25, 60, 85, 86, 89, 95, 102, 105, 135, 143, 157, 159, 163, 168, 169
Adams, Gerry, Jr. 168
Adams, Gerry, Sr. 169
Ag Scaoileadh Sceoil 59
Aitken, Frank 8
Aliens Act 77
Alnwick 29
An Poblacht 14, 171, 172
Anglo-Irish Agreement 13
Ansell, Elsie 92, 100
Anti-Terrorist Bill 74
Arbour Hill Prison 47, 147
Army Comrades Association 12
Arnott, John Corbett 92
Atlee, Clement 158

Baker, Detective Inspector 32
Balsall Heath, Birmingham 46
Barnes, Detective Inspector 32, 98, 103
Barnes, Peter 88, 89, 93, 96, 99, 108–11, 158, 166
Barrows, Major 155
Barry, Tom 14, 15, 17, 30, 58, 143, 164
Barton, Robert 5
Barton-upon-Irwell 30
Behan, Brendan 37–8, 143, 157–8
Belfast Prison *see* Crumlin Road Prison
Birmingham 46, 48, 62, 63, 140
Birmingham Canal Navigation 40
Birmingham Mail 66
Birmingham Post 159
Black Country 40
Blackpool 62, 138
Blake, Constable 54, 55
Blue Shirts 12
Boland, Gerry 147, 148, 152, 154, 164
Boneham, Chief Inspector 98, 104
Borstal Boy 37, 157

Bow St. Police Station 40
Bradford, Gerard 54
Brady, —— 68–69
Brennan, Michael 6
Bridges, Inspector Frank 31, 35, 54
Bridges, Harold 38
Brimsdown power station 32
Brixton Prison 82, 167
Broderick, Joseph 32
Browne, William 45, 46
Brugha, Cathal 5
Buckingham Palace 39
Buckle, Dectective Inspector 32
Bull's Head, Meriden 50
Burgess, Sergeant 67
Burke, Liam 156
Burke, Seamus 167
Burns, Frank 31
Burns, Mike 166
Burton, Montague 40, 160
Byrd, Connie 164
Byrne, Tom 35, 38, 65, 82

Cafferey, Michael 171
Cahill, Joe 156
Cain, Detective Sergeant 35, 73
Callaghan & Co. 39
Campbell, Dr. Malcolm 73–74
Campbell, Michael 31
Campbell, Peter 38, 39, 62, 64, 156
Campbell, Rory 27
Canning, Commander Albert 52
Canty, Jeremiah 16
Carney, John 139
Carroll, Kitty 60
Carson, John 61, 172
Casement, Sir Roger 42
Casey, Charles 27, 42, 43, 171
Casey, Joseph 31

Index

HMS *Castor* 9
Catholic Church 16
Celia's, Coventry 88
Central Criminal Court 35, 42, 47, 54, 62, 64, 73, 132, 171
Chamberlain, Constable 56
Chamberlain, Neville 12, 13, 139
Cherrill, Chief Inspector 42
Cherrington, Henry 50
Cheylesmore 41
Chorlton-cum-Medloc 32
Christle, Joe 168
Churchill, Winston 12, 139
Clady 25
Clann na Gael 17, 47
Clann na Poblachta 155
Clara St., Coventry 86
Clarence Dock, Liverpool 30
Clarke, Joe 83, 146
Clarke, Martin 51, 52
Clay, James 92
Clearey, Michael 27, 30, 34, 42, 43, 61
Cleary, Nick 167
Coffey, Mrs. 65
Coffey, Paddy 142
Cohen, Richard 60
Collins, Joe 23, 50, 58, 59, 156
Collins, Father John 135
Collins, Michael 4–5, 12
Com-Motors, London 53
Confessions of an Irish Rebel 157
Connell, Catherine 47
Connell, Edward 45, 46
Connolly, James P. 35
Connor, Con 142
Conway, Ann 73
Conway, Michael 171
Conway, Rose 73
Coogan, T.P. 163, 168
Cooney, Andy 143
Cooper, Detective Inspector 44
Cooper, Sergeant 32, 100
Cordner, Harry 156
Cosgrave, William 5, 10, 12
Costello, John 153, 155
Costello, Tom 40
Cotter, Garrett 40
Council House, Birmingham 48
Court of Criminal Appeal 44
Coventry 40, 41, 47, 48, 56, 63–64, 82, 85, 140
Coventry Herald 87
Coventry Station 70–71
Covney, Sergeant 31
Cowpe-Pendleton, Detective Sergeant 106
Crane's Hotel, Coventry 48
Crawford, Detective Inspector 90–91

Crompton, Vincent 59, 139, 156
Cross, S.W. 135
Crotty, Daniel 91
Crumlin Road Prison 26, 147, 165
Cumann na mBan 17, 43, 60, 77, 103, 170
Cumann na nGaedheal 10–12
Cunard Line 39
Curragh 47, 143, 149, 172

Dacey, Timothy 34, 44
Daley, Timothy 172
Daly, Jack 39, 141
Darcy, Tony 14, 162
Dartmoor Prison 97
The Dead March Past 157
Defence of the Realm Act 82
Deighan, Joe 27, 29, 58, 59, 75–76, 82
De Valera, Eamon 5, 10, 11, 13, 14, 75, 78, 83, 134, 137, 143, 146, 153, 155
Devil's Deal 160, 168
Deviney, Patrick 31
Devlin, Bernadette 97
Dillon, Joe 25
Dillon, Prof. Tom 19
Dineen, Charlie 60
Dobson, Sir Gerald 39
Donaghue, Donal 18
Donaghy, Patrick 66, 68, 73
Donnelly, Simon 137
Donovan, Seamus 38
Dower, Patrick 53, 54
Dowley, Peter 34, 60
Down Holland 75
Drumond, Tad 40
Dryden, James 49
Duane, Dr. 154
Duffy, Frank 25
Duffy, Luke 154, 155
Duggan, Denis 32
Duggan, John 58–59
Duignan, Leo 24, 38, 39, 62, 156, 163, 171
Duignan, Sean (TV) 166
Dundrum Mental Asylum 153, 165
Dunlea, Laurence 48, 156
Dunlop, Gerard 41, 42, 53, 54, 55
Dupre, Frederick H. 102, 106–7

Earley, Paddy 38
Economic War 14
Edgeworth, Margaret 34
Edward VIII 13
Egan, John 15
Eire 75, 78
Elford, Dr. William 101
Elizabeth II 172
Emergency Powers Act 148

Index

Enfield Arms Factory 29
Ennis, Commandant Tom 7
Evans, John James 91
Explosives Substances Act 57, 77
Express & Star 72

Fabian, Detective Inspector 67, 68, 90
Fairfield, Letitia 128
Falkirk 35, 60
Farrell, Father 159
Ferguson, Mick 17, 21, 137
Fianna Fail 10, 11
Fine Gael 12, 155
Fitzgerald, Frank 18
Fitzpatrick, Daniel 31, 43, 44
Fitzpatrick, Michael 17, 18
Fitzsimons, Sylvester 148
Fleetwood 83
Fleming, Mick 25, 42, 43
Fleming, Patrick 27, 28, 32, 34, 145, 170
Fluke, Samuel 45, 46, 47
Foley, Bob 60
Foley, John 64, 171
Foot, Dingle 80
Four Courts 7, 8,
Franco, General 16
Fretwell, Detective Sergeant 35
Fuller, Sean 27, 51, 171
Furlong, Emily 51, 52
Furlong, Evelyn 51, 52
Furlong, Mary 51, 52

Gallagher, Eddie 154
Gallagher, Molly 34, 43
Gallagher, Sheila 61
Game, Sir Philip 52
Gaughran, William 45, 143
Gaumont Cinema, Birmingham 63
Gavahan, John 32
Genoa 143
Gentle, Rex 92
George II 195
Gestetner Copying 53–54
Gibson, Detective Con. 100
Gibson, John 91
Gill, Edward 61, 172
Gilmore, George 16
Glasgow 61
Glasgow High Court 61
Glasnevin cemetery 49
Glenn, Jack 31, 44
Glenn, Mary 32, 44
Glenn, Nora 32
Goertz, Hermann 144–5
Goodley's Furniture, Coventry 56
Gosford Green 41, 49

Goss, Richard 48–49, 166
Goulding, Cathal 162, 168
Graham, John 156
Grand Union Canal 38, 40
Great Barr, Birmingham 30
Griffin, Denis 163, 167
Griffin, Michael 38, 64
Griffin, Sean 171
Griffin, Tommy 167
Griffith, Arthur 5, 7,
Griffiths, Jackie 59, 64
Grogan, Larry 28, 84, 147

Habeas Corpus Act 77
Halford Cycle Co. 89, 96, 99
Halfpenny, Gina 25
Halifax, Lord 27, 42
Halifax Building Society 64
Hallet, Mr. Justice 134
Hammersmith Bridge 45, 60
Hams Hall 30
Hannigan, Lanty 25
Hannon, James 18, 34
Hannon, John 34, 60
Hannon, Patrick 34, 58, 60
Harlesdon 30
Harrogate 62
Harte, Tom 150
Hasty, James 142
Hawkett, Thomas 67
Hayes, Bill 163
Hayes, Stephen 24, 25, 28, 47, 84, 165
Hayward, Constable Ernest 54
Heal & Son, London 54
Healey, John 32, 39, 42, 43, 45
Heffernon, Myles 83, 146
Henry VIII waxwork 67
Hewart, Lord Chief Justice 4, 134
Hewitt, Joseph 86
Hewitt, Mary 86
Higgins, Mossie 170
Hilbery, Mr. Justice 134
Hinsley, Cardinal 68
Hitler, Adolf 12, 144
Hoare, Sir Samuel 61, 76, 77–78, 80
Holmes, Detective Inspector 73
Hoven, Jupp 143
Hughes, Detective Sergeant 92–93
Humphrey, Dr. John 136
Humphreys, Mr. Justice 42, 43, 44
Hunt, Tommy 23, 48, 60, 150
Hyde Park 25
Hyland, Detective Constable 150

International Brigade 16, 167
IRA in the Twilight Years 167

Index

Irish Club, Kilburn 32
Irish Free State 6, 13,
Irish Freedom 41
Irish Observer 169
Irish Press 58, 59
Irish Prisoners Aid Society 45
Irish Republican Brotherhood 6
Irish Times 144, 170

Jack Jackson Band 71
Jenkins, Douglas 100, 128, 133
Jervis St. Hospital 147
Jones, Constable 57
Jones, Sergeant Evan 31
Jones, Gary 72, 87
Jordan, Daniel 91

Kane, Brendan 31
Kavanagh, John Joe 150, 164
Keane, Ellen M. 64
Keane, John 38, 39, 44, 53, 54, 64
Keane, Sarah 94, 102
Kearns, Jackie 27
Keating, Dan 37, 141, 172
Keating, Sean 22
Keeble, Detective Inspector 31
Kell, Sir Vernon 77
Kelly, John James 25–26
Kelly, Patrick 25
Kelly, Thomas E. 34
Kemp, Anne 73
Kendall, Sir Norman 26
Kenneally, Christopher 138
Kennedy, Samuel 35
Kent, William 74
Kerr, Jerry 25
Kerr, Joe 172
Kilburn, London 40
Killeen, Jim 15
Killiney Castle 23, 147, 171
Kilssmann, Helmut 144
King's Cross Station 40, 73–74, 82
Kings (Liverpool) Regiment 62
Kinsella, Robert 92
Kirk, Gerard 53, 54
Kirwin, Detective 157
Kwayser, P.C. 57

Labour Party 11, 155
La Retraite Convent 164
Law, Detective Sergeant 100
Leeds-Liverpool Canal 29, 75
Leicester Station 38, 71–72, 95
Leinster Gardens 90, 161
Lennox, Detective Sergeant 58
Liddell, Cecil 36

Liverpool 34, 38, 48, 51, 52, 59, 60, 75, 82, 138
Liverpool Daily Post 51
Lloyd George, David 4–5, 7,
Logue, Jack 31
London 41, 65
Lynch, Jack 17, 24, 25
Lynch, Liam 6, 8
Lynch, Tadgh 18
Lyons, Gerard 46, 53,

MacEoin, Uinseann 21, 24, 37, 167
MacNamee, Eoin 21, 27, 51, 167
Madden, John 163
Magill, Tom 44
Magan, Tony 25, 39, 163, 168
Malone, Joseph 54, 143
Manchester 30, 31, 48, 57–58
Manchester Ship Canal 30
Mao, Tse-tung 165
Marble Arch 60
Marks & Spencer 40
Martin, John 45
Martin, Tom 59, 76
Mazengarb, Joseph 92, 100
McAleer, Joseph 53, 54
McAleer, Pat 46, 54
McAleese, President Mary 172
McAllister, Bill 141
McAteer, Hugh 156
McBride, Sean 15–16, 94, 154–5
McBrien, James 9
McCabe, Jack 65, 156
McCafferty, Charles 25–26
McCafferty, Dan 43, 156
McCaffrey, Jack 156
McCann, Robert 44
McCarthy, Charles 35, 43
McCarthy, Daniel 35, 43
McCarthy, Geroid 149
McCarthy, Thomas 35, 43
McCaughy, Sean 24, 154
McCormack, Bertie 148
McCormack, James 86, 87, 117, 158, 166
McCorry, Willie Joe 24
McCready, General 7
McCurtain, Tomas 18, 149, 163, 168
McDermott, Tommy 60
McDonagh-Byrne, Tom 60
McDonnell, Margaret 6, 138–9
McDougal, Detective Sergeant 31
McGarrigle, Cormac 64, 172
McGarrity, Joe 17
McGeough, John 57
McGill, Tom 17, 158, 165
McGillycuddy, Denis 44, 64

Index

McGillycuddy, Joseph 44
McGirl, John Joe 24
McGlynn, Paddy 171
McGowan, Francis 35, 43, 172
McGowan, James 43, 65
McGrath, Paddy 20, 24, 84, 147, 148, 150, 171
McGuinness, Bernard 23
McGuinness, Jim 38, 39, 45, 166
McGuinness, Seamus 27
McGuinness, Willie 2, 26, 27, 39, 84, 147, 163
McKeown, Sergeant 150
McLogan, Paddy 18, 167
McLoughlin, Pearse 17, 38, 39
McLoughlin, Terry 167
McMillan, Bob 156
McNally, Albert 25
McNeela, Jack 21, 25, 162
McNeela, Paddy 157, 163, 167, 171
McNeela, Sean 149
McSherry, Terence 35, 60
McSweeney, Rita 49, 60, 171
Meath Hotel 148
Meriden 50
MI5 20, 36
Midland Daily Telegraph 94, 97
Midland Red buses 50
Milverton Station 70, 196
Mitchell, John 32
Moffat, Clifford 45, 46
Mooney's Bar 22, 142
Moore, Herbert 60, 73
More O'Ferrall, Gerald 15
More O'Ferrall, Richard 15
Morgan, Leo 60
Moriarty, Chief Constable 136
Morris, Frank 156
Mountjoy Prison 147, 149
Mulcahy, Richard 6, 8
Mullingar 159, 165
Mulready, Dick 24
Murphy, Peter 59
Murphy, Seamus 60, 167
Murray, Josephine 171
Murray, Timothy 53, 54
Murrihy, John 44, 64
Mussolini, Benito 12

National Defence Force 14
National Guard 12
Nazi Germany 80, 139, 143
Nelson, Charles 68
Nelson, Thomas 66, 73
Nelson's Column 29
Newman & Co., London 53

News Chronicle 41
"98" 59
Nolan, Maggie 25, 60, 141

O'Bradaigh, Ruair 162
O'Cadhain, Mairtin 26
O'Connell, Denis 21
O'Connell, J.J. 7
O'Connell, Patrick 31, 44, 170
O'Donaghue, David 38, 160
O'Donnell, Paedar 16
O'Donovan, James 18, 21, 23, 59, 65, 68, 152, 156-7, 170
O'Duffy, Eoin 12, 13, 143
Offences Against the State 146
O'Flaherty, Peader 17, 21, 24, 28, 29, 84, 147
O'Hanlon, Jimmy 24
O'Hanlon, Tom 142
O'Hara, Brigit 86
O'Hara, Michael 61, 172
O'Hare, Rev. John 149
O'Higgins, Kevin 11, 12
O'Kane, Michael 85
O'Kennedy, Sam 27
O'Leary, Mick 25, 39
O'Malley, Ernie 6
O'Neil, Jimmy 141
O'Neil, Sean 157
O'Regan, James 91, 156, 165, 167
O'Shea, Michael 32, 42
O'Sullivan, "Joby" 87, 89, 91, 92, 9, 99, 135, 143, 150, 152-3, 159, 163, 164, 165, 166, 168
O'Sullivan, Kevin 157
O'Sullivan, Richard 99
Owen & Owen 40

Paddington Station 40
Paddington Town Hall 142
Page, Superintendent 31
Paramount cinema, Birmingham 63
Paramount cinema, Liverpool 52
Parker, Chief Inspector 99, 105-6, 132
Parkhurst Prison 54, 59, 143
Parliament 74
Paxo 22, 25, 69, 195
Pendleton, Detective Sergeant 56
Perry, Jimmy 156
Perry, Terence 141, 142
Pfaus, Oscar K. 143
Phillips, T.M. 135
Phoenix Park magazine 148
Pierrepoint, Albert 135
Pierrepoint, Thomas 135
Plunkett, George 28, 29, 83, 146
Portlaoise Prison 150, 154, 156
Price, Albert 25, 85, 170

Price, Dolours 170
Price, Marian 170
Price of My Soul 97
Pritt, Dennis 80–81
Public Safety Act 11

Quearney, Christy 24, 28
Queen Mary 38, 65
Queslett Quarry 46
Quigley, Gerard 27

Radio Ulster 142
Red Riding Hood waxwork 67
Rednal 51
Rees, Chief Inspector 74
Reynolds, Jimmy Joe 15, 17, 21, 25–26
Rhodes China, Coventry 56
Rineanna Aerodrome 83
Roche, John 150, 163
Rogers, Inspector 31
Rollins, Constable 56
Rosslare Ferry 40
Rowe, Constable Kathleen 104
Rowlands, Gwilym 92
RUC 17
Russell, Sean 15–16, 17, 18, 20, 22, 25, 27, 28, 34, 37, 47, 83, 143, 144, 156
Ryan, Frank 16, 144, 167
Ryan, Jim 20
Ryan, John 35
Ryan, Roger 150, 164

S-Plan 19–20, 32, 34, 36, 139, 159, 173–183
St. Bricin's Military Hospital 149, 164
St. George's Hospital 74
St. Osburg's Church 41
St. Pancras Hospital 74
Samuel, Ltd., H. 91
Saor Eire 14
Saorise 166, 170
Saul, Constable 67
Savage, Jim 167
Scott, Detective Sergeant 44
Seaforth Barracks 62
Selmer, Ltd., Henri, London 54
Shannon Airport 83
Sheehy, John Joe 18
Simpson, Paddy 156
Singleton, Mr. Justice 99
Sinn Fein 8, 10,
Sloane, Robert 85
Slyfield, Detective Inspector 74
Snow Hill Station, Birmingham 48
Somervell, Sir Donald 42
Somerville, Henry Boyle 15
Southport 62, 83

Southwark, London 29, 30
Spanish Civil War 13, 16
Special Branch 9, 20, 21, 26, 31, 32, 36, 39, 52, 72, 90, 98
Standuin, Mairtin 59, 60, 170
Stannard, George 58
Stapleton, Dan 23
Stapleton, Edward (Ned) 23, 25, 73
Staunton, Martin 23
Steadman, L.B. 42
Steele, Jimmy 156, 165
Stockhausen, Korvetten-Kapitan 144
Strabane 25
Sunday Times 159
Sweeney, Maire 60
Sweeney, Rose 60
Sykes, Detective Constable 104

Talty, Sean 22, 24
Tansley, Inspector 32
Tatler Cinema, Birmingham 63
This Week 166
Thompson, Inspector 31
Timmons, Dick 60, 171
Tipperary Brigade 6
Toms, Mrs. E. 85
Tottenham Ct. Road 38
Tower of London 39
Trainor, James 163
Traynor, Mick 24, 157, 162
Trocadero Cinema, Liverpool 52
Truform Shoe 51
Tubbert, Eileen 170
Tuite, Matty 84
Tussaud's Waxworks 67
Twomey, Moss 13, 15, 20, 25, 143

Ui Mhuimheachain, Caithlin 158
United Irishman 158, 166
Urquart, Marjorie 53

Venn, Charles 71
Victoria Law Courts 57
Victoria Station, London 73, 74

Walker, Joseph 42, 43
Walsh, James Joseph 82
Walsh, Patrick 32
Walsh, Peter 23, 25, 27, 33, 34, 42, 137
Walsh, Una 60
Walton Jail 38, 48
Ward, Mr. 100–1
Webster, Dr. J.M. 49
Wednesbury 40
Welsh, Mick 17
West, Harry 40

Index

West End Cinema, Birmingham 63
West Midlands Forensic Lab. 106
Westminster, Palace of (Parliament) 39
Wharton, Gerard 31, 43–4
White, Alfie 156
White, Harry 25, 37, 39, 64–65, 68, 69, 85, 146, 167
Whitehead, Detective Inspector 33, 44
Whittaker, George 139
Willesdon, London 29, 30, 40
Williams Deacons Bank 30
Wilson, Sir Henry 7
Windle, Lancashire 30
Windsor Castle 39
Winning, T.H. 107
Winson Green Prison 164
Winterbottom, Anne 53
Wolfe Tone Weekly 27, 83, 146, 147
Wolverhampton 40
Wolverhampton Station 72
Wood, Albert 133
Woods, Charles 72, 73
Woods, Ella 72, 73
Woolworth's 40
World War II 139
Wright, Sergeant 56
Wynn's Hotel 20

www.ingramcontent.com/pod-product-compliance
Lightning Source LLC
Chambersburg PA
CBHW032057300426
44116CB00007B/780